This study attempts to clarify the nature and value of rights-language in moral philosophy and Christian ethics. It does so partly by means of a conventional analysis of this terminology, and partly through a relatively novel approach involving the use of models and metaphors. The imaginative metaethics which emerges is seen to be rich in possibilities for both Christian and secular understandings of rights-talk, and demonstrates how – while there is a notable overlap between secular and religious perspectives – a specifically Christian understanding of the nature and value of rights might be constructed.

RIGHTS AND CHRISTIAN ETHICS

NEW STUDIES IN CHRISTIAN ETHICS

General editor: Robin Gill

Editorial Board: Stephen R. L. Clark, Anthony O. Dyson,
Stanley Hauerwas and Robin W. Lovin

In recent years the study of Christian ethics has become an integral part of mainstream theological studies. The reasons for this are not hard to detect. It has become a more widely held view that Christian ethics is actually central to Christian theology as a whole. Theologians increasingly have had to ask what contemporary relevance their discipline has in a context where religious belief is on the wane, and whether Christian ethics (that is, an ethics based on the Gospel of Jesus Christ) has anything to say in a multi-faceted and complex secular society. There is now no shortage of books on most substantive moral issues, written from a wide variety of theological positions. However, what is lacking are books within Christian ethics which are taken at all seriously by those engaged in the wider secular debate. Too few are methodologically substantial; too few have an informed knowledge of parallel discussions in philosophy or the social sciences. This series attempts to remedy the situation. The aims of New Studies in Christian Ethics will therefore be twofold. First, to engage centrally with the secular moral debate at the highest possible intellectual level; second, to demonstrate that Christian ethics can make a distinctive contribution to this debate – either in moral substance, or in terms of underlying moral justifications. It is hoped that the series as a whole will make a substantial contribution to the discipline.

BOOKS IN THE SERIES

RIGHTS AND
CHRISTIAN ETHICS

BY

KIERAN CRONIN

 CAMBRIDGE
UNIVERSITY PRESS

Published by the Press Syndicate of the University of Cambridge
The Pitt Building, Trumpington Street, Cambridge CB2 1RP
40 West 20th Street, New York, NY 10011–4211, USA
10 Stamford Road, Oakleigh, Victoria 3166, Australia

First published 1992

Printed in Great Britain at the University Press, Cambridge

A catalogue record for this book is available from the British Library

Library of Congress cataloguing in publication data
Cronin, Kieran.
Rights and Christian ethics/Kieran Cronin.
p.   cm. – (New studies in Christian ethics)
Includes index.
ISBN 0-521-41889-5 (hardback)
1.   Christian ethics.   2.   Human rights.   I.   Title.   II.   Series.
BJ1275.C76   1992
241'.622 – dc20   92-3126 CIP

ISBN 0 521 41889 5 hardback

To
Robin Gill
and
Sandy McCall Smith

Contents

Contents   xi

General editor's preface

This book is intended as the first of a series in two senses. It is the first book of the series *New Studies in Christian Ethics*. Fundamental to this series is the attempt to bring together recent discussions in philosophy and the social sciences with the very best in Christian ethics. This is meant to be an intellectually challenging series and, as such, it will make heavy demands on contributors. Nothing less is demanded than expertise in both a secular discipline and in Christian ethics.

Dr Cronin fulfils this admirably. He handles difficult philosophical material on the highly important topic of rights with obvious competence. It would be difficult to find another theological work in this area which displays the same level of expertise on this topic. Indeed, it has been an obvious weakness of theologians writing on the topic of rights, that they have seldom shown that they are fully acquainted with what is now a large body of philosophical discussion elsewhere in the intellectual world.

By combining philosophical and theological skills in this way, Cronin conforms very exactly to the aims of the series *New Studies in Christian Ethics*. He attempts to show that Christian ethics can make a distinctive contribution to understanding rights in society at large – not least in providing distinctively religious reasons for acting morally and in suggesting key models for Christian, as well as for secular, ethics. Cronin's understanding of imagination and models in relation to rights is particularly helpful. Whilst he takes seriously the philosophical literature which attempts to define and analyse the nature of 'rights', he does show that a more metaphorical (and then

theological) approach also has something important to contribute to the secular debate.

But I hope that this book is the first of a series in a more
personal sense. Dr Cronin's contribution is a distinctive one,
and will hopefully be followed by many more from him in the
future.

I am delighted to welcome this book as the first of what I hope
will be a very fruitful series in both senses.

ROBIN GILL

Preface

'Try to imagine Nowheresville – a world very like our own except that no one, or hardly anyone... has *rights*.' This is the thought experiment conducted by the philosopher Joel Feinberg at the beginning of his essay on 'The Nature and Value of Rights'.[1] Surely such a world would be a deficient one from the moral point of view. Perhaps it would even be a wicked or iniquitous society, an anarchic place where life is nasty, brutish and short. But let us not jump to this conclusion too readily. Feinberg is quite willing to allow many other moral features of great respectability to exist in Nowheresville. 'In particular, let the virtues of moral sensibility flourish. Fill this imagined world with as much benevolence, compassion, sympathy and pity as it will conveniently hold without strain.'[2]

Go even further, Feinberg suggests. Take into account the Kantians who insist on the idea of moral duty and include such an idea as motive for moral behaviour in our imaginary society. But maybe we have now gone too far. Maybe the introduction of duties has also brought in by the back door the idea of rights, due to the important and widely held doctrine of the correlativity of rights and duties. If people have duties, then there must be corresponding people who can claim these duties. But this does not necessarily hold. Not every duty has a correlative right, as we shall argue later, and the correlativity doctrine is not as tidy as some think. Feinberg considers it possible that the language of duties in Nowheresville would simply mean that there is a law which requires one to act in a certain way but without actually owing this action to someone. One example mentioned by Feinberg is that of a motorist stopping at a red

xiv

light (p. 144). There is a duty to do so required by law, but there is something artificial and strained in saying that other motorists and pedestrians have a strict right to this obedience. Thus, Feinberg insists there can be in Nowheresville the concept of duty without the correlative concept of having a right against someone.

Nor is he finished yet in arranging the moral furniture of this imaginary world. He includes the notion of personal desert, not in the sense that something is due to a person as a reward for something good he has done. This might imply the language of rights again, as in the case of duty. So Feinberg interprets desert not as what is due to another, but what is fitting or appropriate in response to a situation, rather like laughter after a good joke and applause after some performance. Again it is not necessary to say that anyone has a claim to such responses (p. 145).

Therefore, Nowheresville is not the den of iniquity we might have judged it to be at first. Its inhabitants are not necessarily amoral or immoral. But the question remains, 'Is there something missing morally, something significant, in this world without rights?' And Feinberg insists that there is. Since rights involve the activity of claiming, according to this author, its absence from Nowheresville is highly significant morally, since it 'makes for self-respect and respect for others, gives a sense to the notion of personal dignity, and distinguishes this otherwise morally flawed world from the even worse world of Nowheresville' (p. 155).

Feinberg's philosophy of rights will be studied in greater detail later in this work. His thought experiment is highlighted at this initial stage mainly as an example of the distinction that is frequently made in modern moral philosophy and which is germane to this study. That distinction is between 'Metaethics' and 'Normative ethics'. In the Editorial Foreword to P. H. Nowell-Smith's *Ethics*, A. J. Ayer presents this distinction in a brief and succinct manner: 'There is a distinction, which is not always sufficiently marked, between the activity of a moralist, who sets out to elaborate a moral code, or to encourage its observance, and that of a moral philosopher, whose concern is not primarily to make moral judgements, but to analyse their nature. Mr Nowell-Smith writes as a moral philosopher.'[3] It is not absolutely clear if the moralist and the normative ethicist are one and the same. Perhaps the normative ethicist may stop at elaborating moral codes and leave the encouragement of observance to the preacher. In any case, what interests us here is the work of the metaethicist, especially when it comes to analysing the language of rights.

Now Feinberg's essay is primarily a metaethical study rather than a normative one. He is not concerned with telling us what rights we have. His aims are twofold as seen in the apt title he uses. He intends to elucidate the 'nature' of rights, whilst also exploring the question of their 'value' or usefulness. Regarding the first quest, reference to the 'nature' of rights directs one's attention to their essential meaning, and Feinberg tends to focus on the notion of claims and claiming in order to draw this out. Turning to the quest for the 'value' of rights and the language of rights one's attention is directed towards the sphere of justification. Given that we are relatively clear about the meaning of our language when we talk about rights, we must ask whether we are justified in using such language in our ethical discussions.

In Feinberg's essay these two questions of meaning and value are closely related. Once one analyses the notion of rights as claims one comes to see that having a claim or claiming something against someone is not a morally neutral matter. Normative judgements are built into this use of language, some positive, some negative. Feinberg insists, as we have seen, that a world without the facility of claiming would be an impoverished world, morally speaking, and that the language of rights contributes to human efforts to promote human dignity and self-worth. This raises important questions about the relationship between metaethics and normative ethics, leading some philosophers to question the distinction itself. For instance, Gilbert Harman claims that 'arguments by W. V. Quine and other philosophers actually undermined the supposed distinction between meta-ethics and normative ethics by showing that there can be no real separation between questions of substance and questions of meaning'.[4]

I agree with Harman's point that metaethics and normative ethics cannot be separated because of their close links, but I would still insist on a basic distinction, with each subject having its own particular emphasis. In particular with regard to the question of the value or justification of rights-language it is not too difficult to recognise two senses in need of elucidation. On one hand, there is the normative–ethical sense, which Feinberg appears to emphasise in the essay we have been discussing. The language of rights as claims is related to human dignity in so far as this requires that we stand up for ourselves, demanding what is due to us, being self-assertive in a good way, and so on. Actual moral positions regarding human relationships are very close to the surface in this approach to analysis and justification.

On the other hand, there is another approach to the task of uncovering the value of rights which is more typically meta-ethical. This stresses the value of the 'language' of rights or the 'concept' of rights from the more or less logical point of view. We may ask how useful is this form of language as a tool in any kind of ethical discussion. Is it a sharp tool in the sense of being relatively clear, or is it blunt in the sense of being vague and confused? As a tool does it do one job or many jobs? Does it do one job very well and others in a mediocre way? In other words, is our talk of rights a useful kind of moral language in helping to express the complicated and intricate world of morality? Of course we choose tools because we are interested in getting a job done, hence the difficulty in separating the two occupations. Likewise, we have expressed reservations about separating metaethics from normative ethics. However, I would liken the student of metaethics to the tool-maker who knows that the ultimate value of his job lies in the usefulness of his tools in performing skilled work, but who, in practice, concentrates on the production of the tools in themselves. At times he may even forget the customers who will buy his work, but he can never completely ignore that dimension. The tools are for sale, not for remaining on the shelf for his own admiration.

Various images can be used to explain the relevance of the distinction between metaethics and normative ethics. Kai Nielsen likes to refer to the person who does metaethics as 'a kind of conceptual cartographer'.[5] The work to be done is to map out the relationship between concepts. Again I find the image helpful. When we buy a map we often take the cartographer for granted. We have in mind a particular task, to make a journey from one place to another. The map will guide us. But reading a map requires some training. There are codes and symbols which must be understood in advance, otherwise the map is just a series of coloured blobs and crooked lines. So, in order to arrive at our destination we need to understand the meaning of the instructions on the map, and we then need to put them to good use as we travel along. Similarly, with moral language such as the language of rights, we must be trained in the meanings of the terms used if we are to use them to get to our moral destination. Again meaning and value are closely linked. Once one knows the meaning of the codes and symbols one knows their value – in helping to avoid getting lost for one thing. The value of a map depends on what you have in mind. Some people use maps to travel direct to their destination. Others just like the colours and hang them as posters on their bedroom walls. Others still may study maps as professional cartographers, judging them from the point of view of the particular standards of the profession. However, such standards must have some reference to the general public who use maps, as well as having reference to the special interests of cartographers who have more time to concentrate on the niceties of layout.

What relevance has all this for Christian ethics? The most obvious response is that Christians use the language of rights like nearly everyone else, and they are equally prone to abuse moral language by being vague in their understanding of the complex relationships between moral terms. Even Christian theology can be accused of ignoring to a great extent the analysis of the language of rights at the metaethical level. I can find only a handful of Christian ethicists writing in the English language or translated into English who treat of the metaethical issues surrounding the concept and language of rights. It is odd that Christianity has moved from a situation of hostility to this form of language, to one of almost naive and unquestioning acceptance. John Henley speaks of 'the naivete with which some theologians and church leaders concerned about human rights have understood the relation between *theoria* and *praxis*'.[6] And he goes on, 'This has meant that the cause of human rights has been virtually taken for granted in certain circles, especially those of the World Council of Churches, and little critical attention has been paid to such matters as its foundations' (*ibid.*).

In the following chapters I make an attempt to act as conceptual cartographer, charting the territory of rights-language. To vary the metaphor, as a tool-maker, or better, tool-sharpener I try to sharpen this valuable tool by clarifying its meaning and value. The first chapter presents two major analytical approaches. One is the more traditional approach by way of definition. So I will discuss in a basic way the problems we face when attempting to define and pin down the meaning of complex ethical terms. The second approach is, I think, more original, involving an imaginative perspective in relation to metaethics. This is necessary because of the limitations of the definitional approach, and because of the inherent value of the imagination in the work of analysis and justification of moral language.

My second chapter concentrates further attention on the definitional approach to rights-language, examining terms like 'claim', 'entitlement', 'power' and 'liberty' in order to point out some of the controversy surrounding even such basic attempts to find simple synonyms for a 'right'. Some of the complexity of rights-language is underlined from the point of view of legal philosophy and a number of philosophical problems grounded in these distinctions are brought to light, especially the doctrine of the correlativity of rights and duties.

The first two chapters may have a discouraging effect on the reader who never thought that a form of language used so commonly could in fact be relatively controversial. The next two chapters may be even more discouraging as I face up to radical scepticism about rights-language. Some philosophers have even advocated dropping this way of speaking, abandoning it as a useless tool. These chapters, then, present two different forms of scepticism. The conceptual objections tend to be more metaethical in their emphasis. Is this language incurably vague? Is it not redundant in so far as it can be replaced without loss by the language of principles and rules, or the language of duty, or simply by talking directly about human interests? The normative objections come from moral philosophy and Christian ethics. They are more familiar, perhaps, underlining the individualism and egoism inherent in so much of human claiming. Rights language encourages and expresses the adversarial tendency in modern society. Claims have proliferated immoderately. For example, Lisa Sowle Cahill mentions as well as the Quinlan case in the US, where a 'right to die' was in question, the case of 'an eighty-year-old Japanese sandalmaker [who] had won the "right to sunshine" (asserted against the construction of skyscrapers) from the Tokyo District Court, and the Fiji Island gold miners [who] were seeking "the right to a sex break" during their lunch period.'[7]

Clearly a discussion of such scepticism is necessary at the beginning of our treatment of rights-language. There is little possibility of a proper metaethical treatment of our subject without confronting radical scepticism head-on, so to speak, at the very start. While I begin to provide some answer to the sceptics in my third and fourth chapters, a fuller answer is provided, I hope, in the remainder of this work. The last four chapters take up in detail the imaginative approach to metaethics mentioned in my initial chapter. The role of imagination at the metaethical level is brought out in terms of the value of metaphors and models when these are used to elucidate first the meaning of the language of rights and also the value of this language.

I take the concepts of 'freedom' and 'power', which were used in the definitional approach, and I treat them as models of rights. These are elucidated at a humanistic or secular level at first without any reference to religious insights. Later, however, I build on this secular foundation, adding particular Christian insights or understandings of freedom and power. Applying these models to rights I claim that a deeper and richer grasp of the meaning and value of this language is attained. A further step in this imaginative approach takes up two additional models – covenant and image of God – which are more directly religious in inspiration. I relate these in turn to the previous models of freedom and power, presenting all four as complementary metaethical models of rights. From the point of view of Christian ethics my position is that these models, while overlapping with humanistic approaches to rights, provide a specific vision of reality which is ultimately God-directed. Such a vision is a controlling factor regarding the 'content' of morality and provides the Christian with special justifying reasons for acting morally.

I am grateful to a number of people who have helped me to the point of producing this work. Professor Robin Gill and Dr. R. A. A. McCall Smith, who supervised my original thesis at Edinburgh are deserving of thanks, not only for their professional advice and direction, but for their friendship over the past few years. I am particularly indebted to Professor Gill for suggesting that I present a rewritten version of my thesis for publication in this series. This being my first publication, I am sincerely grateful to Alex Wright and the editorial staff at Cambridge University Press for leading me through the task of preparing a manuscript for publication. Such support and encouragement has been invaluable over the last year.

CHAPTER I

Metaethics: meaning and justification

The pages of this introductory chapter focus on two approaches to metaethics as these have bearings on our analysis of the language of rights. Roughly speaking the first half of the following discussion concentrates on one type of analysis, involving the problems of defining relatively technical moral and legal terms. I begin with some very basic ideas on definition, prescinding initially from the specific issues related to the analysis of moral language as such, and relate these ideas to rights-language in use every day. A move is then made to make some hesitant remarks on the evaluative, as opposed to the merely descriptive, meaning of the language of rights, stressing in particular the ways in which aspects of justification tend to be 'built into' our moral and legal vocabulary. The second half of my discussion derives its importance partly from the limitations experienced in trying to reduce the analysis of rights to definition alone. In other words, I begin to recognise explicitly the disadvantages of depending solely on a discursive metaethics. I attempt to complement the discursive approach with a more imaginative metaethical analysis. Where imagination has been advocated in the study of normative ethics, an attempt is made here to use the same valuable tool in the analysis of ethical concepts, such as rights and duties.

In his discussion of metaethics, William Frankena claims that the subject treats of four major questions:

(1) What is the meaning or definition of ethical terms or concepts like 'right', 'wrong', 'good', 'bad'? What is the nature, meaning or function of judgements in which these

and similar terms or concepts occur? What are the rules for
the use of such terms and sentences?

(2) How are moral uses of such terms to be distinguished from
nonmoral ones, moral judgements from other normative
ones? What is the meaning of 'moral' as contrasted with
'nonmoral'?

(3) What is the analysis or meaning of related terms or concepts
like 'action', 'conscience', 'free will', 'intention', 'promising', 'excusing', 'motive', 'responsibility', 'reason', 'voluntary'?

(4) Can ethical and value judgements be proved, justified and
shown valid? If so, how and in what sense? Or, what is the
logic of moral reasoning and of reasoning about value?[1]

Now Frankena suggests that of these four questions, two of
them (1) and (4) 'are the more standard problems of metaethics',[2] and thus devotes most of his attention to a discussion of
the meaning and justification of our ethical terms, judgements
and arguments. This is not to deny the importance of questions
(2) and (3). From the point of view of the language of rights
such questions do have some application.

For instance, with regard to the second question, namely the
moral/nonmoral distinction, we can agree that not all rights are
moral rights. Alan White, as well as recognising the moral
variety, refers to the following types of right: legal, religious,
political, statutory, constitutional, customary or conventional,
epistemological or logical, and allows for still other examples.[3]
The latter are clearly normative; in fact, all rights are normative
– but how do they differ from the moral variety? In other
words, are there such things as nonmoral rights? One can
imagine a normative statement based on aesthetic value, such as
'This painting has a "right" to be included in the exhibition.'
How would this use of the term 'right' be similar to, or
dissimilar from, what appears to be a clear moral use in the
following statement, 'I have a "right" to be included on the
register of voters for this election.' (where we have in mind
perhaps some discriminatory practice obstructing the right
to vote). Or consider the difference between morality and

etiquette.[4] Is the 'right' of a lady to enter the doorway first a right of the same basic type as the 'right' of a woman to equal consideration in the job market? In other words, questions about rights arise in the context of more general discussion of the distinction between the moral and the nonmoral spheres of human life, or where these spheres seem to overlap, as in the complex relationships between law and morality.

The third question involves the analysis of what Frankena seems to regard as secondary moral concepts, or as nonmoral concepts closely related to the moral field. From his list it is not difficult to imagine how their analysis would be important in relation to an analysis of rights language. For instance, are all rights tied to some action, some external form of behaviour, some change in the world about us? If so, is it the right-holder's action that is primary, for example his activity of claiming something? Or do we focus on the activity of the bearer of some correlative obligation? Or is some combination of these activities involved?

Another word requiring analysis, according to Frankena, is 'promising'. This term is important from the point of view of what are sometimes called special moral rights, claims that originate in some form of promise, either explicit (a performative utterance[5]) or implicit (where one gives another some indication, often non-verbal, that she can depend on one for some service). So, the issue of how rights arise from promises is a metaethical question.[6]

Within the compass of normative ethics, distinctions are often made by contemporary philosophers between theory of obligation and theory of value. Usually the former concentrates on act-evaluation, employing the terminology of 'right' and 'wrong', while the latter tends to concentrate on agent-evaluation, employing the terminology of 'good' and 'bad'.[7] Because of the close relationship between rights and obligations and the language of 'right' and 'rights', there is a temptation to study rights language just in relation to the theory of obligation and to ignore the possible connections between rights and the theory of value, especially the ethics of virtue. Can one violate the rights of others by acting from the wrong motive, or if the

consequences of our actions are beneficial, but were not
intended to be so? Once one sees terms like 'motive' and
'intention' one moves into a different area of normative ethics
– the study of character, personal traits and dispositions – and
the question should naturally come to mind, 'Does the analysis
of rights have some connection with virtue as well as with
obligation?' (We include here the question of when one should
waive one's rights – this could be supererogatory. A theory of
virtue thus might control our activity of claiming.)

THE DEFINITIONAL APPROACH

Returning to the central questions underlined by Frankena, we
first examine the issue of meaning or definition of ethical terms,
such as 'right', with its various qualifications: 'human',
'natural', 'special', 'positive' and 'negative', 'inalienable',
'absolute' and so on. Various problems arise initially when we
consider the definition of terms. Let us cover some of these issues
briefly, borrowing from the ideas of John Hospers in his
standard work *An Introduction to Philosophical Analysis* as well as
introducing insights from some other philosophers.[8] As we
proceed we connect these general issues with our efforts to
elucidate rights-language.

The process of defining our terms may involve a number of
different approaches. Most often, perhaps, we try to give an
equivalent word or set of words. This is the dictionary approach
and is particularly helpful when faced with technical terms.
What we need is some method of translating such terms into
'ordinary' language, the language of the layman. We hear an
unfamiliar term or phrase such as 'male sibling' and the
dictionary informs us of a simple synonym – 'a brother'.[9]

Quite often, however, giving a single equivalent word is not
sufficient to pin down the meaning of a term. One way of coping
with this is to regard words as typically designating 'the sum of
the characteristics a thing must have for the word to apply to
it'.[10] We then look for the defining characteristics of an object.
Being three-sided would be one of the defining characteristics of

a triangle, and without this characteristic we refuse to apply the term 'triangle' to some geometrical figure. Thus, one way of defining a term is to distinguish between defining characteristics and accompanying characteristics (contingent facts about an object), giving as comprehensive a list as possible of the former.

Designation of essential characteristics is one approach to definition, but not the only one. Another approach is by way of denotation. Hospers suggests this method for those situations when 'there may be no set of words which are equivalent in meaning to the word for which a definition is requested' (p. 40). We may not be clear about the defining characteristics of an object, say a human being, but at least we can give some examples of human beings by naming known individuals. Each individual to which the word applies is a denotation of the word. 'The entire denotation of a word is the complete list of all the things to which the word applies' (*ibid.*).

One last approach to definition is called ostensive definition.[11] It is non-verbal and, as the name suggests, it works by means of pointing to an object. Learning a foreign language we may grasp the meaning of a word by having some object, a chair for instance, pointed out to us. Colour words are another example where pointing is one of the best ways of learning the meaning of the word. More complicated are experiences such as pain, fear, frustration, where one cannot point to something internal in a person. Instead one points to certain forms of behaviour which are signs or symptoms of the thing in question.

Regarding the language of rights, what definitional approaches should we apply to our basic terms in order to clarify their meaning?

The basic terminology of rights involves a relatively complex technical vocabulary in moral, political and legal philosophy and yet, at the same time, it appears to be used frequently in popular discussions of morals, politics and law. Can we find an equivalent term or set of terms which will provide a satisfactory verbal definition?

Sometimes a technical term is defined in a way that is logically satisfactory but psychologically unsatisfactory, as when we substitute another technical term for the original one. But there is no guarantee that the new term clarifies the one being defined. Thus, we may define rights in terms of claims or entitlements, with the effect of leaving those we are communicating with still unclear about the definition of our original term. Presumably, we wish to replace a relatively unfamiliar term with a relatively familiar one so that others will be able to recognise examples from their experience and may more easily work out defining characteristics. In other words, presenting an equivalent word is an aid to discovering both the denotation and connotation of the term at issue. Thus, by giving 'claim' as an equivalent word for 'right' one hopes that 'the penny will drop', that others will say, 'Now I know what you mean. Claims and claiming are familiar to me, and I think I know the criteria for using these terms.' Of course, the mention of 'claim' may give rise to a blank reaction. Then we have substituted one unfamiliar term with another, and we must try again. Or indeed, it could be the case that a person is more familiar with the word 'right' than with the word 'claim', so that the latter word is the technical one in need of elucidation.

Hospers distinguished two main kinds of definition – denotation and designation. He departs from the more traditional use of the term 'connotation' in using designation. Later in this chapter we will examine what he means by connotation. Traditional logicians tend to equate denotation with extension and connotation with intension.[12] Although distinguishable the two notions tend to go hand in hand. In the case of the term 'right', for instance, its denotation or extension would include the whole class of such objects taken as individuals; each right is a denotation of the term 'right'. Clearly, a person may have little explicit notion of what the defining characteristics of the term are, yet still be able to recognise instances. This is probably due to some implicit grasp of either defining or accompanying characteristics, that is, a rudimentary grasp of a term's connotation or intension. Someone might recognise moral, legal and religious rights as rights while not being able to distinguish them as different types of right, just as someone might recognise wrens, sparrows and blackbirds as birds while remaining ignorant of what makes these birds belong to different species.

In this work an underlying assumption is that people in general, including some scholars, are in this position regarding rights. Their grasp of the connotation of rights is limited. Therefore, a major task of metaethics must be to bridge the gap between denotation and connotation regarding the language of rights. Although in this work we are interested in the analysis of the general term 'right', it is the various species of rights, represented by the qualifying words applied to the general term which provide the material for the deepest understanding of this type of language.

Depending on our interests our definitions may vary. Our concern may be extremely broad – we seek the most general defining characteristics which characterise any right. Or we are interested in a narrower field, such as legal rights where the defining characteristics are limited to that one area.

Our definition of rights may be reportive or stipulative: we may follow the dictionary definition, the given societal or group understanding of 'right', or we may feel that this is imprecise, or inconsistent, or simply misses the point, and want to substitute our own personal definition, suggesting that it be widely accepted in lieu of the commonly held one.[13] Wesley Hohfeld's analysis of legal rights is an example of a set of stipulative definitions within a specific, indeed highly specialised, context, aimed at improving judicial reasoning.[14] Another example would be the attempt to redefine human rights by limiting their scope. For example, Carl Wellman argues that human rights are a type of civil right, belonging to citizens, but held only against the State to which one belongs.[15] According to this stipulative definition, one does not have a human right which is claimable against one's neighbour, though the state may have an obligation to protect one from a neighbour's aggression.

As we study the language of rights we see how controversial their analysis has become, especially at the philosophical level, so that the various stipulative definitions are often more to the point than the reportive type. In fact, one of the uses of stipulative definition comes into play when there is no available definition to cover some specialised distinction. Then we have to coin a phrase or invent a term, which may or may not become widely accepted. An example from the realm of rights is the distinction between 'mandatory' and 'discretionary' rights.[16] The former involve a perfect coincidence of right and duty on the part of the right-holder. I have a right to do x and I also have a duty to do x. The latter implies that one is free to do x but has no duty to act in this manner. (This feature of rights-language is evidence of open-texture, a notion to be discussed shortly.)

DEFINITION AND EXISTENCE

Definition by designation of essential characteristics does not necessarily imply the existence of the object being defined. Or, to put it another way, connotation does not always imply denotation. Hospers gives the examples of the words 'horse' and 'centaur'.[17] The word 'horse' denotes many things, but the word 'centaur' denotes nothing, since no centaurs exist. Yet the meaning of the two words is equally clear in the sense that we know what defining characteristics are required for the application of the words. Fictional objects have connotation but no denotation. What then of the term 'right'? Given it has some connotation, does the term denote anything or is the term the name of some fictional entity?

Alan White reviews some of the opinions given in the past on this matter from the legal or jurisprudential point of view. Bentham, for instance, held that the word 'right' denotes a fictitious object.[18] This was widely agreed on by many nine-teenth- and early twentieth-century jurists, including Hohfeld.[19] But White himself states that:

Clearly 'right' (like 'duty' etc.) does not denote any entity, whether physical, mental, or fictional. Having a right is neither like having a ring nor is it like having an idea. Nor is denying the existence of certain rights like denying the existence of centaurs or of El Dorado.[20]

Yet this is not to deny the importance of rights. For White goes on to say that sentences involving the word 'right' may state facts or express truths (pp. 2–10). And in general White is opposed to the widespread scepticism shown by many philosophers to the language of rights.

Another eminent philosopher, H. L. A. Hart, goes over similar ground in his essay 'Definition and Theory in Juris-prudence'.[21] He finds it quite remarkable that 'out of these innocent requests for definitions of fundamental legal notions there should have arisen vast and irreconcilable theories, so that not merely whole books but whole schools of juristic thought may be characterized by the type of answer they give to questions like "What is a right?"' (p. 23). He goes on to describe the main theories in question, calling them 'a familiar triad'. The American realists[22] tell us that a right is a term used to describe our prophecies concerning the probable behaviour of courts or officials. The Scandinavian jurists,[23] as mentioned by White, insist that rights are not real, but fictitious or imaginary powers. Both theories denigrate the third approach which sees rights as invisible entities that exist apart from human behaviour. Hart himself disagrees with each of these theory types and instead follows the view of Bentham that a functional approach is what is required. With regard to words like 'right', 'duty' and 'corporation' he declares:

The fundamental point is that the primary function of these words is not to stand for or describe anything but a distinct function; this makes it vital to attend to Bentham's warning that we should not, as does the traditional method of definition, abstract words like 'right' and 'duty', 'State', or 'corporation' from the sentences in which alone their full function can be seen, and then demand of them so abstracted their genus and differentia.[24]

The particular function rights-language has, according to Hart, occurs within the context of a legal system which includes a correlativity between rights and duties, with rights involving a power or freedom of choice over another's duty. This is sometimes called the 'Choice Theory' of rights. We have to admit a certain attractiveness attending this point of view, and it is not too difficult to adapt the Choice Theory to the category of moral rights. Presumably, correlativity of rights and duties, choice whether to claim or waive one's legitimate demands, all in the context of a moral system of values, rules and principles, would be central terms in a possible elucidation of the meaning of moral rights.

Both White and Hart appear to represent the modern analytic approach to language, following Wittgenstein[25] and his emphasis on the use of language, rather than formal definition which tends towards an illegitimate reification of rights. In asking for a definition of the term 'right' we may be bewitched by some picture of a right as some object or entity, whereas for many analytic philosophers such assumptions should not be made; rather one should ask, 'How is the term used in a moral or legal system?' Once this approach is adopted, it is argued, the 'existence' of rights becomes less mysterious.[26]

DEFINITION AND THE OPEN-TEXTURE OF CONCEPTS

It must not be assumed that once a definition is agreed upon that its meaning is settled once and for all. Hart, whose admiration for analytic jurisprudence has just been noted, reminds us in another essay of the important concept developed by F. Waismann, a disciple of Wittgenstein, entitled 'the open-texture of concepts' (*Porosität der Begriffe*).[27] The value of this concept, Hart argues, lies in its stress on the fact that most empirical concepts, not merely legal concepts, are such 'that we have no way of framing rules of language which are ready for all imaginable possibilities. However complex our definitions may be, we cannot render them so precise that they are delimited in all possible directions such that for any given case we can say definitely that the concept either does or does not apply to it.'[28]

Waismann provides a number of examples of unusual situations where we would be uncertain how to apply a common concept or term. For instance, 'Suppose I come across a being that looks like a man, speaks like a man, behaves like a man, and is only one span tall – shall I say it *is* a man?' In response to the objection that such things don't happen, Waismann answers, 'Quite so; but they *might* happen, and that is enough to show that we can never exclude altogether the possibility of some unforeseen situation arising in which we will have to modify our definition.'[29] Hart agrees with this feature of definition, saying that 'We can only redefine and refine our concepts to meet the new situations when they arise.'[30] Hospers states the same point with his remark that 'a definition must be adequate to the *possible* as well as the actual cases'.[31]

It seems natural to admit that the concept of rights partakes of this open-texture. This is seen, I think, in the more controversial attempts to extend the concept to animals,[32] natural objects such as trees,[33] future generations,[34] potential persons[35] and even aliens. How, for instance, might we analyse the status of a claim that a person has a right to have his dying wishes respected after death? Can dead people have rights?[36] Since it is widely held that fundamental human rights focus on essential needs of humanity, such as food, shelter, education, health, and so on, and since it is also commonly accepted that human rights are possessed by each person equally, the issue as to whether the starving of the world have a strict right to food raises questions at the level of the analysis of rights.[37] If rights are necessarily linked to duties as the correlativity theory states, do the relatively comfortable inhabitants of the world have a duty to feed starving strangers? What if this duty is highly impractical or even impossible? What kind of right would this involve? One reply, that of Joel Feinberg, bestows the label 'manifesto rights'[38] on these claims. The need is obvious and its importance is accepted, but the alleviation of the need, the actual practice of the correlative duty is problematic. Here is a prime example where the open-texture of the language of rights is evident. Furthermore, the relative vagueness inherent in this use of the language of rights is damaging to the whole process of clarification. It leads to accusations that the language of rights involves mere rhetoric and wishful thinking. Therefore it seems imperative that we be prepared to redefine and refine our concepts to deal with these situations.

CAUSAL DEFINITION

We have recognised that our definitions of terms and concepts may change over time. In the process of refining and redefining we may grasp the meaning of, say, the language of rights in a deeper way.

Hospers shows how definitions can be improved in technical

fields such as medicine. The example of the disease 'syphilis' is given as evidence of how 'definitions change in the light of our advancing knowledge'.[39] Part of the definition of 'syphilis' includes mention of its cause, namely the spirochete that causes the symptoms to occur. 'Before the discovery of the spirochete, no definition of "syphilis" involving this microscopic creature could have been given' (*ibid.*). Hospers does not say that causal definitions are essential for our understanding of the meaning of terms. He mentions the term 'headache' which is readily understandable without reference to its 'bewildering variety of causes'. Sometimes we distinguish between the technical causal definition and ordinary meaning, as in the case of the colour term 'red'. This can be defined in terms of wave-lengths of light – 'any colour within the range 4000–7000 Angstrom units'; but we do not wish to deny that the millions of non-physicists among us have some idea of the meaning of 'red' as we go about our daily activities.

Although a definition in terms of causes is not always essential for an understanding of basic meaning, it is arguable that such an approach may be quite helpful in many cases. Would it be helpful to us as we attempt to elucidate the meaning of rights? I believe there may be some advantage in exploring the underlying context of the use of the language of rights. We have seen Hart placing the function of rights within a legal system of rules, and have suggested that moral rights should be similarly understood in the context of a moral system of values, rules and principles. Why are these systems in place at all? Presumably, because of our human condition. We need moral and legal systems to ameliorate our human predicament as G. J. Warnock might say. For Warnock, 'the object of morality' consists of a positive response to the dual problem of 'limited intelligence' and 'limited sympathies'.[40] Rights have value and derive some of their meaning from the situation of conflict in which we find ourselves in social relationships. If we never had to face differences of interest, scarce resources, animosity, then the language of rights would simply have no application.

From the point of view of Christian living and theology we might naturally say that the terminology of rights has application precisely as a response to human sinfulness. Sin and moral wrong-doing, then, form the fundamental context for the language of rights. It is because people harm and wrong one another that claiming entitlements makes any sense. Sin 'causes' rights, not in the sense that the spirochete in Hospers' example causes syphilis and is part of its definition, but in the sense that sin causes (or is itself) a form of 'illness' (moral/ spiritual) which seems to require rights as an antidote or form of treatment. And, extending this analogy, there is a degree of ambiguity in claiming that rights are an antidote to sin or wrong-doing in so far as there are some people who argue that in many cases claiming rights brings a cure which is worse than the original disease.[41] This position, held by those who oppose the language of rights on moral grounds, could well lead one to regard sin as a causal definition of the term 'right'. Claiming rights in this context would be a symptom of a disease rather than an antidote. In either case it remains an open question whether or not we should include the conflictual nature of human life as part of the set of defining characteristics of the term 'right'.

DEFINITION AND JUSTIFICATION

Frankena states that the two most important features of metaethics are the clarification of moral terms and their justification. Usually, the justificatory aspect of metaethics is of a general sort. The student of metaethics wishes to see whether normative ethics is possible. One of the major issues under discussion is the ongoing debate between the position of moral realism and that of non-cognitivism, that is whether we can speak of moral statements – having a truth value, being true or false – or whether we should speak of moral utterances (as opposed to statements) which are said to be appropriate or inappropriate rather than true or false. In this work I assume a position of moral realism, following the mainstream of Christian ethical writers.[42] What then of the justification of rights-language? My argument is that justification takes place within a particular normative system of ethics or law and that within such a system elements of justification seem to be built into our definitions and analysis.[43]

Take, for example, our discussion of causal definition, where moral conflict was regarded as the context for the appearance of the terminology of rights. We could almost say that badness and evil 'causes' the existence of rights and makes that form of language have meaning. We even used an analogy from medicine, suggesting that claiming rights is in some circumstances like an antidote (though like all medicines we must be careful in using them according to due specification). But to say that x is an antidote for y is in some sense to justify x. In other words, to call something an antidote is not merely to describe it, but to evaluate it in a positive light. Likewise, to see rights as an antidote to the bad effects of human moral conflict is to evaluate and even justify their use, with the usual qualifications as to appropriate use.

Consider yet another example of how definition and justification appear to come together in a particular use of the language of rights. Notice how popular the qualification 'human' has become in association with 'right'. The association is so popular in fact that we often forget that not all rights are of this type. Many rights are of the special moral type, tied to specific relationships between people.

The language of 'human rights' is quite modern. It gained a great deal of its respectability only in this century, especially through the Charter of the United Nations and its Declaration of Human Rights. It is a successor to the more traditional language of 'natural rights'. Jeremy Waldron argues that there has been a shift in meaning from this traditional use of the phrase 'natural rights' and the 'rights of man' to the modern phrase 'human rights'. He talks about 'a loss of faith in our ability to justify rights on the basis of truths about human *nature*'.[44] And he adds that 'To call them *human* rights is now to characterize the scope of the claims being made rather than hint at anything about their justification' (*ibid.*). In other words, the more traditional definition of what are now called human rights included elements of justification in terms of a metaphysical/anthropological theory of human nature, which now causes such embarrassment in many circles that a new terminology has been embraced, involving a change of meaning (by dropping the aspect of justification). Just because the qualification 'human' has been divested of its aspect of justification by some does not mean that such a move is imperative. It is, after all, a form of stipulation which we may wish to accept or reject. We cannot deny a priori the possibility of retaining the aspect of justification contained in the older terminology of 'natural' rights, and transferring this to the more modern usage of 'human' rights. We may debate whether this change is an improvement on the old terminology and, indeed, we may raise the related question, how far we can go in defining moral/legal terms without involving controversial moral/legal normative theories (and their associated anthropologies)?[45]

Waldron points out one disadvantage of the shift as follows:

The term [human] refers to universality and a commitment to equality and non-discrimination, particularly across races and peoples. But unlike, 'natural' it leaves open the question of justification or, worse still, takes the mere existence of a broad consensus on these matters to be a sufficient reason for avoiding the task of justification altogether.[46]

This criticism is levelled at the lazy option of adopting a terminology which avoids the difficult work of justification while trying to cover over this defect at the level of rhetoric. Of course, it is one thing to claim a justification for rights as part of our analysis or definition of the terminology, it is another thing altogether to establish the justification.

To recap on some of the main issues discussed so far:

1. The first step in definition is often to find an equivalent word which leads us to identify some reality and to discover its defining characteristics. Although it is often easier to ask people to give examples of different rights in everyday use, i.e. denotation or extension, connotation or intension is the more important quest in relation to the term 'right'.

2. We learn more about the defining characteristics of rights if we are willing to both broaden and narrow our focus on rights-language. We must be concerned with the

general criteria for understanding what all rights are like, but the most interesting questions are to do with the various categories of rights and the qualifying language – moral, legal, human, special, absolute, inalienable, manifesto, mandatory, discretionary, etc.

3. We should not expect our definitions to be free of controversy. After all they come in the context of some normative theory, and few such theories go unquestioned in moral philosophy. As such we should regard our definitions as largely stipulative and questionable. Related to this point is the so-called open-texture of our moral concepts which refers to the temporary and conditional nature of our definitions and analysis. There is constant need for vigilance lest we neglect the necessary refinement of our definitions. Still, this should not lead us to the Socratic fallacy of thinking that ignorance of the once-and-for-all definition of a term precludes us from any clear understanding of its meaning. What is required is a healthy agnosticism, not a mean-spirited cynicism.

4. Definition in terms of connotation does not entail the existence of the featured object. Sometimes, however, our questions about existence may lead us down the wrong path. One possible way of avoiding 'the bewitchment of our intelligence by language' is to adopt a functional approach. Ask not whether rights exist, but how the language of rights is used.

5. It is not always clear where we should stop in giving definitions. Some definitions are highly technical and appeal to the 'experts', while others are relatively untechnical, suited to the 'ordinary person'. Sometimes definitions include explanations of contexts and causes. They may even include aspects of justification.

CONNOTATION: ANOTHER INTERPRETATION OF DEFINITION

The traditional interpretation of connotation concerns what Hospers calls 'designation', but this author underlines another sense of connotation which is important. 'The connotation of a word or phrase consists of the associations it has in the minds of the people who use it.'[47] Thus the word 'snake' designates defining characteristics of being legless and reptilian; denotes all the snakes existing on this earth; and *connotes* (in the minds of many) characteristics of being slimy and revolting.[48] Whether this sense of connotation is directly related to meaning is highly controversial. It has been argued, for instance, that the emotive connotations of a word reflect the effect of the word upon the hearer rather than the meaning of the word.

Hospers makes a distinction here between 'semantics' and 'pragmatics'. 'The semantics of a word is concerned with the relation of the word to its meaning, and the *pragmatics* of a word has to do with its effect upon its users, both speakers and hearers.'[49] Moral realists tend to play down the pragmatic aspect of meaning in favour of a semantic approach. For instance, in saying that 'torturing children is wicked' the truth of this utterance is independent of the emotive effect it evokes. A non-cognitivist, on the other hand, would, typically, deny the truth value of the utterance and stress instead the use of this kind of sentence in moulding attitudes and behaviour.[50] One compromise solution might be to accept the distinction between primary and secondary meaning, associating the pragmatics of a word with secondary meaning and semantics with primary meaning. Thus, if we say of a person that he is a 'snake', our primary sense of meaning is to convey that the person is an unsavoury character, untrustworthy, devious. Our secondary sense of meaning conveys our negative attitude towards the person which may include a desire to warn other people to avoid him.

In relation to the study of rights-language the distinction just made may also apply. We may wish to insist on primary, semantic meaning, concentrating on defining characteristics and denotation, while recognising that ordinary usage of the language of rights, in claiming certain goods or benefits for instance, reveals elements of secondary, pragmatic meaning. When we demand that our rights be respected we want others to have a 'pro-attitude'[51] towards us and to act favourably on our behalf. Our use of the term 'right' is partly chosen because it is likely to have such effects.

Hospers' examples of the main types of connotation of a word are instructive. Emotive connotation is just one example, but we should not ignore the others, in particular, 'Pictorial Meaning' and 'Poetic Meaning'.[52]

Pictorial meaning consists of the mental pictures evoked in the mind of the hearer or reader. We hear the word 'elephant' and perhaps a picture of an elephant comes to mind. Such an approach to meaning has some difficulties, as Hospers himself realises. Most obviously, there are some people who have very few mental pictures of words, yet still seem to grasp the meaning of these words. Thus, a person might have no mental picture of elephant, yet be able to give its defining characteristics, recognise various denotations of the word and even give a clear verbal definition. Again, it would appear that mental pictures are effects of the use of certain words, effects which vary widely from person to person, as well as depending on the word used – whether it is abstract or concrete. Pictorial meaning, if it is a form of meaning at all, would be part of the category of secondary meaning.

Similarly with regard to another form of connotation mentioned by Hospers – 'Poetic Meaning' – it is claimed that a special effect is intended, though the actual poetic utterance can be translated into bald prose. One wonders, however, whether what we have called secondary meaning is not in fact the thing of primary interest in writing poetry. We tend to feel that in the process of translating poetry into precise and concise prose something basic in terms of meaning has been lost.

It could be a wise move to delve further into the relevance of so-called 'pictorial' and 'poetic' meaning, by, for instance, questioning its secondary status. One question that comes to mind asks if Hospers is correct in stating that such meaning is purely the effect a word has on us when we hear it spoken or see it in print? I have no doubt that some words do evoke special effects and that our main intention in using certain words or terms is to move others in a specific way. However, I would question whether pictorial or poetic uses of language function in this way alone. I would suggest that pictorial and poetic approaches to language can actually bring out a deeper and richer meaning than a bland definition in ordinary prose. This would apply especially in the case of poetic meaning, where it is questionable whether we can translate metaphorical and symbolic terms precisely, without remainder. Hospers presents an example of a poetic utterance from Macbeth, 'Canst thou not minister unto a mind diseased?' and suggests as a translation 'Can't you help a lunatic?' (p. 50). Clearly the poetic effect has been ruined in the translation, but Hospers seems to suggest that we have lost an element of meaning as well. 'Lunatic' is only an approximation of 'a mind diseased', and 'help' misses out on the rich nuances of the phrase 'minister unto'.

What pictorial and poetic meaning suggests, I feel, is that there is a role for imagination in the definition and analysis of terms and concepts. Such an approach is widely advocated by religious writers where the role of definition is limited in the face of mystery, but there are strong arguments in favour of this approach in ethics as well.

THE ROLE OF IMAGINATION IN ETHICS

In her work on *Metaphorical Theology*, Sallie McFague[53] suggests a distinction between primary and secondary religious language. Primary religious language is essentially metaphorical and symbolic (p. 22). Secondary religious language is essentially conceptual, though she immediately qualifies her distinction saying that 'most primary religious language is implicitly conceptual and most secondary religious language is latently imagistic' (*ibid.*). The two forms of language are distinct, but not radically separate. As our author expresses the point:

Conceptual language tends toward univocity, toward clear and concise meanings for ambiguous multi-levelled imagistic language. In this process something is lost and something is gained: richness and multivalency are sacrificed for precision and consistency. (p. 26)

But, anxious to avoid the radical separation of the two forms, she hastens to add that:

The relationship, however, is symbiotic. Images 'feed' concepts; concepts 'discipline' images. Images without concepts are blind; concepts without images are sterile.[54]

I can see no reason to avoid applying a similar distinction and relationship between primary and secondary language in ethics. In fact, the language of rights seems to be open to the application of such a distinction. It may be the case that images precede concepts in metaethics, so that a proper analysis of our ethical terms requires some examination of the process of development from image to concept. If concepts 'discipline' images, as McFague suggests, a certain price has to be paid in terms of loss of 'richness and multivalency' so that a return to the underlying images could be highly profitable, suggesting other avenues we might travel towards conceptualisation. We might find, for instance, that the disciplining of certain imagery was over strict and that these images would richly reward any effort to revisit them. Or, again, using McFague's terminology and adapting the metaphor slightly, if images 'feed' concepts, then we starve ourselves by remaining stuck at the level of concepts. No wonder that a purely discursive metaethics seems so emaciated.

Note the difference between this position and Hospers' position on pictorial and poetic meaning. Hospers argued that these forms of meaning function in terms of a special effect which is supposedly created in the presence of certain words, and that such effects often seem to be of secondary value because they are so subjective. Different people have different capacities for imagining pictures related to words. Some people find it hard to picture at all. But my position here, following McFague, is that a special effort has to be made to uncover images which may be the foundation of many of our concepts. No claim is made that this comes naturally or is an automatic effect of the use of our concepts, be they technical or everyday common-sense concepts and terms. This special effort is a major part of the work of those engaged in metaethics. And it is primarily the work of our imagination, 'playing' with our terms and concepts.[55]

I have hinted that the language of rights may be open to an application of the distinctions between primary and secondary, imagistic and conceptual, language. This theme will be explored later in greater detail, but here we might mention in a general way how the common verbal definitions of 'right', such as claim, power, liberty, while having a strong conceptual appearance also have strong associative images. The activity of claiming, with its image of standing up for oneself or for others, is a good example of a definition which straddles the distinction between primary and secondary ethical language. Likewise, the term 'liberty' has a vital experiential base and conjures up images of release from slavery, dropping off shackles and bonds, openness to the future, hope and joy. Such words are not cold, precise definitions, but have immense suggestive power touching the heart of human existence.

IMAGINATION AND NORMATIVE ETHICS

The role of the imagination in ethics has received some attention from scholars in recent years, though the trend has been to apply moral imagination in the normative field rather than in the field of metaethics. The Roman Catholic moralist Philip S. Keane has written a full-length treatment of the influence of the imagination on normative ethics, but the concentration is mainly on the ways in which this faculty aids us in deepening our grasp of moral principles.[56] For instance, imagination may help in applying in a critical way principles such as those involved in the just war theory in relation to modern warfare, especially nuclear conflict. Keane declares that:

While Christians may not come up with formally different moral principles, Christians can articulate their principles through Christian symbols and stories. These symbols and stories can give Christians an ongoing imaginative way of developing their insights into and applications of moral principles, even though Christians hold these principles in common with other persons.[57]

Likewise, from within the Protestant moral tradition we find Stanley Hauerwas using the category of imagination in the context of a normative theory of virtue or character. In one of his works, *The Peaceable Kingdom*, he includes a chapter entitled 'Casuistry as a Narrative Art', where we find remarks of this kind: 'Casuistry is the reflection by a community on its experience to test imaginatively the often unnoticed and unacknowledged implications of its narrative commitments.'[58] Taking up a position enunciated by John Howard Yoder,[59] Hauerwas criticises as lacking in moral imagination the presentation of quandaries which promise a tragic scenario unless one equally tragic option is embraced. Such an approach, Hauerwas insists, 'is an attempt to still the imagination by accepting the "necessities" of certain descriptions. Moreover, those "necessities" too often simply assume the givens are the limit of my community, and never think of suggestive ways in which the community and myself might be asked to change our lives' (p. 124). Thus, moral imagination grounded in the particular tradition of a community, for instance the Christian tradition of martyrdom, may lead us to act in a novel fashion. Maybe we should not accept too quickly the option of self-defence when we are attacked, but at least consider imaginatively the option of sacrificing one's life.

These views on the value of moral imagination in normative ethics, both at the level of theory of obligation and theory of value, are important insights which add richness to normative theory. However, my emphasis on moral imagination stresses instead the metaethical dimension of our moral thinking and the role imagination plays in elucidating the meaning and justification of key ethical terms such as 'rights'. I suggest that a metaethical treatment of rights must embrace an imaginative approach which relates concept to image (metaphor and model), as well as the traditional discursive approach which relates concepts to one another.

My argument attempts to establish that both normative ethics and metaethics must for the sake of completeness embrace discursive and imaginative aspects, and that in each branch of ethics we will move back and forward between these aspects recognising their complementarity and also the healthy tension inherent in the distinction. Let me give one further example of the usefulness of an interplay between an imaginative approach in normative ethics and the metaethics of rights.

Judith Jarvis Thomson is noted for her fertile imagination in constructing interesting moral dilemmas and thought experiments. In one of her essays, 'Self-Defense and Rights',[60] she first takes an uncontroversial example of self-defence, where an aggressor driving a tank is going to run down a victim. Clearly, she says, the victim has a right to kill the aggressor to save himself. But what happened to the right to life of the aggressor – a right which is a human one or a natural one possessed unconditionally by all? Well, one answer is that by launching an attack on his victim the aggressor 'forfeited' his right to life. Imagine, however, Thomson asks us, that the tank breaks down, the aggressor dismounts – even breaking his ankles in the process. Obviously, this person is no longer a danger to the original victim. Is the person who was threatened with being run over now allowed to kill the tank-driver? Our intuitions now run in a different direction. The answer is negative, the reason being that the aggressor's right to life has returned. But now we must be puzzled about such rights, a puzzlement which must in turn impinge upon our efforts to define and analyse what a 'right' is. How can rights come and go so readily? What is forfeited in one instant is regained a minute later. How odd? Further, if the right to self-defence is a human right, possessed simply in virtue of our humanity, it is hard to see how it can be forfeited unless and until we stop being human.

This is not the place to argue the issue out. The example is presented with the intention of showing how a section of normative ethical theory, the doctrine of self-defence, when treated in an imaginative way challenges us at the metaethical level to be equally imaginative in our analysis of the meaning of the type of right said to be involved. To put it another way, when we examine moral dilemmas, of which more and more develop each day, as in the area of artificial reproduction and bioethics for instance, we come up against the open-texture of our moral concepts. And the response must involve a willingness to redefine or refine our concepts and definitions.

CONCLUSION

This introductory chapter has presented two major approaches to an analysis or elucidation of 'rights'. The first approach we may call the discursive mode, with its emphasis on concepts and their logical relations. A whole group of important issues was introduced which will reappear throughout this work. For instance, the complexity of the language of rights is largely due to the complexity of the job or function it is called upon to perform. One way of expressing this simply is to refer to the 'open-texture' of our normative concepts. On one hand we want to describe and evaluate normative relationships at a very general level using the terminology of 'human rights', while using an essentially similar form of language when highly specific normative relationships – special rights – are in question. Sometimes our use of language blinds us to central features of our moral concepts, as is seen in the tendency to use the possessive form of 'claim'. Thus, we are tempted to reify rights. Often, too, our normative positions push us to invent new terminology to support our moral judgements, as when we talk of 'manifesto rights'. Because we feel that the starving millions of our world ought to be fed, we want to apply the language of rights, even if this means developing a new category of claims or entitlements, which many find unsatisfactory. In a similar way, the doctrine of the correlativity of rights and duties is so complex that we have to revise our language with terms like 'discretionary' and 'mandatory' rights.

The second approach we may label the imaginative mode with its emphasis on images and the ways in which they are connected and interpreted. While this approach is being used more often in the development of normative ethics, its use at the metaethical level is relatively new. This, I have argued, is appropriate in the light of the interdisciplinary interest shown in the category of the imagination in recent years. In ethics or moral philosophy this approach is most appropriate, especially in view of the fact that moral language does not consist merely of bald descriptions of human behaviour, but is essentially evaluative. From the point of view of Christian ethics there is a further aspect of mystery and transcendence which only imagination can begin to grasp in so far as morality is said to involve an intimate relationship with God. The second half of my work concentrates almost exclusively on this imaginative approach to metaethics in terms of models and metaphors. But before we embark on that course let us return to the more discursive approach, beginning with attempted verbal definitions of rights by means of relevant equivalent words or synonyms.

CHAPTER 2

Initial elucidation of rights-language

INTRODUCTION

This chapter attempts to clarify the language of rights from the
point of view of a more discursive approach to metaethics. In
other words, the emphasis will be on the major questions
regarding definition and justification mentioned in an introductory way in the first half of the last chapter. I begin by
examining some terms which are widely regarded as being
practically synonymous with rights – 'claim', 'entitlement',
'power' and 'liberty'.[1] These terms should lead to a preliminary
grasp of the defining characteristics of all rights, legal or moral,
human or special, and so on. The focus is relatively wide or
general.

From this general level I proceed to elucidate the language of
rights at a more specialised level – that at which mostly legal
philosophers and some moral philosophers discuss the terms just
listed above. Thus, I devote some space to the work of Wesley
Hohfeld, whose distinctions concerning the language of rights in
the law have developed, according to some, a paradigmatic or
classic status. Hohfeld's analysis is then adapted to fit the moral
field through the interpretation of Carl Wellman. At this stage
it should have become clear that clarity in elucidating rights-
language does not automatically do away with controversy.
Indeed it will be seen how debate on this subject involves
differences of opinion at the metaethical, as well as at the
normative, level. Or, to put it another way, there is disagreement not merely regarding the answer to the question
what rights people have (a typically normative issue), but also

regarding the proper analysis of the concept of 'right' (a typically metaethical issue). It will be seen that reportive definitions of rights have limited usefulness, and that one is faced with a multiplicity of stipulative definitions at the jurisprudential and moral levels of analysis.

Some discussion follows on a set of basic difficulties connected with the Hohfeldian distinctions, all of which are, to an extent, interconnected: the doctrine of the correlativity of rights and duties, the value of liberty-rights (Hohfeldian privileges), and the important debate between those who advocate the 'Choice Theory' of rights and those who argue for the 'Benefit Theory'.

GENERAL ANALYSIS OF RIGHTS-LANGUAGE

Rights as 'claims'

It is quite common in moral and legal philosophy to associate rights with 'claims'.[2] The work of Joel Feinberg is especially significant here and is worth examining in more detail. In his article, 'The Nature and Value of Rights', Feinberg distinguishes different uses of the terminology of claiming. For instance, a person may 'make a claim to something'. Or someone may 'claim that' something or other is the case. Or then again an individual might, according to Feinberg, 'have a claim'.[3]

Feinberg presents typical examples of these usages. 'Making a claim to', for instance, is typified in those situations where a right-holder demands his due; often when something is acknowledged to be his – 'something borrowed, say, or improperly taken from him' (p. 150). Frequently a person makes a claim in such circumstances by presenting a chit, or IOU, in order to prove the basis of the claim or right. Feinberg further characterises this usage as 'performative claiming'.[4]

The second usage mentioned by Feinberg is given the title 'propositional claim'[5] and is clearly thought to have a weaker force than 'making a claim'. Again a homely example brings out the difference, 'Anyone can claim, of course, *that* this umbrella is yours, but only you can actually claim the umbrella'

(p. 150). For Feinberg, thinking of legal rights, making a legal claim to something has special legal force, while claiming that something is the case may be 'a mere piece of descriptive commentary with no legal force' (*ibid.*).

The third usage underlined by Feinberg, that of 'having a claim' is explained as follows: 'I would like to suggest that *having a claim consists in being in a position to claim, that is, to make claim or claim that.*'[6] In speaking thus Feinberg is actually introducing a note of criticism, for he goes on to remark: 'If this suggestion is correct it shows the primacy of the verbal over the nominative forms. It links claims to a kind of activity and obviates the temptation to think of claims as *things*, on the model of coins, pencils, and other material possessions which we can carry in our hip pockets' (*ibid.*).

Over all then, Feinberg's position on rights as claims stresses the activity of claiming, the 'performative' sense in which people actually demand their due. We shall see again the value of 'being in a position to make a claim', which is part of the description of one's having a 'justified or valid' claim. And we will encounter too the valuable link between the activity of claiming and the notion of human dignity.

Rights as 'entitlements'

For the understanding of the notion of rights as entitlements we enlist the aid of the Australian philosopher, H. J. McCloskey.[7] He rejects the association between rights and claims, and insists instead on the close link between rights and entitlements.

What is wrong with thinking of rights as claims? According to McCloskey, a right may provide a ground for claiming something, but it is not a claim in itself. He takes the example of the legal right to marry: 'My legal right to marry consists primarily in the recognition of my entitlement to marry and to have my act recognised. It indirectly gives rise to claims on others not to prevent me so acting, but it does not primarily consist in these claims.'[8]

Another example found in McCloskey's work concerns the fundamental right to life. This, he says, is not a right against anyone, though it may imply duties on the part of others to refrain from killing me. 'But it is essentially a right of mine, not a list of claims, hypothetical and actual, against an infinite number of actual, potential, and as yet nonexistent beings.'[9] In this way McCloskey appears to think of rights as entitlements in the sense of possessions, in opposition to Feinberg's emphasis on the verbal form of claiming. In effect, McCloskey's entitlements are closely akin to Feinberg's third meaning of claim – 'having a claim'.

I feel it is important at this stage to question this distinction between rights as claims and rights as entitlements. Surely these terms are closer in meaning than McCloskey is willing to admit. Feinberg and Wasserstrom tend to treat these terms as practically synonymous. For instance Wasserstrom uses them interchangeably in the following statement: 'Perhaps the most obvious thing to be said about rights is that they are constitutive of the domain of entitlements. They help to define and serve to protect those things concerning which one can make a very special kind of claim – a claim of right.'[10] And consider Feinberg's declaration: 'Generally speaking, only the person who has a title or who is qualified for it, or someone speaking in his name, can make claim to something as a matter of right. It is an important fact about rights (or claims), then, that they can be claimed only by those who have them.'[11]

So Feinberg has to make a further distinction between mere claims which are lacking in justification or validation, and justified or valid claims. This should answer the anxiety of those who object to the unqualified use of 'claim' which could include demands made without any moral or legal foundation. Helpful here is Alan White's distinction between 'making a claim' and 'having a claim'.[12] The former has no necessary relation to justification, whereas the latter has. The difference between the two, he argues, is like the difference between our 'making a point' and our 'having a point' in the course of an argument. Only the latter has a link with the notion of justification.

Perhaps we can defend Feinberg by giving him some credit for his attempt to distinguish between a claim understood as a mere demand and a valid claim where the demand has some

normative backing. Doubtless, however, he should have
brought out in a clearer way the ambiguity inherent in the idea
of 'making a claim'. Only on some occasions does a person who
makes a claim have a claim. Certainly in the quotation given
above he would have been more accurate in saying that 'It is an
important fact about rights (or claims), then, that they *may* be
claimed only by those who have them', and not merely that
'they *can* be claimed only by those who have them'. He should
have specified the normative sense of 'can' in this sentence,
something which the term 'may' includes.

Therefore it seems reasonable to identify 'entitlement' with a
particular form of claim – a 'valid' or 'justified' claim. The
notion of entitlement is not to be seen as starkly opposed to the
notion of claim. Nevertheless 'entitlement' has the advantage of
clearing up the ambiguity found in the language of claiming.[13]

Before passing on to another term used to elucidate rights, I
should mention an additional aspect of Feinberg's treatment of
rights as claims which can be seen as an improvement on
McCloskey's interpretation of rights as entitlements. Feinberg
insists that claims are always 'to' something *and* 'against'
someone.[14] McCloskey's analysis appears to play down the
second element of rights in favour of the first, that is, he places
the stress on what we have rights to, and tends to undervalue the
role of others in helping us to achieve the goods or values we
seek. The problem with this approach is that it tends to
undermine the important doctrine of the correlativity of rights
and duties which is one of the keys to understanding the nature
and value of the rights concept. However, McCloskey's viewpoint does underline one of the major problems in that doctrine
of correlativity, namely the 'untidiness' of our normative
relationships, of which more will be said shortly.

Rights as 'powers'

There is a long philosophical tradition which equates rights
with powers. S. I. Benn and R. S. Peters refer to this in their
discussion of positivist theories of rights, mentioning in particular the writings of Hobbes, Spinoza and Austin.[15] Clearly the

emphasis in legal positivism is on the sanction which gives backing to the exercise of rights, but there are serious problems in attempting to identify a right with the power to threaten some form of punishment if a correlative duty is not performed. Just what type of power might be involved in possessing rights?

Turning to McCloskey again, we note his opposition to any identification of rights with power. He insists that the right to vote, for example, is an entitlement to vote, but does not necessarily imply the actual 'power' to vote. Think of a laxly policed state, he suggests, where the 'power' to vote is merely notional and cannot be exercised.[16]

One way to respond to this objection is to distinguish between 'having a right' and 'exercising a right'. In the case of voting in an anarchic or insecure political system citizens have a right to vote, but find it difficult to exercise that right. In one sense of the term 'power' they are not (physically/psychologically) capable of arriving safely at the polling station, but in another sense they still have the 'power' to vote, that is a moral/legal status which cries out for recognition and protection. This point is well made in the following words of Michael Bertram Crowe:

A man's right to life can be described as his *moral* power to claim or demand that no one takes his life away. Normally, of course, a man is able to support this claim by physical force; he may repel an attack, using physical force to fight off his attacker. But we would easily recognise that the ability to fight off an attack is not the basis for his right to life. A champion boxer or a trained commando may be well able to use physical means to defend his life. But a handicapped or otherwise defenceless person, an infant, an old person, one who is paralysed for example, although unable physically to defend himself, has every bit as much a right to life as the strong man. What both the weak and the strong have in common is the *moral power* (that is, the right). And this moral power is far more important than the difference in their physical strength.[17]

This quotation harmonises quite well, I think, with our previous attempts to bring together entitlements and justified claims, for in Crowe's words a right is a moral power to claim some action or forbearance. The 'power' lies in the appeal of reason contained in the claim. 'Entitlement', 'valid claim' and 'moral/legal power' appear then to be practically synonymous on this analysis.

Rights as 'liberties'

As in the case of powers there is much historical backing for seeing a connection between rights and 'liberties'. White points to this linkage in a summary fashion:

> The plausibility of an equation of rights and liberties is strengthened by the fact that most of the famous Bills of Rights from Magna Carta to the United Nations Declaration of Human Rights mention and list, seemingly indifferently, both rights and liberties. Furthermore, the history of most struggles for human rights is largely an account of a fight for freedom against oppressive laws and governments.[18]

When discussing the relationship between rights and 'liberties' or 'freedoms' it is essential to distinguish between liberties as the objects of certain rights, and liberty or freedom as part of the elucidation of the concept of rights. (Similarly, powers can be the objects of rights and part of their elucidation.) It makes sense to say that people have rights to certain liberties or freedoms, for example freedom of conscience, freedom of association, and so on. But in this section I am more interested in liberty or freedom as an aspect of the elucidation of the nature and value of rights-talk. Having a right is in this light a fundamental freedom on which other aspects of freedom build as their foundation.

I tend to understand the concept of liberty in a way that is very close to my understanding of the other terms used to elucidate rights. For example, returning to McCloskey's discussion of the 'right to vote', this right can be understood equally as a 'liberty', not necessarily in the sense of having *de facto* physical freedom to exercise one's franchise, though this freedom is also sought, but as a moral or legal freedom having a special power of its own, if only to challenge the consciences of others. Where a person's freedom or liberty in a particular sphere is justified, that person is free to claim, has a power to claim, and is entitled to claim, some value or good.

This section of general clarification and elucidation has been an effort to show important links between the various terms used to express the meaning of rights. Although some philosophers have their preferences for certain specific usages, and are critical of others, my position has involved an attempt to harmonise these different approaches, so that the various terms in use are found to be complementary.

The language of 'claiming' and 'entitlement' is narrower in its focus than the language of 'power' and 'freedom'. To refer to rights as entitlements has a special advantage of underlining the justificatory element in claiming something, though on its own the term 'entitlement' sounds rather technical and abstract. The language of claims and claiming in turn suffers from some ambiguity until one qualifies it, adding the aspect of justification – valid or justified claim. The possessive usage of the language of claims was found to be defective in so far as it encourages a false image of rights as things on the analogy of physical possessions. However the verbal form is a helpful corrective, stressing as it does the activity of claiming. In addition, this verbal form is enlightening in its implication that rights are held against others as well as being related to goods or values needed by the moral agent.

Connecting rights with 'powers' and 'liberties' brings about a change of focus to a more general level of analysis. The most obvious drawback of using these terms is that they are not synonymous with rights, as valid claim and entitlement appear to be. Having a right may involve having a power or a liberty, but the language of rights presents only a limited grasp of the rich texture and application of these concepts. We find ourselves in a position, then, in which a relatively limited concept – rights – is being elucidated with the aid of a relatively wide concept or concepts. Therefore, we have to discern the specific aspects of freedom and power that have a direct relationship with rights, distinguishing these from other aspects that have a more tenuous relationship.

Such wide-ranging concepts as power and freedom can cause confusion in our project of analysing rights, though it must be admitted that the linkage may help in pointing out new horizons for our study. Furthermore, the language of freedom and power has the advantage of being relatively familiar, albeit a deceptive familiarity at times, concealing as it does a depth of meaning in need of exploration. These terms are also to an extent evaluative, and therefore play a valuable role in the justification of the terminology of rights. Freedom and liberty in particular have positive connotations in modern society, so that associating rights with these notions tends to give a degree of respectability to the language of rights. Power, however, is a different matter, being more ambiguous from the moral point of view. Still, when it is argued that rights as powers imply an enablement of the oppressed to live a decent and dignified life, then rights seen in this perspective again achieve a degree of respectability. In later chapters I intend to concentrate in a deeper way on the rich meaning of freedom and power in order to draw out the meaning of rights. For the moment though I shall continue on my course to elucidate rights-language discursively by dwelling on a more specific analysis of rights-talk at the level of jurisprudence.

SPECIFIC ANALYSIS: HOHFELD'S DISTINCTIONS

It is a major aim of mine to suggest that Christian ethics can benefit greatly from paying close attention to the detailed analysis of rights-language which is found in moral philosophy and jurisprudence. This is one reason why this chapter has been so heavily analytical. My next step is to take some of the terms discussed above and to look at them in a more specific, technical light. First, I shall note the limited meanings given to the terms 'claim', 'liberty', 'power' and 'immunity' within the legal sphere, especially in the work of the distinguished American jurist Wesley Hohfeld. Then I shall refer to one attempt to translate these specialised terms to the moral sphere, since it is the reality of moral rights that most concerns us.

Among those impressed by the Hohfeldian distinctions is T. D. Perry who suggests that this analysis of rights-language is 'a paradigm of philosophy'. 'A paradigm', he argues, 'gives exactness of analysis and solving or illuminating power'.[19]

What exactly is paradigmatic about Hohfeldian analysis? One answer is provided by Samuel Stoljar in this summary statement:

Hohfeld was certainly not the first to recognise 'right' as a very ambiguous word, but his was the first attempt to sort out the meanings systematically. Arranging rights according to their various correlatives and opposites, he divided them into two squares: one based on claims and liberties, the other comprising powers and immunities.[20]

It is generally held that, for Hohfeld, the square consisting of claims and liberties was of primary importance. 'Claims' are in fact 'rights' in the strict sense, and must be distinguished carefully from 'liberties' as well as from the other fundamental legal concepts, 'powers' and 'immunities'. A person has a claim to something against another in so far as the other person has a duty to the right-holder regarding that object. John Finnis expresses this in a technical way when he states that, 'to assert a Hohfeldian right is to assert a three-term relation between one person, one act-description, and one other person'.[21] Another way of stating Hohfeld's formulation of 'claim-rights' is to say that here he holds the strictest form of the correlativity of rights and duties.

If claim-rights are rights in the strict sense, what then of the other half of the square – liberty-rights, or what Hohfeld called 'privileges'? Stoljar explains the difference:

In the case of a liberty, the respective incidents are different. Instead of asserting a right in x together with a duty in y, we rather assert, Hohfeld thinks, that x has a right to do p in the sense of having a liberty to do what he is doing without x having any corresponding claims against y since y is under no correlative duty toward x.[22]

Let me give some examples of each kind of right to illustrate the differences between them. A typical claim-right would be any so-called 'special right',[23] those rights which arise from entering into an agreement with another person, say, by promise or contract. If I borrow some money from a friend and agree to repay it within a certain period, then I give my friend a (special) right to expect the return of the loan. He can claim against me, and, correlatively, I have a duty to repay the sum as I promised.

In other words, I have no liberty not to repay the money as long as my friend holds me to my duty. My freedom is strictly limited by my friend's claim-right. Similarly, in the category of 'human rights'[24] the values involved are so important that the link between right and duty is usually regarded as quite strict. In fact, human rights are often said to be 'inalienable',[25] that is they cannot be waived by the right-holder, and the correlative duty-bearer cannot be released from his duty or obligation.

Turning now to liberties one recognises at once that the connection between the right-holder and relevant others is much looser than in the case of claims. For instance, my right to look at my neighbour over the garden wall is a common liberty-right. I have no duty in ordinary circumstances to refrain from looking at him. However my neighbour has no correlative duty or obligation to make himself available to be looked at by me; he can stay indoors if he so wishes. Furthermore, my neighbour can, within reason, obstruct my liberty to look at him by, for instance, erecting a garden fence or screen. Other examples of liberties involve situations such as when two persons see a sum of money on the ground, each has a liberty-right to pick it up, and neither person is obliged to give way to the other in the attempt to possess the object.[26]

This last example is important since it points to a category where liberty-rights have some utility, namely economic competition. As Hart puts it, 'The moral propriety of all economic competition implies this minimum sense of "a right" in which to say that "x has a right to" means merely that x is under no "duty" not to' (*ibid.*). Consider, for instance, the competition between shopkeepers. If I should open a shop in a certain line of business near another shop involved in the same trade, I may (if I am efficient enough) damage my fellow shopkeeper's business. But I have a liberty to do this, given the rules of fair competition. Presumably, of course, one has no intention of damaging another person's welfare in a malicious manner; one simply goes about one's own work, with the consequence that other enterprises in the vicinity suffer due to one's legitimate efforts. Competitors cannot complain that fellow-competitors are failing in their duties in the very activity of being in competition because ordinarily there is no such duty to avoid competition. So, paradoxically, there is a right possessed by people which in certain circumstances actually permits them to harm others in going about their legitimate business.

It was in fact an example from this sphere which Hohfeld discussed when criticising the legal confusion between claims and liberties. In the case of *Quinn v Leathem* (1901)[27] the plaintiff, Leathem, was a butcher who had been pressurised by a trade union (represented by Quinn) to sack all non-unionised employees in his shop and to replace them with union members. The union tried to achieve this aim by putting pressure on one of Leathem's customers not to deal with him, as a result of which Leathem suffered financial damage, and for which he demanded and received compensation.

Lord Lindley's judgement in favour of the employer was based on the general right everyone has to pursue whatever lawful business or employment he or she chooses. In his opinion, this right implied a correlative duty on the part of others not to interfere in another's legal business without lawful justification.[28] Hohfeld, however, argued that the 'right' in question was not a claim but a privilege or liberty. Thus the defendants had no right against Leathem that he refrain from going about his lawful business, but this did not include a positive duty committing them to non-interference.

Stoljar explains the fallacy Hohfeld considered had been made in this judgement as follows:

Hohfeld's view was that the court here confused the plaintiff's liberty with his right to carry on business; the court committed a *non sequiter* in concluding that because the plaintiff undoubtedly had a liberty to pursue his business, he therefore had a right to pursue it; the fallacy was to transform a liberty, the correlative of which was only a no-right, into a right with a corresponding duty not to interfere.[29]

There is some doubt whether Hohfeld was correct in his interpretation of the court's decision, but I shall allow his criticism to go unchallenged, simply presenting this case as an example or illustration of the legal distinction between claims and liberties.

As well as distinguishing between claim-rights and liberty-rights Hohfeld presented another square which focuses on the distinction between 'powers' and 'immunities'.[30] Again, as in the square of claims and liberties, this involves a set of jural correlatives and opposites. Claims are correlative with duties, and are opposed to 'no-rights'. Liberties are correlative with no-rights and opposed to duties. What then of powers and immunities?

In his book, *Legal Philosophies*, J. W. Harris gives a brief account of the elements of this second square:

To say that A has a power entails that he can by his voluntary act change the legal relations of some other person, B, who has a correlative liability; and that it is not true that A has a disability as against B's legal relation, correlating with an immunity of B.[31]

The main example of these relationships suggested by Harris is that of a man, A, sending a letter to B. The context of this letter from A to B is a previous letter from B to A making A a specific offer. A's letter is an acceptance of the offer in the form of a contract. In this way, A has a power to enter into the contract and B has a correlative liability to have certain contractual relations created. It also follows that if A has a power to enter into a contract, he must not suffer from any disability in doing so – this is one of the jural opposites. And if B has a liability correlative to A's power, B cannot have an immunity against A. Unless one voluntarily enters into a contract or makes a promise, one has an immunity-right against others not to take on the contractual relations. This right protects one in particular from the paternalistic interventions of others.

AN ETHICAL TRANSLATION OF THE HOHFELDIAN DISTINCTIONS

The question now to be faced is how the legal distinctions just discussed can be translated into the moral sphere? After all, this work is mainly concerned with moral rights, though much of the analysis so far covers material which is a basic common denominator underlying all rights-talk. Can the Hohfeldian distinctions be applied morally? One philosopher who answers affirmatively is Carl Wellman. Here is a brief summary of his approach to this question:

Just as a legal right is a complex system of legal advantages, so an ethical right is a complex system of ethical advantages, a cluster of ethical liberties, claims, powers and immunities. At the centre of every ethical right stands some unifying core, one or more ethical advantages that define the essential content of the right. Thus, at the centre of my ethical right to dress as I please is my ethical liberty of wearing in public any decent clothing I wish, and the core of my ethical right to protection of the laws is my ethical claim against the state that its legal system afford me just as much protection as it affords any other individual subject to it. Around the core of any ethical right cluster an assortment of associated ethical liberties, claims, powers and immunities. What ties these ethical elements together into a single right is the way in which each associated element contributes some sort of freedom or control to the possessor of the right. Because freedom and control are two aspects of autonomy, any ethical right can accurately be thought of as a system of ethical autonomy.[32]

The terms 'core' and 'cluster' bring out the central features of Wellman's theory. A situation which involves rights cannot usually be reduced to one legal or ethical relationship, but typically I may isolate some core concept or relation which is primary and around which the other legal or ethical relationships cluster in support. The core concept of a right tells me the kind of protection I can expect for my interests in that area. Thus if someone owes me a sum of money, the core right is a claim against that person. Then if that person refuses to repay me, I may exercise my ethical power to seek compensation, either through the legal system or through moral suasion. Furthermore, I can argue that no other party has the ethical power to stop me from claiming or using my ethical power to seek redress – this is what is called an ethical immunity. Then again, I may have the ethical liberty to waive the payment of the sum of money.

Each of the Hohfeldian distinctions, with its correlative and opposite, can be translated into the ethical sphere. Ethical claims are correlative with ethical duties, and their opposites are no-rights. Ethical liberties are correlative with no-rights, and their opposites are duties. Ethical powers are correlative with liberties, and opposed to disabilities. Immunities are correlative with disabilities, and are opposed to liabilities. In these cases it becomes clear that the essence of a right is some kind of relationship of advantage before another. No wonder Wellman can say that

No one who has studied Hohfeld can imagine for a moment that the content of the right to life is simply life. He forces us to ask whether the right to life is essentially the liberty to defend one's life when under attack or the claim against being killed by another or the power to sue in the courts for legal protection of one's life or all of these or none of them.[33]

Yet often when one reads literature on the subject of rights the impression is given that the content of rights is simply the good or value in need of protection, when the emphasis should be placed on the kind and degree of protection that is sought, and the appropriateness of such protection for that particular value. This point will be made again and again in this thesis; in fact, it has already been made a number of times, as in Feinberg's insistence that rights are both claims to something and claims against somebody; and recall Finnis' remark that rights assert a three-term relation between one person, one act-description, and one other person.

SOME CONTROVERSIES IN THE ANALYSIS OF RIGHTS

Already in our section on the general analysis of rights-language, some disagreement was noted concerning the appropriateness of certain common terms used to elucidate rights. In the more technical analysis of rights-language – the Hohfel-dian distinctions – I held back from including the disagreements on the appropriateness of these legal and ethical concepts. This was done in order to avoid making the section too long and to avoid confusion over technical terms. At this stage, however, it may be worthwhile to mention a few difficulties regarding the analysis of rights and rights-language given so far.

The correlativity of rights and duties

The centrality of this doctrine in discussions of rights-language has been hinted at already. Feinberg's 'claims against' seem to suggest some binding force concerning others in relation to one's interests. Hohfeld's 'claim-rights' are said to be rights 'in the strict sense', and are defined in terms of another's obligation or duty. Downie and Telfer state that 'rights and obligations are opposite sides of the same coin: if there is a duty to treat people in a certain way they thereby have a right to be so treated.'[34] There are many other examples of both philosophers and theologians taking this correlativity for granted.[35] However, this doctrine has also been heavily criticised in recent years.

Before actually discussing some of the problems of correlativity I must warn the reader of further complications which arise from the point of view of duties and obligations. In first place, some philosophers distinguish between 'duties' and 'obligations'. For instance, C. H. Whitely[36] argues that the moral philosophical sense of both duty and obligation is related to the right thing to do in the sense of the best thing to do, or what a virtuous man would do. But, he argues, there is another sense in which duties and obligations are related to particular roles; think of the duties of one's station or one's state in life, what society expects of one. The two meanings are not synonymous, since there is no contradiction in saying that a person ought not to do his duty in one sense of that word. This is the case because sometimes what is expected of people in certain roles is judged to be morally wrong.

To make matters more complicated, Alan White insists that one make further distinctions between 'having an obligation', 'being obliged' and 'ought'.[37] Feinberg, in one of his studies of the correlativity of rights and duties, reminds the reader of the complexity of the concept of duty as well as that of right, since he gives nine different types of duty, and attempts to relate them to rights.[38] Hart, too, recognises the need to distinguish between 'duty' and 'obligation'. He declares that '"duty", "obligation", "right", and "good" come from different segments of morality, concern different types of conduct, and make different types of moral criticism or evaluation'.[39] For my purposes here I shall ignore the distinctions between duties and obligations, and between the notions of 'ought', having an 'obligation', and 'being obliged', as they are not central to the kinds of criticism I shall be mentioning with regard to correlativity of rights and duties.

The strictest correlativity between rights and duties would hold that for every right there is a duty and for every duty a right. I think that such a doctrine would be difficult to defend. In my opinion, the stronger correlativity lies between rights and duties rather than between duties and rights. In other words, all rights involve some duty on the part of another or others, but not all duties entail rights on the part of others.

What duties do not entail correlative rights? One example might be duties of beneficence or of charity. These are sometimes called duties of 'imperfect obligation'. John Stuart Mill explains this reality:

Now it is known that ethical writers divide moral duties into classes, denoted by the ill-chosen expressions, duties of perfect and of imperfect obligation; the latter being those in which, though the act is obligatory, the particular occasions of performing it are left to our choice; as in the case of charity or beneficence, which we are indeed bound to practise, but not towards any definite person, nor at any prescribed time. In the more precise language of philosophical purists, duties of perfect obligation are those duties in virtue of which a correlative right resides in some person or persons; duties of imperfect obligation are those moral obligations which do not give birth to any right.[40]

It seems to me that Mill's distinction applies well enough to the relationship between citizens of developed lands and their poorer brothers and sisters in the so-called 'developing countries'. Those who are reasonably well-off in the Western World seem to have some duty to share at least part of their surplus earnings with the poor of the Third World, but given the number of people and the number of regions in need at any one time, it is practically impossible to situate a strict relationship of duty and right between a householder in Britain, say, and a refugee in the Sudan or Ethiopia. The only exception

I can think of to this rule would be in cases where a wealthy country developed its wealth partly from a poor country during an imperial era, and now owes some restitution.[41]

There are other examples, too, of duties which do not appear to be correlated with rights, though some of these cases are controversial. One might argue for instance that humans have duties to animals, while denying that animals have rights. Some philosophers have stood in favour of the 'rights' of animals, while others have opposed this move.[42] One way of getting around the duty/right correlation here might be to use McCloskey's distinction between 'duties to' and 'duties concerning'.[43] I can have a duty to someone, but not to an animal. Here, the 'duty to' concept involves a personal relationship which is characteristic of the duty/right correlation. However, I can have a duty concerning an animal (and McCloskey includes things, for example paintings and art) which would not entail a correlative right, because of the impossibility (by definition) of having an interpersonal relationship with an animal.

Other examples of duties without correlative rights are given by White, some of which are decidedly odd and unconvincing. Thus, he says that the judge has a duty to punish an offender, but this does not entail a correlative right. True enough, it would be odd to say that an offender has a right to be punished, but it is quite sensible to say that a judge has a duty to punish someone, which is correlative to the rights of citizens to be protected from criminal elements.[44] He also says that a prisoner of war's duty to escape does not imply his captor's right to help him to escape, but this is to miss out on the fact that the escapee's right is most likely against fellow prisoners who might be opposed to the escape plan and in favour of submitting to the enemy regime.

Perhaps there is more sense in his example of a duty to bury the dead – with no correlative right on the part of the dead? And he thinks that a person's duty to himself does not have a correlative right. If one has a duty to oneself, does this mean that one can waive one's right against oneself? This seems very odd indeed. Nevertheless, such examples do suggest that there will be difficulties often in correlating duties with rights, at least in a one-to-one correspondence.

From the point of view of rights correlative with duties, there have been some voices of dissent from the strict view that all rights entail duties. One such voice has been that of David Lyons,[45] who points out that correlativity works well enough in cases of Hohfeldian claim-rights, but not so well in cases of Hohfeldian liberty-rights.

For Lyons, claim-rights are exemplified in contracts and promises which give rise to special moral rights. These rights are the paradigm of correlativity, according to Lyons, because of the relation between the content of the right and the content of the duty:

Rights and duties not only connect ordered pairs (or sets) of persons; they also have contents. By 'contents' I mean, *what* it is that A has a right to and *what* it is that B has a duty or obligation to do. These also must have a definite relation if we are to be able to infer the right or the obligation from the other directly, and *a fortiori* if rights and duties are to be regarded, even in this limited class of cases, as conceptual correlatives.[46]

An example of the connection between the contents of a right and a duty is where one person owes a sum of money to another. In a case like this Lyons would say that 'the content of the right is related to the expression of the content of the obligation as the passive is related to the active voice' (p. 48). In respecting the right of A, B gives the money to A (active voice), and A receives the money from B (passive voice), who thus discharges his duty to A.

Once the paradigm of correlativity is understood, Lyons considers cases that fall away from this paradigm. Most obviously this occurs, he thinks, in the case of liberty-rights. He takes what he considers to be a typical liberty – the 'right' to freedom of speech. A liberty-right is defined in terms of a person having no duty not to do something, and the correlative entails that others have no right that the right-holder refrain from so acting if she wishes. But Lyons' point is that the freedom to speak is not supported by a real right against others, since others have no duty to listen to a stranger speak.[47]

In fact, the general possession of this liberty seems to allow for others to heckle and interrupt one's speech if they so wish. Surely there is some protection of this liberty in terms of correlative duties? Surely, a person speaking in public in ordinary circumstances cannot be gagged forcibly? Indeed, a person has a right not to be gagged or assaulted; in fact, this is a strict claim-right rather than a liberty. The point about this, however, is that such a claim-right has little to do directly with the liberty-right to speak freely. Lyons argues that the right not to be gagged or assaulted is part of a general right not to be attacked, and this could conceivably remain as a right if the right to freedom of speech were withdrawn. So there seems to be no strict duty correlative to the right of freedom of speech as such, and the content of that liberty-right is not mirrored by the content of a particular duty towards the right-holder, as is supposed to occur for strict correlativity to exist.

In reply to Lyons, David Braybrooke makes a number of points. In fact, the title of his article, 'The Firm but Untidy Correlation of Rights and Obligations' reveals something of his basic position on this question. He says of Lyons' position:

There are clear signs in Lyons's work of a tendency to take for real the tidy consequences that would be features of social life if men's actions and institutions fulfilled certain ideals of logical economy.[48]

Braybrooke insists that Lyons has missed out on the 'open texture' of the concept of the correlativity of a right and an obligation. For instance, in relation to the right to freedom of speech, there are corresponding obligations that can be worked out in a normative ethical system. And these obligations are not simply to refrain from assault; they also could include the duty to avoid extravagant heckling, or jamming loudspeakers. He asks if flying a sky-writing aeroplane might not be considered as a violation of this liberty-right, or, in the case of an indoor meeting, turning up the thermostat?[49] Braybrooke argues that this open-texture with regard to the content of obligations correlative with rights may redound to our advantage by allowing further precedents to be introduced to the legal system. Clearly, rights like that of freedom of speech are more complicated in their operation than the right to be repaid a loan. In the latter case either the sum of money is repaid or withheld, whereas in the former case the freedom to speak may be respected or not respected in various degrees, simply because each person has an equal right, a fact which leads to the problem of arbitrating between conflicting freedoms or liberties.

It is worth noting here Braybrooke's argument for the firm correlation between rights and duties, a correlation which remains firm in spite of the untidiness of the connection. Any right must involve some protection for the right-holder, and duties provide such a protection. Consider, he says, a person testifying that N has the right to do x, for example to speak in public freely. The witness is asked to consider all sorts of actions interfering with N's right: threats, assaults, extravagant heckling and so forth. In every case she denies that people acting in that way fail in their duty to N. In effect, the witness refuses to agree that they ought to refrain from interfering with N. But in saying all this she makes the original claim concerning N's right empty (p. 361). Hence every right must have some correlation with some duty, even though the exact correlation may be difficult to establish.

Earlier, I mentioned duties of beneficence or of charity and the difficulty of linking these to individual rights. Looked at from the perspective of rights this also presents a problem of correlation. Feinberg, for instance, argues that statesmen often use the term 'claim' in a special sense, a 'manifesto sense' of 'right'. As he puts it,

The manifesto writers on the other side who seem to identify needs, or at least basic needs, with what they call 'human rights,' are more properly described, I think, as urging upon the world community the moral principle that *all* basic human needs ought to be recognised as *claims* (in the customary *prima facie* sense) worthy of sympathy and serious consideration right now, even though, in many cases, they cannot yet plausibly be treated as *valid* claims, that is, as grounds of any other people's duties.[50]

I am not sure that I agree with Feinberg when he says that these 'manifesto rights' are not valid claims. It seems to me that they are valid, but that these rights cannot be exercised at present. Morally speaking basic human needs ought to be fulfilled, and, in so far as they are not at present fulfilled, it is arguable that human injustice is a contributory factor. It seems quite appropriate to me that manifesto rights to food in the face of starvation entail some duties on the part of the so-called 'Superpowers' who spend so much human resources on weapons of destruction. And if this remark sounds too general, I think it may be made more specific and applied to individual citizens of the developed countries – to put pressure on politicians to consider the poor of the world, and not just narrow national issues. If democracy means anything, surely it requires this kind of responsibility. However, all this said, it will have to be recognised that many of the poorer inhabitants of the world will not be able to exercise their manifesto rights for some time, due in part to the unwillingness of people in the developed lands to recognise correlative duties. It takes some degree of wisdom to see how individual duties here in the West are correlated with rights in the Third World.

The value of liberties

The sense of 'liberty' I want to discuss here is again the technical Hohfeldian one, whereby a party has no-duty-not-to do something. The correlative is usually seen as a 'no-right', in the sense that others have no claim against me if I act in accordance with my liberty. The shopkeeper next door has no right against me if I start a business in competition with his; each of us has an equal liberty-right in the eyes of the law, and it is simply a question of co-existing or 'Let the best man win'.

There have been some criticisms levelled at this statement of 'liberty-rights'. First, Hohfeld is often criticised for entitling liberty-rights 'privileges'. Glanville Williams explains that in the usual sense of the term a privilege is a permission given to a single person or to a few people, it cannot be given to all; but a liberty may be possessed by all, for example freedom of speech.[51] Second, the correlatives and opposites mentioned by Hohfeld regarding liberties/privileges have been corrected. Where Hohfeld stated that a liberty was correlative with a no-right and opposed to duty, Williams corrects this, saying that the correlative of liberty is in fact a 'no-right-not', while the opposite of liberty is not necessarily a duty, since a party may have a liberty to do his duty (p. 1135).

An example of the correlation between liberty and no-right-not is a father's right to chastise his child. This is a liberty-right in that the father has no duty not to chastise his child. But the correlative to this in the case of the child is that the child has no right not to be chastised. Regarding the relation between liberty and duty, it is not always the case that these are opposed. Williams tells his readers that there is a different use of the term 'liberty' between law and philosophy. In legal circles a liberty may not involve any choice: 'the lawyer can accept as a liberty what is simply an absence of duty to act otherwise' (p. 1139). And he insists that it follows that there is a liberty to perform a legal duty.

I believe that in moral philosophy and in Christian ethics there may be a similar liberty to do just one thing, the right thing, and that this involves the basic choice between good and evil. In fact, by definition, a liberty involves having no duty not to do something, and this is perfectly compatible logically with having a duty to do the same thing. My duty to respect the life of others is compatible with my having no duty not to do this. Thus, there seem to be two different senses of liberty: one is the usual sense in which it does not matter whether I do x or not; the other being the sense in which I must do x if I am to respect my moral and/or legal freedom. If this sounds rather abstract, let me mention another example from Williams to make the distinctions concrete.

When a prisoner has completed his sentence, the warden may say to him 'You are at liberty to go.' On one hand, this means that the prisoner has no duty not to leave; he will not be committing a criminal offence by leaving. But in addition to this he has no right to stay on at the state's expense. He is not free to stay. In such a case liberty is not opposed to duty but implies both absence of duty (to stay) and positive duty (to leave).[52]

This discussion of claims and liberties brings me to a more basic problem – the value of liberties in the first place. If rights are supposed to protect one's freedom to act or not to act, what protection do liberties really give? The legal case just discussed brings into question the value of liberties as protection. If my liberty means that others have no real duty of non-interference in my regard, and even have permission to harm me indirectly in following out their own projects, what advantage is there in calling a liberty a right.

Some efforts have been made to attach protection to liberties. H. L. A. Hart, for instance, has suggested that liberties have a 'protective perimeter' which gives some 'security against the cruder forms of interference,' for example assault or trespass.[53] He mentions Bentham's distinction between 'naked rights' and 'vested/established rights': the former are liberties without the perimeter of protective obligations; the latter are liberties with this perimeter (p. 181). A somewhat similar distinction is found in Williams' article. There he distinguishes between a 'protected liberty' and a 'bare liberty': the former is exemplified in situations where a statute expressly enacts that it will be lawful to do something; the latter refers to situations where the statute book simply refrains from forbidding the conduct in question.[54] In the legal world, then, the language of liberty is used in a strong and a weak sense from the point of view of limiting the freedom of others.

The danger here, it seems to me, is that the strong sense of liberty may easily become a claim-right with correlative duties, while, on the other hand, the weak sense loses the meaning of a right altogether because of the absence of any real protection for the liberty-holder. Still, there is some sense in maintaining the language of liberties, for application to situations of competition and conflict where each party is justified in pursuing his or her own projects to the detriment of others. It is very much a *laissez-faire* type of legal and moral reality, since my liberty offers me a minimum of protection *vis-à-vis* others. However, this minimum is still important; it amounts to a basic claim against others to permit me to carry out my project within set limits. It does not, however, amount to a claim that others positively help me in my projects, or that they refrain from harming me indirectly in their own pursuit of similar goods.

I would like at this stage to introduce two basic theories of the essence of rights with the help of a further criticism sometimes levelled against Hohfeld. In the words of Harris:

In particular, it can be urged that Hohfeld's analytic squares fail to bring out the essence of the concept of a legal right. He says that we should distinguish four senses in which the word 'right' is sometimes used – right, privilege, power, immunity – but does not pose the question whether there is some underlying idea which explains all these uses. He does not take sides in the time-honoured debate between those who favour a 'will' or an 'interest' conception of 'right'. These schools are represented in modern British legal philosophy by Professor Hart and Professor MacCormick.[55]

The Choice Theory

Hart presents his 'Will' or 'Choice' theory as follows:

The idea is that of one individual being given by the law exclusive control, more or less extensive, over another person's duty so that in the area of conduct covered by that duty the individual is a small-scale sovereign to whom the duty is owed.[56]

And he then goes on to declare that the fullest measure of control over the duty of another comprises of three elements: (1) The right-holder may waive or extinguish the exercise of the right or leave it in existence by refusing to insist on the performance of the correlative duty. (2) In the case of a breach of a right or its threatened breach, the right-holder may leave it unenforced, or it may be enforced by, for example, suing for compensation. (3) The party may waive or extinguish the right to have due compensation paid (*ibid.*, pp. 192–3). The emphasis, then, is on control of another's duty, such that duties with their correlative rights 'are a species of normative property belonging to the right-holder'.[57]

A major advantage of this approach to rights is that it allows some flexibility in the normative relationship between persons, segments of whose lives are joined by rights and duties. The concept of waiving a right is of utmost importance in the context of normative relationships between persons, especially in view of the reality of frequent conflicts of rights. Often the ability to waive a right is a greater sign of moral character than the insistence on claiming our due.

Unfortunately, however, the disadvantages of the choice theory are also evident, so much so that Hart has to some extent distanced himself from this position in recent years.[58] Some of these disadvantages have been listed by G. Marshall.[59] For one thing, Hart's theory seems to apply more to the sphere of civil law rather than to the sphere of criminal law – in the latter one's freedom to waive rights is quite limited as public order may require one to apply the full rigour of the law to offenders. Another example comes from the sphere of games and their specific regulations. Thus, the football player cannot waive his right not to be tripped. There are some things, then, which one does not feel ought to be a matter of free choice. There are values which one must respect in one's own life and in the lives of others, and which form the content of rights we have called mandatory and inalienable.

Finally, there is the problem for Hart of how to cater for the so-called rights of children and the severely handicapped, individuals with little or no capacity to control the duties of others towards themselves. Carl Wellman takes the choice theory to its logical extreme in his discussion of consent to medical research on children when he denies that very young children have moral or human rights. He holds instead that parents' consent to research in this matter is really a case of their waiving their own right against others interfering in the process of caring for their children.[60]

The Benefit/Interest Theory

Associated with the names of a number of philosophers and legal thinkers,[61] its essence is summarised in these words of D. N. MacCormick:

To ascribe to all members of a class c a right to treatment т is to presuppose that т is, in all normal circumstances, a good for every member of c, and that т is a good of such importance that it would be wrong to deny it or withhold it from any member of c.[62]

MacCormick uses the example of children's rights to illustrate the theory. He is of the opinion that 'at least from birth, every child has a right to be nurtured, cared for, and, if possible, loved, until such time as he or she is capable of caring for himself or herself' (*ibid.*, p. 305). But what of the Choice Theory which claims that talk of the 'rights' of children makes no sense because of their inability to release others from correlative duties? Could there be a case for children's rights based on the idea of proxy waivers? MacCormick points out that the British legal system has the power to take children from parents who do not fulfil their duties of care towards them.

But this is not an example of the state waiving the children's right to care, or releasing the parents from their duty, since the parents may in fact be punished for not carrying out their duty, and, anyway, in all cases it is the interests of the children that are in question, not the question whether the children can release their parents from their duties. A strong case can be made out for the state claiming rights for children in place of their parents, but the case for the state and for others to waive the rights of children is more difficult to establish. Indeed, it may be that children, like adults, have some inalienable or even absolute rights which no one can waive or extinguish. MacCormick insists that 'powers of waiver or enforcement are essentially ancillary to, not constitutive of, rights...' (p. 314).

The benefit or interest theory of rights appears to avoid many of the faults associated with the choice approach. It seems less arbitrary in so far as it stresses the particular goods due to persons rather than an abstract freedom to accept or reject certain values. The benefit approach can accept the existence of inalienable rights. It is more plausible in its acceptance of the common-sense intuition regarding the possession of rights by children and the mentally incapacitated.

Still, the benefit or interest theory of rights does present at least one disadvantage. This occurs in relation to the problem of moderating claim-rights on the part of all who stand to benefit from the fulfilment of a duty. The question is whether one person's duty to another also gives third parties some right, since they benefit, sometimes indirectly, from the performance of the duty? And what then of fourth and fifth parties who may benefit?[63] All that one can do here, I feel, is to take this problem into account at the normative level when one seeks to nominate the person or persons who are to be the beneficiaries of a particular duty. In the case of special moral rights, for instance, established through promise or contract, the beneficiaries should be named clearly in order to avoid undue expectations arising. In more informal arrangements between persons such distinctions may be more difficult to draw.

I do not wish to give the impression here that the choice or will theory is totally discredited. True enough it seems to be limited to the sphere of discretionary rights and has difficulty with mandatory or inalienable rights.[64] But its emphasis on control of the freedom of others, by insisting on, or waiving, one's right to performance of a duty, is of key importance in a moral theory of rights. That each person is in some sense 'a small-scale sovereign' with power to limit the freedom of others with regard to his or her basic interests is an important aspect of human dignity.

CONCLUSION

The second part of this chapter began with an introduction to the stipulative definitions of rights found in the jurisprudence of Wesley Hohfeld. Once again, terms like 'claim', 'power' and 'liberty' turned up, but now with narrower application than in our chapter's opening discussion. The basic distinction in the Hohfeldian scheme is one between claim and liberty, and is based on the relationship each has to duty. In the case of a claim-right the correlativity between the claim and duty is very strong, while the correlativity between liberty-rights and duties appears to be either very weak or non-existent. The examples from economic competition show that in some cases we are permitted to harm or hinder the plans and projects of others, whilst others have the same freedom towards us. Yet, liberty-rights must be relatively few in reality and must be directed towards the protection of relatively unimportant goods. The more important the interest, good or benefit, the more likely the right is to be a fully-fledged claim. The notion of a liberty-right is essentially parasitic on the stronger notion of a claim-right, since often liberties require a protective perimeter of claims which are taken for granted. It is also difficult to see how powers and immunities with their correlatives, liabilities and disabilities, are radically different from claim-rights. A power or capacity to change another person's legal or moral position is really a part of the meaning of having a valid claim against another.[65] The term liability looks very like another name for a duty, or a potential or latent duty. Similar arguments can be employed regarding immunities and disabilities.

Whether or not we accept the Hohfeldian distinctions, together with Wellman's application to the moral sphere, will depend a great deal on our practical interests. Rights have to be practical instruments for protecting the interests of people. Thus claim-rights with clear-cut correlative obligations which are enforceable are valuable political, moral and legal tools. Liberty-rights with little or no protection presented to the right-holder may amount to no more than empty rhetoric, especially when one is dealing with a situation of great inequality and oppression. The example of two shopkeepers in competition gives a picture of more or less equal parties in conflict. In this situation liberty-rights may well be sufficient protection for each party. But the situation may change radically if a large supermarket chain enters the area. Now we have inequality of a type which may require more than liberty-rights to protect the weaker party, in this case the small shopkeeper. In underdeveloped countries it is hard to see the practical value of liberties in giving protection against the high-powered economic policies of the First World. At least negative claim-rights would seem to apply in such cases. By this is meant that, even if a positive duty to alleviate hunger and give development aid is rejected, a negative duty to refrain from doing further economic, social or cultural damage would be justified and could be validly claimed. The assumption underlying the concept of a liberty is that parties in competitive relationships are basically strong enough to fend for themselves and thus have minimal claims against one another. But such situations are relatively rare, and when they exist have no guarantee of remaining in such healthy equilibrium. Nevertheless, there is some possibility that a situation of equality or relative equality could depend for some time on liberty-rights, until some radical change came about in the situation, causing an imbalance or inequality which would call for greater protection for the weak. Then claim-rights might be the order of the day.

It would appear then that our decision on the use of claim-rights or liberties depends on the importance of the good in need of protection, and the ability or inability of those whose good is in question to assure themselves of its enjoyment. Human rights tend to be important because the goods they protect are fundamental for human flourishing. Problems in relation to such rights occur especially in Third World countries (but not only there) because often the majority of their inhabitants do not have the ability to enjoy basic goods through their own efforts and are not in a position to make effective claims against those in a privileged position. This is why human rights tend to be claim-rights rather than liberties. But there is one further assumption that must be made: for human rights to be truly claim-rights and thus to have a strict correlativity with duties imposed on named individuals and groups, there must be a widespread acceptance of the normative relationship stemming from one's sharing in a common humanity. After all one can recognise that some goods are basic for everyone; one can recognise that some people have no chance of achieving such goods unaided; and one can still say 'What is that to me? Why should I have an obligation to do anything for these people?' Thus, the strongest doctrine of rights implies a strict correlativity with duty based on an acceptance of a relationship with others, which can be general or special, but which calls on one to respond to their valid claims.

The doctrine of correlativity gives us one of the major defining characteristics of rights. This is clearest when we are dealing with claims, but also applies to the other terms we have been studying such as powers and immunities. Hohfeldian liberties have a more distant relationship to duties, but the wider term 'freedom' is still useful in describing one of the essential aspects of rights, according to Hart and Wellman, namely autonomy or control of one's life by means of the control rights give one over the duties of others. The Choice Theory needs to be supplemented by the Benefit Theory, however, since it is particular goods which give us a justification to limit the freedom of others, and the relative importance of the benefits tell us whether we should waive or claim our rights. I would suggest that this analysis applies in general to all rights – legal, moral, religious, political, constitutional, etc. Human rights and special moral rights are found within these various categories, so that legal rights may involve human and special rights; likewise with moral rights – some are human, others are special. And there will be considerable overlapping of these categories and types. Yet all must consist of some normative relationship where some person or persons have claims or entitlements against other persons to some benefit (or something considered beneficial), the claim or entitlement being correlative to some duty or obligation borne by another or others.

CHAPTER 3

Conceptual scepticism and rights

The last chapter introduced some of the philosophical and legal literature on the concept of rights and the use of rights-language. The idea there was to clarify and elucidate that concept and language, partly as a response to an initial kind of scepticism which would accuse rights-language of being incurably vague and indeterminate. The clarification and elucidation of rights-language is of importance in philosophy and in theology, given the regular use of this kind of language. Obviously if moral arguments are to hinge on the concept of rights, that concept must be clear and determinate.

In this present chapter, I continue to face up to arguments against the value of rights-language, in particular those arguments which hold that the concept of rights is 'logically redundant or epistemologically ungrounded or both'.[1] It seems to me that Christian ethicists have not paid much attention to this question, but have taken for granted the basic logical respectability of the rights concept.[2] Obviously, if philosophy could establish that the use of this concept is logically redundant or epistemologically ungrounded, this would cause some embarrassment in moral theological circles. It is my task here to examine the arguments for conceptual scepticism in order to show how they fail, and in order to establish the logical and epistemological respectability of rights-language in general.

In the following pages I shall deal with these questions of scepticism mainly as they are presented in Alan Gewirth's essay 'Why Rights are Indispensable?'. He deals with two kinds of scepticism in this article – conceptual and moral – but I limit myself to the conceptual type in this chapter.

THE CORRELATIVITY OBJECTION

The doctrine of the correlativity of rights and duties was discussed at some length in the last chapter, but how does this doctrine lead to conceptual scepticism about rights in general? Gewirth shows how the correlativity objection runs. If right and duty are simply different names for the same normative relationship, depending on the point of view from which it is regarded, then surely one of them is redundant? If the language of rights adds nothing extra in the way of content to the language of duty and obligation, then, arguably, the language of obligation and duty should be preferred to the language of rights.[3]

In reply to this objection, Gewirth argues thus:

...even though claim-rights and strict duties are correlative, this does not mean they are identical. Instead, they have different normative contents and a different valuational status, in the following way. Rights are to duties as benefits are to burdens.[4]

Note here how Gewirth adopts a position close to that held by Feinberg and by Benefit or Interest theorists. For Gewirth, rights are 'justified claims to certain benefits' (p. 333). A duty, on the other hand, is a justified burden, restricting the freedom of the duty-bearer 'in ways that directly benefit not himself but the right-holder'.[5] In this way Gewirth's position is similar to that of Neil MacCormick as well, for MacCormick has argued that, at least in certain cases of legal rights, rights are prior to duties. In his article on children's rights already cited,[6] MacCormick refers to the Succession Act (1964) in Scot's law, where children have a right to parental property if a parent dies intestate. This right is possessed even before the executor is named who will bear the correlative duty. According to Gewirth, rights are prior to duties 'in the order of justifying purpose or final causality, in that respondents have correlative duties *because* subjects have certain rights'[7]. Rights-language is not redundant, then, because rights are the 'justifying basis' of duties.

Ronald Dworkin appears to support the main point of the

non-redundancy of rights-language in his famous distinction between 'right-based', 'duty-based' and 'goal-based' moral theories. Dworkin adopts a view close to that held by Braybrooke, discussed above, that the correlativity thesis is untidy but firm:

In many cases, however, corresponding rights and duties are not correlative, but one is derivative from the other, and it makes a difference which is derivative from which. There is a difference between the idea that you have a duty not to lie to me because I have a right not to be lied to, and the idea that I have a right that you not lie to me because you have a duty not to tell lies. In the first case I justify a duty by calling attention to a right; if I intend any further justification it is the right that I must justify, and I cannot do so by calling attention to the duty. In the second case it is the other way around.[8]

Dworkin's stress on derivation rather than correlativity does not undermine his general position of 'taking rights seriously', for at least some rights would appear to be prior to duties in his approach. His first aim, of course, is to oppose both right and duty-based theories of morality to goal-based theories, the latter being exemplified in Utilitarianism[9]. 'Rights are best understood as trumps over some background justification for political decisions that states a goal for the community as a whole.'[10] However, given that right-based theories of morality protect individuals from utilitarian reasoning which might demand unjust sacrifices from them, Dworkin also distinguishes between right-based and duty-based theories. Although both theory types put the individual at the centre of attention, each treats the individual differently. Duty-based theories, for example Kantian morality, are more concerned with the quality of acts reaching a certain standard (whatever the consequences). On the other hand, 'Right-based theories are, in contrast, concerned with the independence rather than the conformity of individual action. They presuppose and protect the value of individual thought and choice.'[11]

If Dworkin is correct in his analysis of rights-language, not all rights can be reduced to the language of duty, since some duties are derivative from rights, and, secondly, because the language of rights forms a theory-type which stresses the important moral value of individuality. Here again the relationship between metaethics and normative ethics is seen clearly. The language of morals is found first in everyday talk concerning moral issues, and the analysis of this language must take into account what people think is important in the moral life. Thus, if people are worried that communal advantage will swamp the legitimate interests of individuals, such an anxiety may well come to be situated in moral theory in the language and concept of rights.

A further defence of the language of rights against reduction to the language of duty is found in another argument presented by David Braybrooke in his article on the 'firm but untidy correlation'. In response to Lyons' position he makes this important point:

There is an interpretation of Lyons' which makes the entailment between rights and obligations logically superfluous, because a set of clear obligations exist anyway. But logical superfluity does not imply practical superfluity. People, for instance, might first learn about their obligations from being educated about rights. The connection might be kept for fear of unforeseen lapses in following obligations.[12]

This 'pedagogical' argument for maintaining the language of rights is partly a metaethical argument and partly a normative one. From the normative point of view, the interest is in getting people to respect rights in the most effective way. And one way may be as Braybrooke suggests, to look at obligations from the angle of rights, rather than looking at obligations on their own separate from the claims of others. But, learning to look at the normative relationships between people involves a metaethical aspect, some 'concept' of the different angles one can look at what binds people together morally, namely, rights and duties.

Finally, I can mention once again the key element in the 'Choice' or 'Will' Theories of rights – the control one has over the duty of another. Sometimes this control implies a firm claim against others to act or refrain from acting; sometimes control means the capacity and freedom to waive or to relinquish one's right, with the corresponding release of another from his or her duty. Now, it seems to me, that any reduction of rights-language to the correlative language of duty will miss out on this important function of control over duty. One might argue that in the place of waiving rights one could create a hierarchy of duties, with accompanying rules telling one when a duty no longer applies; but all this does is to transfer the power of waiver to the persons who frame the particular rules. It is furthermore doubtful whether an agreed hierarchy of duties and obligations could be constructed. And, finally, the faculty of waiving is such a personal one, taking in the area of supererogation for instance, that general rules for bypassing certain obligations or duties would be relatively unhelpful, if not totally useless.

THE INTERESTS OBJECTION

The interest/benefit theory of rights holds that the essence of rights lies in nominating the beneficiaries of certain duties, in order to protect their interests or assure their benefit in a special area. The objection now is that human agents can easily recognise the importance of respecting interests without having to mention having rights to them. In this way, rights are only so much 'excess baggage'.

R. Frey has insisted on this point, arguing against the value of rights-language from a utilitarian perspective. He suggests that:

What is wrong with torturing or killing someone is not the violation of some right of his, but the sheer agony and suffering he undergoes, the snuffing out of his hopes, desires and wishes, and so on... In short, there is no need to postulate moral rights as intermediaries between pain and agony, or thwarted hopes, desires, and plans, or ruined lives and the wrongness of what was done.[13]

Gewirth's response to this objection seems remarkably weak. He just says that rights add something indispensable to the situation, that is, a moral justification for the protection of an interest. Then he says, rather lamely in my opinion, that one could have an interest in murdering someone and even be protected in furthering this by unscrupulous friends, but this would not amount to a moral right.[14] However, I am sure that Frey is not thinking of making just any 'interests' morally right simply by adding some protection to the agent. Frey, as a utilitarian, can argue that his moral theory is perfectly well-suited to distinguish morally between interests.

Frey's argument then, to have any chance of success, must begin with interests that are moral. There are, after all, natural disasters which cause agony and suffering, snuff out hopes and desires, and so on, but the ways in which events touch personal interests is not in question here. What is in question is human action which affects the interests of others; and Frey's argument assumes the basic moral position that persons ought not to cause others suffering, other things being equal, or without clear justification. Surely anyone can see this, is Frey's reaction, and there is no need to complicate matters by introducing rights as 'intermediaries'. In some cases no doubt people do what is right and avoid what is wrong without considering the 'rights' of others; there can be an intuitive reaching out to the victims of suffering without much, if any, conceptualisation of right and wrong, or of rights and duties. But this does not mean that nothing further can be learned about the moral realities of such situations, and that rights are redundant from the explanatory point of view.

The basic problem, I think, with Frey's reductionist approach is that he assumes too quickly a normative connection between the interests of persons and the activity of others in fulfilling these interests. Granted that another person is suffering in some way, the question remains 'What is this to do with me?'. Many people suffer in this world, but I cannot help everyone. In many cases I have an obligation to help those with whom I have a special relationship, for example family and friends, and this leaves me comparatively little time and resources to help others down the road, and even further afield. How do I distinguish between various suffering people and decide on my strategy?

Surely one answer is that I should consider the rights of others. And it usually turns out that certain people have more of a 'claim' on me than others. Moreover, if I fail to recognise the justified claims of those closest to me, I may well cause a specific form of suffering – betrayal – because of the special expectations that arise from 'special moral rights'. So it appears that rights often do help in directing agents towards the relief of human suffering, and they explain some of the further intensity of suffering caused when those with most claim on others are ignored or betrayed.[15]

It is opportune here to reiterate one of the main points of my thesis, namely, that rights-language concentrates not merely on interests and benefits of persons in isolation, but on the 'claims against' and 'powers over' others which these interests and benefits provide. To conclude this section I present a quotation from Charles Fried, who takes up a position on rights and interests similar to Dworkin's emphasis on rights as trumps over utilitarian attempts to maximise values or interests. I hope that these words will be self-explanatory, and a partial summary of what has preceded.

Yet it is the case that rights are *also* interests, or at least they protect or express interests. Indeed, in consequentialist analyses rights appear only as interests, more specifically as those interests which in a particular or general striking of the balance have ended up as carrying the day over competing interests. In the system I propose, rights have a prior status. When a person asserts a right he is doing more than announcing an interest to be taken into account. After all, every interest must at least be taken into account. And since an interest is a potential pleasure or pain, the utilitarian must always consider it, just as a businessman must consider any potential revenue or cost. The assertion of a right is categorical. Thus a right is not the same as an interest, though there is an interest behind every right.[16]

THE JUSTIFICATORY OBJECTION

Joel Feinberg situates the grounds of rights in certain rules or principles. He states that:

A man has a legal right when the official recognition of his claim (as valid) is called for by the governing rules. This definition, of course, hardly applies to moral rights, but that is not because the genus of which moral rights are a species is something other than *claims*. A man has a moral right when he has a claim the recognition of which is called for – not (necessarily) by legal rules – but by moral principles, or the principles of an enlightened conscience.[17]

Robert Young[18] takes up these ways of grounding rights, and highlights the complexities underlying such seemingly innocuous remarks, with particular reference to moral rights (legal rights being relatively determinate in contrast to moral rights). The main issue here, according to Young, is the pluralism of moral principles and the difficulty of finding widespread agreement on moral matters. It appears that the foundation of rights will be rather unsound, especially if one does not hold the existence of objectively correct moral principles. Given such a moral epistemology, one has to adopt a conventionalist understanding of moral rights, as established by community consensus. This will make the whole question of universal human rights a difficult one to settle in practice.

Raymond Frey likewise holds that the pluralism of moral principles undermines the theory of the value of rights:

If moral rights are put forward on the basis of unagreed moral principles, we will not agree on whether there are such rights, whereas if they are put forward on the basis of agreed moral principles, they appear unnecessary, since our principles will already be leading us to behave in what the rights' proponents see as the desired way.[19]

I shall answer the objection that rights can be reduced to moral principles in the next section; here I must answer the objection that rights are redundant precisely because principles are so varied and conflicting.

The first point must be rather obvious: the existence of rights does not depend on their being recognised by everyone, though their exercise requires widespread recognition, especially in the case of human rights. Arguably, some special moral rights may be exercised so long as a small group of people (sometimes just one other person) recognises the normative bond. One might deny the existence of objective moral values just as one might deny the existence of God, but this denial would not necessarily do away with either rights or the Deity.

In second place, it may be argued that moral pluralism regarding rights has been grossly exaggerated by thinkers like

Young and Frey. One can point to the existence of the United Nations Declaration of Human Rights, as well as other international agreements, as a sign of a general degree of basic agreement on fundamental interests which can be claimed in international law.

Sean MacBride, for instance, has argued that the UN Declaration 'was not when it was adopted, a binding legal document, but it has now acquired the status of being enforceable as part of international customary law'.[20] Such an agreement is rather surprising in view of the different ideologies expressed by the world's different governmental systems.[21] Where there are conflicts of interests, some rights are subordinated to others, but often such subordination is either hidden for reasons of embarrassment, or justified in terms of other rights. In this way, most states reveal a degree of unanimity regarding the value of rights, in spite of different interpretations of these rights in practice.

Nor do I agree with these attempts to load all the blame for present-day moral pluralism and indeterminacy on the shoulders of the concept of rights. It seems as if rights-language is being made a scape-goat bearing moral indeterminacy out into the desert. Unfortunately for the sceptics, this use of language and the concept underlying it has a tendency to wander back to haunt them. In my opinion, rights-language is not indeterminate in itself, it simply reflects the indeterminacy of the many competing moral theories in vogue today. In this way, rights-language seems no worse off than any part of moral language, for instance, the language of duty or the language of rules or the language of virtue. None of these hangs in the air untouched by moral pluralism, so why single out moral rights as the main culprit? Granted that some of the claims made to various personal interests have been immoderate, this provides an argument only for moderation, not for the redundancy of rights-language.[22] If the sceptics are to be consistent in their analysis of moral language in relation to pluralism, they should be equally despairing of the language of duty and obligation.

Therefore, I am not convinced that moral pluralism undermines the foundations of rights-language, though I recognise that concern must be voiced over moral pluralism's effect on the exercise of many rights.

In the following sections I move away from the treatment of conceptual scepticism about rights as treated by Gewirth, and begin to treat of further types of conceptual scepticism. The justificatory objection spoke of the importance placed on moral principles as the grounds of moral rights, and then tried to weaken reliance on rights-language by pointing out the degree of moral pluralism with regard to those principles. A further step might be to simplify matters by returning to the principles themselves, using them as a substitute for talk of rights.

Before any attempt is made to make rights-language redundant in favour of moral principles, it should be noted how the philosophical treatment of moral principles is not without controversy. For instance, there is the question of the distinction between moral principles and moral rules. Regarding this distinction, Marcus Singer remarks that,

It has generally been recognised that there is a distinction of some importance between moral rules and moral principles. Yet the distinction has not generally received explicit formulation, and there is no general agreement on just what it is.[23]

So, straightaway there is the problem of whether the reduction of rights is going to be in favour of principles, or rules, or some combination of these. Singer favours the view that moral principles are more general than moral rules, though not so general that they lose their action-guiding force. Principles have a role, for instance, in limiting the content of moral rules. Thus, an example of a moral principle would be the 'Generalization Argument' or principle of justice/impartiality. This states that 'What is right for one person must be right for any similar person in similar circumstances.'[24] Such a principle, according to Singer, is exceptionless. Also it sets limits to any moral rule if it is to lay claim to being a 'moral' rule. Moral rules, on the other hand, are specific, for example 'Stealing is wrong', 'Everyone ought to keep their promises.' Such rules are specifically action-guiding, but they are so specific that they must allow for exceptions, according to Singer. However, there is a general principle which states that exceptions to rules must be justified. This is a further example of a principle guiding the content of rules.

More recently, the American philosopher, Daniel Maguire, has reacted to this distinction between principles and rules, arguing that in practice these terms are interchangeable. Thus, what is often called the 'Golden Rule' could just as easily be called the 'Golden Principle' because of its generality. Or take the example of the so-called 'Principle of Double Effect', which might well be called 'a set of rules for situations where an action brings forth good and bad effects'. Maguire comes to the conclusion that 'The effort to render ethics unnecessarily tedious by distinctions that do not hold up in usage is both pedantic and unkind.'[25]

Whatever the merits of these different approaches to principles and rules, it appears that all of the authors who discuss these terms agree on their action-guiding nature or function. A person interested in being morally good cannot afford to ignore moral principles or moral rules, either at the general or at the specific level. Thus, it seems to me, that the language of moral principles and moral rules is very close to the language of duty and obligation. One is not meant merely to consult principles and rules, but to follow and obey their direction. Thus, the advice to reduce rights-language to the language of moral principles brings me back to the correlativity objection, which insisted on the priority of duties over rights. And, it follows that the response made to that objection will apply again here.

In addition, some further arguments can be made for the retention of the language of rights, showing that the language of principle performs different functions in moral argument from the language of rights. Thus, for instance, Jeremy Waldron, argues that the language of moral principles and moral rules refers moral agents to the right thing to do, what they ought to do. The language of rights, on the other hand, does not always refer to the right or obligatory action, but often enough to actions which are merely permissible. Such permissible actions have already been covered under the category of 'discretionary rights'. So, my right to do x does not entail that there is always a moral principle or rule commanding me to do x, though it usually implies such principles or rules on the part of others who have the correlative duty to protect my freedom in this area. In fact, in some cases persons have a 'right to do wrong' against others. There may be a principle or rule forbidding a certain action, but others have no freedom to impose the principle or rule on others. The common example here is in the sphere of 'personal morality', of what 'consenting adults do in private'. Here, persons may act wrongly, but still have a right to non-interference in the matter. Non-interference is often a correlative duty because interference might cause a greater wrong than the wrong performed by the right-holder.[26]

Another argument which distinguishes principles/rules from rights is that only the former give reasons to act on every occasion. Having a right does not always give one a reason to act. An obvious example is the ordinary right to marry; having this right against others does not force me to prove its existence by trying to marry. Rights, then, do not necessarily justify moral actions on the part of right-holders, though usually there is the assumption behind valid claims that the interests sought are good, and the actions posited are right ones. (Thus, even in the case of the 'right to do wrong', right-holders either believe that they are acting rightly, though in fact their conscience is erroneous, or they are acting in bad faith but conceal this from others, pretending that they are following conscience.)[27] There is, however, a strong connection between rights and reasons for acting, in so far as valid claims or entitlements presuppose reasons for duty-bearers to respect the interests of right-holders. Sometimes, too, right-holders have duties to claim their rights and are obliged not to waive or alienate rights. These 'mandatory rights' have been mentioned already; they are a perfect coincidence of right and duty in the life of the same person, but one should note that it is the aspect of duty here that gives the reason to act, not so much the aspect of right.

It is important for a proper understanding of rights that the correct relationship between rights and justified action be noted. I have already stated that rights do not necessarily justify the action of the right-holder, though they do usually justify the actions of duty-bearers. However, in talking of the action of the right-holder a further distinction must be made, between an agent pursuing a particular interest and an agent claiming either the help or the non-interference of others. Having a right does not necessarily justify the former, but it necessarily justifies the latter, since the connection between having a right and claiming against others is analytic or conceptual.

To illustrate this distinction, consider the basic right to take up lawful employment. Suppose I have an offer of a job and someone asks 'Are you justified in seeking employment in that position?', the reply, 'I have a right to take on this job', is not the proper answer. That reply – 'I have a right to take on this job' – is really the appropriate answer to the question 'Why do you expect me to help you to get this job?', assuming that the right-holder is looking for positive help, for example a reference, or negative help, for example an assurance from another that he or she will not compete for the same position. The 'right' to take on a particular job is not necessarily a justification of the agent's decision to do just that, rather it concentrates on the control one has over the activity or forbearance of others. There is much sense, then, in the following words from Glanville Williams:

No one ever has a right to do something; he only has a right that some one else shall do (or refrain from doing) something. In other words, every right in the strict sense relates to the conduct of another, while a liberty and a power relate to the conduct of the holder of the liberty or power.[28]

It is probably a bit extreme to say that 'No one ever has a right to do something'. I think there is justification in using this form of speech in ordinary affairs, so long as its usage is accompanied by the proper interpretation, i.e. that rights turn on what I can expect others to do for me, legally and/or morally, regarding what I wish to do or not to do.

Finally, in my attempt to show that the language of rights should not be replaced by the language of principles, I cite the interesting article by Stephen Toulmin, 'The Tyranny of

Principles'. Toulmin is worried about 'the revival of a tyr-
annical absolutism in recent discussions about social and
personal ethics'.[29] For instance, in the debate on abortion,
'much of the public debate increasingly came to turn on
"matters of principle." As a result, the abortion debate became
less temperate, less discriminating, and above all less resolvable'
(*ibid.*, p. 32). A further example given by Toulmin of the
growing reliance on rules and principles is worth quoting at
length:

My perplexities about the force and value of 'rules' and 'principles'
were further sharpened as the result of a television news program
about a handicapped young woman who had difficulties with the local
Social Security office. Her Social Security payments were not sufficient
to cover her rent and food, so she started an answering service, which
she operated through the telephone at her bedside. The income from
this service – though itself less than a living wage – made all the
difference to her. When the local Social Security office heard about
this extra income, however, they reduced her benefits accordingly: in
addition, they ordered her to repay some of the money she had been
receiving. (Apparently, they regarded her as a case of 'welfare
fraud.'). The television reporter added two final statements. Since the
report had been filmed, he told us, the young woman, in despair, had
taken her own life. To this he added his personal comment that 'there
should be a *rule* to prevent this kind of thing from happening'.

Notice that the reporter did not say, 'The local office should be
given discretion to waive, or at least bend, the existing rules in hard
cases. 'What he said was, 'There should be an *additional* rule to prevent
such inequities in the future.' Justice, he evidently believed, can be
ensured only by establishing an adequate system of rules, and injustice
can be prevented only by adding more rules. (p. 32)

Toulmin goes on to explain how humanity has come to this
emphasis on rules. Looking at Roman law, he remarks that rules
were not explicitly used in the Roman legal system for the first
three centuries of its history. This was due to the small and
relatively homogeneous character of daily life. Legal conflicts
were solved by the 'College of Pontiffs', a set of judges who
adjudicated cases set before them. They did not have to give
reasons for their judgements, since the citizens trusted their
judgement and allowed them wide discretion in judgement.

This changed when Rome grew into an empire, the case-load increased and had to be adjudicated by junior judges. These judges had to be trained in the practice of the law, and this involved passing on rules to deal with different situations. Less discretion was allowed, as Toulmin mentions, 'Discretion, which had rested earlier on the personal characters of the pontiffs themselves and which is not easy to teach, began to be displaced by formal rules and more teachable argumentative skills' (p. 33).

In general, Toulmin argues that the reign of rules and principles reflects the growth of the 'Ethics of Strangers'. As communication, especially travel, developed, people who were used to dealing morally with others in the personal and intimate way of small communities, now had to deal morally with groups of people who were unknown to them – strangers. Tolstoy's notion of morality is cited by Toulmin as an example of a system that has largely passed away, and which needs to be revived in some ways.

As he saw matters, genuinely 'moral' relations can exist only between people who live, work, and associate together: inside a family, between intimates and associates, within a neighbourhood. The natural limit to any person's moral universe, for Tolstoy, is the distance he or she can walk, or at most ride. By taking the train, a moral agent leaves the sphere of truly moral actions for a world of strangers... (p. 34).

Once one begins to deal morally with strangers, an element of distrust enters, and the role of strict rules and principles is supposed to give some confidence in dealings with such people. Furthermore, since those who run the legal system are also strangers, they must be controlled by strict rules as well. One cannot afford to allow them too much discretion.

Toulmin's warnings about the tyranny of rules and principles are basically a call for a return to the value of equity, which requires an important element of discretion in the legal and moral system.[30] Treating the moral world as a world of strangers only gives rise to a morality of rules stressing equality, but this complex world of different personalities with different needs demands equity to temper the rigidity of equality. In the ethics of intimacy, of the 'friendly society', individual needs and differences are taken into account, and this model should be restored so far as is possible.

Toulmin does not mention the role of rights in his article, so I am not sure what he would have to say about their role in morality. Some may argue that they too are an expression of the 'ethics of strangers'. But my arguments have stressed the fact that rights-language is more flexible than is sometimes thought, and certainly more flexible than the strict language of principles, rules, obligations and duties.[31] The fact that at least some rights are 'discretionary' and that rights can be waived or relinquished in some cases is indicative of the flexibility of this kind of moral and legal language. On the other hand, rights can also participate in the categorical nature of rules and principles, especially when vitally important values are at stake – hence the usefulness of notions like 'inalienable', 'absolute' and 'mandatory', rights.

SCEPTICISM AND 'HUMAN RIGHTS'

Scepticism concerning rights usually concentrates on moral rights rather than on legal rights. Frequently when people think of moral rights they identify these with the category of 'human rights'.[32] However, this is a mistake since not all the rights of human persons are 'human rights'. If I promise to meet a friend at the cinema this evening, I give him a right to expect me to keep my promise, but this right is not a human right in the strict sense.

The main characteristics of a human right are given by Richard Wasserstrom:

First, it must be possessed by all human beings, as well as only by human beings. Second, because it is the same right that all human beings possess, it must be possessed equally by all human beings. Third, because human rights are possessed by all human beings, we can rule out as possible candidates any of those rights which one might have in virtue of occupying any particular status or relationship, such as that of parent, president or promisee. And fourth, if there are human rights, they have the additional characteristic of being assertable, in a manner of speaking, 'against the whole world'.[33]

Clearly, the third characteristic mentioned above eliminates my example of promising to meet a friend from the sphere of human rights. Human rights are universal in the sense of being possessed by all in virtue of their common humanity. However, nearly all the characteristics mentioned by Wasserstrom are controversial, and some of the arguments against human rights may engender scepticism about the many claims made in their name. Indeed, some may feel that the category should be eliminated totally. Let me mention some of the problems faced by this category of 'human rights'.

Kai Nielsen has criticised the concept of human rights as epistemologically ungrounded[34] The concept, he argues, depends on certain built-in normative assumptions that have not been proved, assumptions mainly to do with equality between humans. If the moral point of view is characterised in terms of prescriptivity and universalisability, then Nietzsche's 'Slave Morality' qualifies as a moral system. There are some superior individuals in the human race, and rights and duties apply to them in the full sense. The *Ubermenschen* need not recognise the rights of weaker men and women because they are not equal. According to Nielsen, then, one begs the question of the moral point of view by building-in equality and then assuming that everyone is in fact equal. It is quite obvious to everyone that in many areas of life human beings are unequal, so the equality spoken of by human rights theorists must be of a 'special' kind. Usually this involves statements about 'intrinsic worth', but this type of language is rather hard to pin down. According to Nielsen, it appears to be related to some dubious metaphysical and theological doctrines.[35]

If 'intrinsic worth' is related to some distinctive endowment of human beings, for example their rationality or their ability to value interpersonal relationships, then there will be some 'humans' whose 'intrinsic worth' will be in question. There may then be severely mentally handicapped people who cannot be accorded 'human rights'. If 'intrinsic worth' simply means being a member of the human race in the sense of being born of human parents, then holders of such a position may be accused of 'speciesism'.[36] This charge criticises the arbitrariness of respecting the human species by according it special rights as against other species. Why should not gorillas be given special rights because they are born of gorilla parents?

It is clear that Nielsen has made some important points in his criticism of the concept of 'human rights'. Ultimately, I feel that the notion of 'intrinsic worth' can only be understood in metaphysical or theological terms, (of which more will be said later). However, I am not sceptical, as Nielsen is, about the possibility and value of either metaphysics or theology. Moreover, I believe that Nielsen's point about having to build in equality into the concept of human rights is well taken. The concept of universal human rights involves an ultimate evaluative position concerning humanity. The concept is not a logical discovery which binds everyone by fear of contradiction if one were to deny it, it is a moral discovery which grounds one's normative ethics. And from here it passes into metaethics. When one refers to the basic equality of human beings as requiring special respect to be shown for all, one is not saying that all humans are equal in their talents and in their actual participation in earthly goods. One is saying that at the deepest level all human persons have equal worth, a worth which demands action to bring the less fortunate of the species up to a satisfactory level of participation in the goods which make human worth obvious to the naked eye. It remains open to people whether they want to use this concept or not, just as it is open to people to accept or reject the notions of inalienable and absolute rights. One can understand the meaning of these concepts as one understands the concept of unicorns and ghosts, yet deny the actual existence of these realities. One can accept their connotation while denying them denotation.

A further problem with the concept of human rights arises once again in the area of correlativity, this time in relation to the scope of the right. Human rights are said to be universal rights, possessed by everyone and against everyone. But this is not agreed upon by everyone. In the last chapter, I cited the work of McCloskey on the notion of rights as 'entitlements'. Remember his argument that the right to life (a typical human right in most normative systems) can hardly be seen as a list of claims against every single person in the world. After all, I am not likely to be in touch with a large proportion of the world's population during my life-time, so why should I be in need of some normative relationship regarding such strangers?

One solution to this problem of human rights implies that universal human rights are possessed by all, but not against all. Instead they are rights of citizens against their state. This is how Carl Wellman expresses the point:

Traditionally, human rights have been thought of as those ethical rights that every human being must possess simply because he or she is human. Thus, human rights are the rights any individual possesses *as* a human being. Although this seems to capture current usage pretty well, I propose a more narrow conception of human rights. I define a human right as an ethical right of the individual as a human being *vis-à-vis* the state. Excluded by this definition are the ethical rights one has as a human being that hold against other individuals or against organizations other than the state.[37]

Wellman explains the reasons why he wishes to narrow the concept of human rights. Firstly, the tradition of natural rights and the major declarations of the rights of man tend to have as their 'primary and definitive purpose' the proclamation of the rights of individuals 'in face of' the state. Secondly, there must be a difference between the relationship holding between the individual and the state and that which holds between the individual and other individuals and organisations, 'just because the state is a special sort of organisation with a distinctive role to play in human affairs'.[38]

There is much to be said for narrowing the concept of human rights in line with Wellman's thesis, especially when the concern is with exercising rights in a positive way. Because of the state's power and resources, individuals more readily look to the state for positive help and for non-interference than to other individuals. The state's control over health services and social services in general are cases in point. But, at the same time, I am reluctant to eliminate the wider notion of human rights as being held, at least in some circumstances, against everybody. Of course the positive aspect of this is not of first importance. I cannot expect perfect strangers to help me in many cases where

I am pursuing some project. But the negative aspect of human rights is important, in so far as it gives a general sense of confidence that a wide circle of individuals recognise my need not to be disturbed. Thus, D. D. Raphael makes a useful distinction between human rights in the 'strong' sense and human rights in the 'weak' sense.[39] The 'strong' sense refers to rights held against everyone; while the 'weak' sense corresponds to Wellman's narrowing of the concept to social or civil rights. I feel that both senses have some validity in moral and legal discourse.

Finally, regarding the difficulties with the concept of 'human rights', there is the connection between these rights and the traditional 'natural rights'. The modern term 'human right' tends to hide some of the essentialist assumptions included in the concept of 'natural right', as we noted earlier in our discussion of justificatory elements built into our definitions of rights. Is there some common 'nature' which all humans possess and which acts as a basis for deriving fundamental rights? Or are human rights to be understood in a more conventionalist sense, with reference to generally accepted values, but without metaphysical assumptions?

In a seminal article on the subject of 'Natural Rights', Margaret Macdonald argues that natural rights are in the category of values rather than facts, and as values they are a matter of decision or choice, not a matter of discovery. In the light of this non-cognitivist approach to morality, she holds the position that:

In short, 'natural rights' are the condition of a good society. But what those conditions are is not given by nature or mystically bound up with the essence of man and his inevitable goal, but is determined by human decisions.[40]

Inevitably, then, Macdonald is a critic of the view that there is a fixed human nature from which can be derived 'natural' or 'human' rights. She calls the attempt to do so 'the Aristotelian dream of fixed natures pursuing common ends', and she lampoons a modern version of this in the work of J. Maritain, where he uses the analogy of different pianos, all geared towards the production of attuned sounds.[41] According to Macdonald, 'Men do not share a fixed nature, nor, therefore, are there any ends which they must necessarily pursue in the fulfilment of such nature.'[42]

One can sympathise with Macdonald because the position she opposes is so extreme. Of course it sounds ridiculous to compare human persons to pianos, and to speak of fixed natures in that sense. It is also dangerous to try to deduce in detail rights, rules and principles from human nature.[43] But I cannot see how one can escape from some notion of a human nature that is fixed and also normative in some way. How can one talk of human beings unless there is some set of characteristics that distinguishes the species from other species of animal? Not that all human characteristics divide men and women from the rest of nature in an absolute way. Clearly there are points of contact, especially between human needs and those of animals; but there is also a sense in which being human imprints something special regarding the experience of those needs, so that they become conscious values to be promoted.

In recent times, the category of the 'personal' appears to have come to the fore in much 'natural law' thinking, such that the older idea of 'fixed nature' has moved into the background.[44] This may be a good thing, since it is important to recognise the individual ways in which human nature is experienced. Thus, human rights must take into account the variety included in individual experience of personal nature. However, this makes respect for human rights more complicated.

CONCLUSION

This chapter has taken up some of the controversial points surrounding the analysis of rights-language which were studied in the last two chapters, and has added to these points in order to make clear the case for conceptual scepticism with which one can confront this form of moral language. The underlying question here has been, 'Given the difficulties of analysing rights and the language of rights, is it truly worthwhile to maintain the usage of the concept and the language?'

In general the conceptual objections presented in this chapter have been part of a reductionist enterprise regarding rights-language. I have given a number of reasons why this form of moral language should not be abandoned. For instance, rights often appear to be prior to duties in the sense that duties are for the sake of rights as burdens are for the sake of benefits. Then there is the advantage of flexibility in moral language based on the possibility of waiving rights or relinquishing them voluntarily. The distinction between 'discretionary' rights and 'mandatory' rights in particular, reveals how the language of rights can be strict at certain times and flexible at other times. It was argued that even if it were the case that rights were logically superfluous, there would still be a pragmatic argument for retaining them, for instance, for pedagogical purposes, in order to remind people of their duties. Sometimes moral positions become clear by looking at normative relationships from different angles.

I argued that rights cannot be replaced by talk of interests, because the language of rights deals with the fundamental question of how the interests of others bind persons in normative relationships. Again the essential point is that rights are relational realities, and they help to discriminate between different moral and legal relationships. Regarding the justification of rights and the unavoidable moral pluralism of modern society, I argued that moral pluralism should not be exaggerated, and that there was at least a general agreement on the value of the language of human rights. No state wants to have the name of being a human-rights violator, even if violation of rights is performed in secret in so many places. In any case, the argument for moral pluralism seems to apply equally to the use of other moral concepts, whether it be duty or obligation, or rules or principles. The concept of 'right' should not be made into a scapegoat in this way.

On the subject of the possible reduction of rights-language to the language of rules and principles, I tried to show first of all that the relationship between rules and principles is not very clear. Then I argued that rules and principles are directly connected with 'right action', which is not the same concept as 'having a right to do something'. If an action is the right thing to do then I have a moral reason for doing it, and, other things being equal, I ought to do it. But 'having a right to do x' does not necessarily give me, the right-holder, a reason to do x, as in the case of the right to marry. Rights thus protect freedom in general, whereas rules and principles seem to function in directing human freedom along particular lines. Since moral principles and moral rules do not perform the same function as the language of moral rights, it seems unlikely that the former can take the place of the latter without remainder.

As a parting shot, I introduced the views of Toulmin, who associates the language of moral principles and rules with the 'ethics of strangers'. This form of language tends towards absolutism, lack of trust in others, unwillingness to allow discretion and equity. The language of rights, I think, can allow readily enough for the flexibility required in an 'ethics of intimacy' as well as helping men and women to cope in a world of strangers.

Finally, I dealt with some of the difficulties connected with the language of 'human rights'. Again the problem of correlativity between rights and duties came to the fore, and I had to distinguish between 'strong' and 'weak' senses of human rights. I accepted that certain moral assumptions of an ultimate kind, for example equality of intrinsic worth, should be built into the concept of a human right, and that no one is logically compelled to do this. And I argued that the concept of a fixed human nature is a necessary element in the analysis of human rights, all the while qualifying this by underlining the variety of individual participations in the common human nature. This qualification is a warning against a derivation of a rigid set of rights from a fixed human nature. Such a rigid set of rights of the 'mandatory' kind would be little improvement on the language of principles, rules, duties and obligations.

In his book, *Ethics and the Limits of Philosophy*, Bernard Williams puts the question:

If there is such a thing as the truth about the subject matter of ethics – the truth, we might say about the ethical – why is there any expectation that it should be simple? In particular, why should it be conceptually simple, using only one or two ethical concepts, such as *duty* or *good state of affairs*, rather than many? Perhaps we need as many concepts to describe it as we find we need, and no fewer.[45]

This is precisely the question I have been attempting to ask and answer in this chapter. I believe that the language of rights has a valuable role to play in moral language, and I have shown that reductionism with regard to rights-language is unhelpful. If the language of rights is used carefully, it is highly respectable from the moral point of view.

In my initial introduction to this book and in the first chapter, I underlined the point that metaethics consists of two main activities – analysing the meaning of our moral language and justifying the use of that language. One form of justification takes place at the conceptual level, a level we have explored in depth in this chapter. In answering conceptual scepticism concerning the language of rights a move is made towards justifying that language. An attempt has been made to show that talk of rights is logically respectable and that it provides us with a generally useful tool for discussing some important aspects of the moral life. And all this is prior to the choice of any particular normative system. Only the most general moral views are assumed as a context for the analysis of rights-language.

My next chapter remains with the problem of establishing the respectability of moral rights, but this time the scepticism in question is of the normative kind. In answering this form of scepticism another level of justification is involved, namely normative justification, in which more specific moral positions are assumed. At this stage I begin to introduce some theological themes relating to scepticism about rights.

CHAPTER 4

Moral and theological scepticism

Having defended the language of rights in the face of conceptual objections which question the value of the underlying concept, I now turn to another form of attack on the language of rights, a two-pronged attack from the point of view of normative moral theory in both secular and Christian ethics. There is a certain overlap between these objections, since Christian ethicists and theologians have tended to echo some of the normative moral objections of secular moralists and moral philosophers. I also grapple with more radical moral theological objections which have some connection with mainstream moral philosophy.

I begin, then, with some rather obvious arguments why the language of moral rights is said to be not really morally respectable. First, the language of rights tends towards individualism and egoism, and tends to play down social solidarity and the common good. Second, the exercise of rights, especially the use of the faculty of 'claiming', is a sign of a growing adversarial trend in modern life which sets people at loggerheads, and does little for social harmony and peace.

From here I pass on to a more radical form of moral scepticism which has a clear theological reference as well as a secular moral one. I consider what may be called an 'anti-naturalist' position connected with the question 'Can a good man be harmed?' This position is radical indeed, in so far as it practically refuses to see much of ordinary human suffering, including what comes through injustice, as 'harmful' and as the object of rights. The only value of worth is the development and maintenance of moral character; therefore, so much of the language of rights is merely a distraction from this one aim.

From the theological point of view, this radically exposed
situation is made possible by a kind of faith in one's 'absolute
safety' in the hands of a greater power. In the light of such
protection, much of the language of rights is distracting,
concentrating as it does on forms of 'harm' that are hardly
worth considering according to this point of view.

Since the last position may sound quite bizarre, I go on to
discuss some religious positions which appear to share something
of this single-mindedness and lack of care regarding the suffering
which this world can throw up. Thus, I treat of the early
Franciscan tradition and some pacifist stances. Such minority
stances are strikingly attractive, but are often felt to be too
utopian to be put into practice on a wide scale for any length of
time. Furthermore, these stances often appear to be justified in
terms of highly original callings discerned by special individuals,
so that it is almost impossible to universalise their moral aspect.

I hope to show that the moral and theological objections fail
and that the language of rights is respectable morally and
theologically, once due care is taken with the use of this
language.

THE EGOISTIC OBJECTION

Alan Gewirth describes this objection as follows:

Since a right involves a claim that a person makes for the support of his
or her own interests, it evinces a preoccupation with fulfilment of one's
own desires or needs regardless of broader social goals; hence it
operates to submerge the values of community and to obscure or annul
the responsibilities that one ought to have to other persons or to society
at large. The insistence on one's rights may also, in certain circumstances, violate duties of generosity and charity, as when a land-
owner evicts a needy family in the depths of winter for non-payment
of rent.[1]

The egoistic objection is closely related to the charge of
individualism which is often brought against the concept of
rights, especially in view of the history of the development of the
'Rights of Man'.[2] Note how this point is expressed by Eugene
Kamenka:

The concept of human rights is a historical product which evolves in Europe, out of foundations in Christianity, Stoicism and Roman law with its *ius gentium*, but which gains force and direction only with the contractual and pluralist nature of European feudalism, church struggles and the rise of Protestantism and of cities. It sees society as an association of individuals, as founded – logically or historically – on a contract between them and it elevates the individual human person and his freedom and happiness to be the goal and end of all human association.[3]

Historically, perhaps the most radical example of individualism and egoism regarding the rights concept is associated with Hobbes and his notion of a 'Right of Nature'. In *Leviathan* he describes such a right as:

the liberty each man hath, to use his own power, as he will himself, for the preservation of his own nature; that is to say, of his own life; and consequently, of doing any thing, which in his own judgement, and reason, he shall conceive to be the aptest means thereunto... And because the [natural] condition of man... is a condition of war of every one against every one... and there is nothing he can make use of, that may not be a help unto him, in preserving his life against his enemies; it followeth, that in such a condition, every man has a right to every thing; even to one another's body.[4]

The major problem with a 'right' of this kind is that it is not really a right in the modern sense, because it gives no protection to an individual by means of a correlative duty. And Hobbes himself recognises this when he states 'But that right of all men to all things, is in effect no better than if no man had right to anything. For there is little use and benefit of the right a man hath, when another as strong, or stronger than himself, hath right to the same.'[5] In other words, a right which is just a physical liberty to do something is worth little or nothing. The legal and moral concepts of right insist that certain actions have some protection in relation to others, in view of the judgement that 'might is not always right'.

Another way of criticising the Hobbesian theory of natural right is by means of D. D. Raphael's distinction between 'rights of action' and 'rights of recipience'.[6] A right of action, according to Raphael, is rather like Hohfeld's liberty-right, defined in terms of absence of obligation on the part of the right-holder; a person may act in such a way if she wishes. On the other hand, the person has no claim against others to either help her to act or to refrain from interfering in her activity, as was noted earlier. A right of recipience, however, does involve obligations or duties on the part of others; one can expect something, some service, perhaps, from others. Hobbes' right of nature is a right of action not a right of recipience. If it is a basic protection and promotion of human needs, especially of the needs of weaker human beings, that makes the concept of human rights important, then they must be rights of recipience as well as rights of action.

For the other great populariser of the concept of natural rights or the 'rights of man', John Locke, such rights are indeed rights of recipience as well as being rights of action (though he did not use this form of language). Macpherson shows how Locke is an improvement on Hobbes with regard to the analysis of natural rights:

The grounds for claiming Locke as a genuine natural rights man are apparently clear: (1) His natural rights are presented as effective rights, rights which others have a natural obligation to respect. (2) His natural rights, being less wholesale than Hobbes's, are more meaningful and more specific (e.g., the right of private appropriation and the right of inheritance). (3) Locke uses natural rights to establish a case for limited government, and to set up a right to revolution.[7]

However, for all the impressiveness of such an expression of natural rights, Locke ruins his reputation, in Macpherson's opinion at least, by overriding one of the limits of natural rights (with regard to property acquisition), 'thus removing the equality of natural rights'.[8] Because of this justification of inequality regarding the accumulation of property, the basic individualism of the theory of natural rights shines through even in Locke. 'Locke's natural man is bourgeois man: his rational man is man with a propensity to capital accumulation. He is even an infinite appropriator.'[9]

D. D. Raphael, while accepting that Locke's natural rights are rights of recipience as well as rights of action, admits that as rights of recipience they are largely negative. The natural rights to life, liberty and property are essentially the right to be left free to live, left free to do as one chooses, left free to enjoy the fruits of one's labours (p. 211ff.). The positive rights to aid from others were hardly developed at all, unlike the modern concept of human rights. As Kamenka insists:

The demand for rights in the seventeenth and eighteenth centuries was a demand *against* the existing state and authorities, against despotism, arbitrariness and the political disenfranchisement of those who held different opinions. The demands for rights in the nineteenth and twentieth centuries becomes increasingly a *claim upon* the state, a demand that it provide and guarantee the means for achieving the individual's happiness and well-being, his welfare.[10]

Though freedom from despotism and oppression is of importance, it seems clear that the rights of the seventeenth and eighteenth centuries were of more value to some groups than others. The benefit to those who already had property, education and a reasonable quality of life must have been greater than to the poorer sectors of human society. Thus, natural rights which favour the relatively strong members of society and leave the weaker members to 'go to the wall' are a clear sign of individualism and egoism.[11]

The theoretical criticisms of natural rights theory so far presented are further supported by the historical evidence of the practice of respect for rights in the American and French Revolutions. The equal rights of all men in the American Declaration of Independence to 'Life, Liberty and the Pursuit of Happiness' did not extend to slaves. In fact, the contemporary American constitution did not contain a Bill of Rights; Americans had to wait until 1791 for this. The Reign of Terror in France disappointed many of the European liberals who had expected so much from the Declaration of the Rights of Man and the Citizen (1789).

The moral criticism of the language of rights in the wake of the French Revolution seems to have come equally from liberals, conservatives and socialists, to use the rather crude labels of popular political science. From the liberal point of view, Jeremy Bentham attacked the doctrine of natural rights in his *Anarchical Fallacies*. Part of his criticism was conceptual. As a legal positivist, Bentham only had time for rights which had the sanction of law. Hence, 'natural rights' were a nonsense. But he also criticised the language of natural rights from a moral angle. On this point Jeremy Waldron states that 'by the mid-1790s he [Bentham] was convinced that talk of natural rights was not merely nonsense in a good cause, but "terrorist language", "mischievous" and "dangerous nonsense"'.[12] Bentham associated the Terror of the 1790s with the fall away from law legitimised in part by the rhetoric of natural rights. According to Waldron, Bentham was of the opinion that human life without positive law would be characterised by the warlike situation described by Hobbes as life 'before' the social contract. The Reign of Terror was ample evidence of the disastrous results of moving away from pragmatic legal sanctions used to control social life. Moreover, the language of rights, Bentham thought, could be used to obstruct much needed social reform which enlightened government might be expected to introduce. This might happen as a result of appeals to inalienable and imprescriptible natural rights belonging to individuals. What was needed as the moral standard for political reform, in Bentham's opinion, was the utilitarian principle of the greatest happiness of the greatest number.

Edmund Burke's *Reflections on the Revolution in France* represents a conservative reaction to rights-language. Again one can say that Burke's critique of the language of natural rights is partly conceptual and partly moral and political. Conceptually, Burke attacked the French Declaration of The Rights of Man for its generality and for its 'metaphysical abstraction'. For Burke, slogans like 'Liberty, Equality, and Fraternity' could not be depended on to organise political life. Instead, what is required is a careful study of the circumstances of each 'civil and political scheme'.[13] Morally and politically, Burke felt that the French Revolution had more or less 'thrown out the baby with the bath-water'. He admitted that the *ancien régime* was in need of reform, but he believed that the Revolution had done away with many of the good things in the traditional political system. The important values in his political morality were, according to Waldron, 'conservatism, caution and respect for establishment' (p. 88). Instead of building on sound foundations such as these, the abstract theorists of the Revolution had given way to the anarchy of individual interpretations of rights. And even if the majority of citizens agreed on certain interpretations of rights, such a democracy only served to make Burke fearful of the tyranny of the majority, whereby the rights of minorities would be violated. Burke preferred the notion of a political elite ruling the nation, guided by, and judged by, the value of service to the common good.

The socialist critique of rights-language as found in the writings of Karl Marx concentrates on the fundamental contradiction between the 'Rights of Man' and the reality of capitalist society in which these rights are supposed to be implemented. Marx held that capitalists traditionally utilised the concept of rights to break down the feudal system, in order to insist on the alienability of land and the equality of the right to possession and acquisition. In practice, however, the language of natural rights tends to be used in an ideological way as a protection of the 'interests' of a minority group or class. As in Bentham, Marx felt that talk of rights can easily become a smoke-screen either to support the status quo or to hide the refusal to bring about radical egalitarian reform. According to Marx, it is in the interest of the bourgeoisie to encourage the doctrine of rights at an abstract level, whilst the basic corruption of the social structure, which obstructs the implementation of the true doctrine of equal rights, is concealed.[14]

Christian theologians have frequently recognised the individualistic and egoistic nature of the traditional doctrine of the rights of man. David Hollenbach, for instance, cites the work of Macpherson in studying the rights doctrine of Hobbes and Locke. The conclusion is that 'the liberal rights theory is compatible with the presence of extreme want in a society, even when the resources necessary to eliminate it are present'.[15] This state of affairs is made possible by the liberal emphasis on negative freedom and defensive rights. Jose Miguez Bonino says of the eighteenth-century rights proclamations: 'Human rights are defined in this stage in the perspective of the individualism that characterises modern thought. There is, no doubt, a primacy of the economic dimension of this individualism.'[16]

Wolfgang Huber is yet another theologian to study the history of the concept of human rights, and he has this to say about the American and French revolutionary movements: 'Human rights were demanded equally for all; their formulation was not, of course, entirely free from the limitations of class consciousness, and their content bears the stamp of an attitude of bourgeois *possessive individualism.*'[17]

All in all, then, the history of the concept of rights tends to have an inbuilt bias towards individualism and egoism. Often the kind of individualism and egoism hidden in the proclamations of the rights of man was of the group or class variety, since there can be a group egoism or selfishness just as easily as there can be the self-centred preoccupation of single individuals.[18] But the question remains whether this tendency gives sufficient reason for eliminating rights-language from present day moral vocabulary? Do the points made in preceding pages undermine the moral respectability of the language of rights?

Let me begin my response to the objection above with Gewirth's own answer. This involves what he entitles the 'Principle of Generic Consistency', which when applied to rights appears in the form: 'Act in accord with the generic rights of your recipients as well as of yourself.'[19] This principle is a version of the principle of universalisability or of generalisation, which is widely held to be a necessary principle of morality. Dorothy Emmet has called this principle a 'constitutive rule':

A constitutive rule in morality would be a necessary condition for a practice being called a moral practice at all. One candidate for such a constitutive rule has been called by Mr Hare and others 'Universalizability.'[20]

Emmet goes on to explain this point. It involves the rule 'treat like cases alike, and different cases differently', or put more precisely, 'if it is right to treat A in a certain way, it is right also so to treat others who resemble A in the relevant respect' (*ibid.*). The practical value of this formal criterion of ethics is that 'it exclude arbitrariness in the sense of inconsistency in the application of a principle' (*ibid.*, p. 62).

Now Gewirth shows that human rights as moral concepts necessarily involve the criterion of universalisability or the principle of generic consistency. Thus, all humans must seek to respect the basic rights of others as well as claiming them for themselves. One cannot accept that there are other humans in the world besides oneself, but refuse to accord these others human rights one claims for oneself. One could argue this point from a purely prudential position, that one will not get far in having one's interests protected if one fails to recognise a corresponding duty to respect and protect the interests of others. However, a more satisfactory argument appeals to the general relationship that must exist between individuals sharing the same basic nature. Being a member of the human race involves a kind of kinship which demands some level of altruism in living a human life. The language of human rights reflects this altruism of kinship in theory, though in practice humanity tends to be distracted by what has been called above the 'ethics of strangers'.[21]

The notion of equality which was seen to be a necessary assumption of the theory of natural or human rights is a difficult assumption to accept in practice. If it were accepted in practice, so many of the duties and obligations which are now thought to be related to charity or beneficence would be included in the category of strict justice. Because the hungry of the Third World are equal with the people of the First and Second Worlds only in terms of their abstract humanity, their interests are not strictly respected. If the poor of the world could be seen as human in the sense of being part of the human *family*, then their 'rights' in justice could be truly respected.

I think that W. Huber is highly perceptive when he makes this comment on the famous slogan of the French Revolution:

It is interesting to note, however, that the third element of the slogan, fraternity, did not find its way into the human rights documents of the Revolution. Fraternity is not a claim before the law but rather an attitude, a 'virtue' in the classical sense of the term.[22]

A conclusion following from this remark is that the theory of human rights has long remained on the abstract level, accepting in an abstract manner the equality of all human beings, but missing out on the heart of this equality in the concept and virtue of fraternity. In other words, the concept of human rights, of respecting the basic interests of all humans requires some serious effort to see oneself as part of a universal family in more than a rhetorical or sentimental sense. Thus, there is an antidote to the historical individualism and egoism associated with the liberal human rights tradition in the almost forgotten, but central, aspect of fraternity, without which the concept of a human right remains abstract and without a heart. In a sense, the doctrine of human rights has not failed, it just has not been tried or implemented as it should, by taking into account the challenge presented by its originators to see those far away as brothers and sisters rather than as strangers with little or no claim on one. The real challenge of the human rights tradition is to widen the circle of those regarded as equal and to see equality in a personal rather than in an abstract way. The abuse of the doctrine of human rights does not lead to an elimination of that doctrine as morally disreputable, since there is still a core truth which, once recognised, is at the heart of human moral endeavour.

There is some danger in admitting that the history of the doctrine of human rights is characterised in part by ethical individualism. The reason for this is that 'Individualism' is by definition a negative concept with heavily pejorative meaning.[23] So, admitting the charge of individualism is a bit like admitting to the charge of murder (another negative concept), and then trying to justify oneself. Steven Lukes opines that:

Ethical individualism is a view of the nature of morality as essentially individual. In the seventeenth and eighteenth centuries this may be seen as having taken the form of ethical egoism, according to which the sole moral object of the individual's action is his own benefit. Thus the various versions of self-interest ethics, from Hobbes onwards, maintained that one should seek to secure one's own good, not that of society as a whole or of other individuals.[24]

I think I have shown already in a satisfactory way that the deep theory of human rights involves elements of altruism, equality and fraternity. The fact that the language of rights can be used in a reactionary way does not take away from the basic aspirations deeply embedded in the concept of universal human rights. I accept fully the statement of Alan Falconer of the Irish School of Ecumenics: 'Rights, however, do not solely emerge in the conflict to secure the protection from interference by other individuals or groups. They also emerge as an aspiration. Human rights are values to be protected or encouraged.'[25] This should not be surprising in the light of Christian insistence on the sin of humankind. Just as rights arise because of human conflict, a conflict which is often destructive, so the attempt to overcome such conflict can itself be infected with the sin of the world.

In spite of the dangers of individualism and egoism associated with the language of rights, it is important to note that individualism is in fact a perversion of a closely related value, namely 'individuality'. The American Roman Catholic theologian Daniel Callahan has written in praise of individuality, arguing that Roman Catholics must avoid two extremes, one of complete 'docility to authority combined with conformity to the prevailing piety of the Catholic community', the other of 'pure self-direction...a refusal to accept any part of the collective whole'.[26] Callahan then states that 'it is only as a unique individual that one can be a Christian' (*ibid.*). Another theologian, Thomas Ogletree, recognises that in Christian ethics 'in shifting the locus of origination in moral experience from the dynamics of self-integration to the call of the other, the moral subject appears to lose all rights before the other'.[27] And in response to this threat he speaks up for 'being good to self', or as he puts it 'The first word may be: enable enjoyment, and not: be responsible to and for your neighbour. Grace is prior to commandment.'[28] Jurgen Moltmann is highly critical of Christian apologetics for defaming the 'will to self-actualisation as irreligious', but he insists that there is a kind of self-actualisation that has nothing to do with egoism but is part of the love commandment 'love your neighbour as yourself'.[29] This is applied directly to the notion of claiming one's own rights. It is part and parcel of God's command to love self properly.

Note how some modern authors have stressed that human rights are really protections for individuals against the state. And recall Dworkin's concept of rights as trumps against utilitarian considerations of general welfare. Consider, too, the emphasis in Marxist states on social and economic rights rather than on individual freedom of speech and conscience. Given these positions, there is still a need to protect the individual human being against group tyranny.[30] There is a richness which individuals bring to the notion of human nature in practice which must be respected by the language of rights, as has been noted already in the last chapter's discussion of Macdonald's critique of natural rights.

Does respect for individuality mean that the common good of society is thereby harmed? Not necessarily. It is difficult to see how the common good can be based on the violation of individual rights; indeed, this is one of the common arguments against cruder forms of act-utilitarianism, that it is willing to sacrifice individual basic goods for what it considers to be the general welfare. There must not be an exaggeration of the tension between the good of individuals and the good of groups, including the state. In fact, humans often have a desire to co-operate in communal activities.

John Finnis devotes the sixth chapter of his book *Natural Law and Natural Rights* to showing this general desire to act with others in ways that bring about individual well-being as well as the well-being of others. Very often, in fact, the individual well-being fades into the background as co-operating actors concentrate on some shared good, as in 'play'. As Finnis puts it, 'the central feature and good of play is that the activity or performance is valued by the participants for its own sake, and is itself the source of their pleasure or satisfaction'.[31] In other words, it is a mistake to think of all people acting all the time from motives of personal satisfaction. Clearly, Finnis believes that humans can be altruistic in many situations, especially in relationships of friendship and family. But, interestingly, he insists that altruism, the going out of oneself in service to others, requires that one has something individual to give.

[O]ne can give nothing to a friend unless one has something of one's own to give. One cannot even have him to dinner if one has no food save one's own ration. You say, let him bring his own food, it is the sharing that counts. But what am I sharing with him? *My* shelter, warmth, living-space. You say, have dinner together in the communal eating place. But still I have to give him *my* company, my attention and interest, which I thereby deny to someone else.[32]

If the common good is to be served, then, the individual contributions of the community must be protected in the first place.[33] The common good is built on the riches of the individual personalities making it up.

Finally, in defending the concept of rights against the charge of individualism and egoism, one can underline the various movements in recent times which struggle to obtain respect for the rights of different oppressed groups. In other words, not all rights-claims are self-centred and egoistic.[34]

THE ADVERSARIAL OBJECTION

This objection may perhaps be seen as an extension of the preceding one. Recalling the notion of rights as claims, or as entitlements which enable one to claim, the present objection is that such a possibility of claiming tends to thrust people into adversarial and 'potentially coercive relations whereby each seeks to impose burdens on others for his own benefit'.[35]

The Christian moralist, Stanley Hauerwas, has pointed out the adversarial tendency of claiming rights. In his work, *Suffering Presence*, Hauerwas discusses the appropriateness of references to the rights of children, and is heavily critical of this approach to their welfare. But his dissatisfaction with the application of the language of rights to children is part of a wider dissatisfaction with the language of rights in general. He sees the language of rights as a reflection of society's individualism and goes on to say that

Rights are necessary when it is assumed that citizens fundamentally relate to one another as strangers, if not outright enemies. From such a perspective society appears as a collection of individuals who of necessity must enter into a bargain to insure their individual survival through providing for the survival of the society.[36]

From this point of view, Hauerwas suggests, one can see, how inappropriate it is to speak of children having rights, for it assumes that children are merely another interest group in need of protection from other interest groups, 'including their parents'.[37]

Moreover, the morally jarring effect of claiming one's rights is reminiscent of Stephen Toulmin's attack on 'the tyranny of principles'. Toulmin speaks of 'the stresses of lawsuits' in the United States – 'the homeland of the adversary system' – all the time seeing this as a symptom of the 'ethics of strangers'.[38] When persons are in the habit of claiming their rights at a moment's notice, is not this a sign of the 'ethics of strangers'? Nevertheless, Toulmin recognises that there are limits to the adversarial system in practice in the US, which takes some of the bite out of the adversarial objection:

Even in the United States, the homeland of the adversary system, at least two types of disputes – labor-management conflicts and the renegotiation of commercial contracts – are dealt with by using arbitration or conciliation rather than confrontation. This is no accident. In a criminal prosecution or a routine civil damage suit arising out of a car collision, the parties are normally complete strangers before the proceedings and have no stake in one another's future, so no harm is done if they walk out of court vowing never to set eyes on each other again. By contrast, the parties to a labor grievance will normally wish to continue working together after the adjudication, while the disputants in a commercial arbitration may well retain or resume business dealings with one another despite the present disagreement. In cases of these kinds, the psychological stress of the adversary system can be quite destructive.[39]

I feel that this example provides some answer to the adversarial objection and the morally jarring quality of claim-rights. There are in certain circumstances ways of claiming rights, involving more or less peaceful arbitration, which accepts that some kind of harmonious relationship beneficial to all parties in the dispute is to be maintained afterwards. In other words, the morally jarring quality of rights as claims is limited to those situations where the persons claimed against remain as strangers, outside the circle of one's intimacy. And in so far as one makes an attempt to draw strangers into that circle of intimacy, one has to show greater care in claiming in an adversarial sense. In fact, ideally the adversarial sense of rights as claims should be relegated to situations where relationships between persons have broken down to such an extent that they have to be separated, each receiving what is due as a result of the life of the relationship. I am thinking here in particular of marriages and friendships which break down. I envisage the language of rights in such circumstances as a way of salvaging some justice from the situation. In other words, I accept that there will be some situations in which rights-language must be used against a background of bitterness and hurt; but I insist that this use need not be the primary use of the language of rights. People can accept that conflict is a part of life and that mutual rights in such situations can be negotiated and upheld.

The adversarial objection appears to be related more to the language of claiming rights than to the language of having claims and entitlements. The presumption of this objection seems to be that all rights must be claimed and that all right-holders will naturally spend their time taking their neighbours to court. But, of course, this presumption is false. In a number of cases of possessing rights, claiming is inappropriate because of the circumstances. For instance, Robin Downie, in his discussion of the 'right to criticise' mentions the case of the tutor who has the right to criticise a student, but should not exercise the right in certain cases. For example close to an examination, when such criticism might seriously undermine the confidence of the student.[40] Claiming the right to criticise would be singularly inappropriate at such a time.

Another way of expressing the limits to claiming rights is by reference to the distinction made already between mandatory and discretionary rights. Where a right is discretionary the right-holder is permitted to waive her claim more or less at will. Indeed, whenever the emphasis on claiming rights becomes too insistent, it needs to be supplemented by the emphasis on the power to waive claim-rights. Sometimes, in order to avoid the bitterness of adversarial proceedings, right-holders' waiving of rights may amount to acts of supererogation. Needless to say, the power to waive a right is severely limited in the case of mandatory rights (and does not exist in the case of inalienable rights), and whenever a right is waived the motives and reasons of the person should be examined, since waiving rights may be an easy option for some, rather than having to face up to necessary (though ultimately positive) conflict which comes with claiming.

I should also mention the limits to claiming associated with manifesto rights as described by Feinberg. These 'claims' refer to basic needs of persons which for various reasons cannot be fulfilled in the foreseeable future. Feinberg gives the example of young orphans in the Third World and their needs as a case of possessing such a right.[41] It is inappropriate for the poor children of Latin America to claim a right not to be poor, since the immediate possibilities of alleviating their poverty are non-existent. As a long-term goal, respect for the rights of the poor of the Third World, in the sense of individualised, specific needs, regarded as basic in the developed lands, is something to be encouraged. But attempting to claim the impossible or the utopian makes little or no sense. Claim-rights should be kept as specific and as practical as possible if they are to be correlated with workable duties or obligations.[42]

In spite of the adversarial objection, then, I prefer to follow the example of Feinberg and stand by the value of claiming:

Even if there are conceivable circumstances in which one would admit rights diffidently, there is no doubt that their characteristic use, and that for which they are distinctively well suited, is to be claimed, demanded, affirmed, insisted upon. They are essentially sturdy objects to 'stand upon,' a most useful sort of moral furniture ... This feature of rights is connected in a way with the customary rhetoric about what it is to be a human being. Having rights enables us to 'stand up like men,' to look others in the eye, and to feel in some fundamental way the equal of anyone.[43]

CAN A GOOD MAN BE HARMED?

This question comes from the title of an essay by the philosopher Peter Winch.[44] Indirectly, the question and the article present a further kind of radical scepticism about the rights people ordinarily claim. If Winch's argument is successful, so many of the claims humans make today will have to be set aside as unimportant, or worse, as morally distracting.

'HARM' AND THE GOOD MAN

Winch presents a number of examples of the thesis that a good man cannot be harmed, but feels 'absolutely safe'. Let me mention just one of these examples. In modern times, Wittgenstein has noted an experience which he says is not uncommon, namely, 'the experience of feeling absolutely safe'.[45] What sense can one make of this remark?

It appears that Wittgenstein regarded such safety as being a possible feature of one's fitting into the moral language game, within which an absolute value is given to the pursuit of the 'Good'. For Wittgenstein the moral language game commits the participator to certain values which bind him or her uncompromisingly. One can see how binding moral values are by contrasting two uses of the term 'ought'. If I am a mediocre tennis player and someone challenges me saying 'You ought to play better', there is no obligation to heed this advice or command. There is nothing wrong in saying, 'I am quite happy playing at this level.' On the other hand, if I behave badly, by lying for instance, I cannot set aside the criticism 'You ought to be truthful', by saying 'I am quite happy being a liar.' To say something like that is to fail to understand the moral language game and to put oneself outside of it.

Thus, within the moral language game the language of duty and obligation in relation to the pursuit of the 'Good' has an absolute status. As long as one pursues the 'Good', one cannot be harmed. In other words, according to the line of argument I am following, the good man can be harmed only when he gives in to 'sin'. His fall from grace is the only real tragedy from the moral point of view.

How is scepticism about the language of rights derived from the notion that the good man cannot be harmed? The immediate answer is that so much of the language of rights is directed towards protecting people from harm in the ordinary sense of pain and suffering and deprivation. In fact, claims to be protected from suffering have proliferated to a bewildering extent, distracting humanity from the 'one thing necessary' – pursuing the Good. To give serious attention to any 'harm' other than moral harm may be in itself harmful. It seems to me that this objection works best in conjunction with the two previous objections of individualism/egoism and the adversarial trend of modern society, perhaps even adding further a kind of 'slippery slope' argument.

When persons begin to claim all sorts of rights to what might be called 'pre-moral' goods (that is goods or values seen in the abstract apart from particular situations of choice by moral agents), for example health, education, employment, participation in government and so on, there is a real danger of undermining one's moral character through entering into conflict with others, making false claims, exaggerating one's needs. It is so easy to be drawn into sin by the power which claiming gives the individual. According to this point of view, even seemingly unselfish claims for the sake of others must be viewed with some suspicion, since fighting for the rights of others can be just as damaging morally as fighting for one's own rights. In both cases the 'fighting' or 'struggle' can be harmful in the true 'moral' sense.

The approach so far described can be applied in practice in at least two ways. On one hand, one could adopt a high Stoical approach which counsels a radical detachment from the goods of this world. This would allow a person to minimise the pain of losing his or her participation in such goods, and there would be less temptation to make claims which add to the conflict and disharmony of moral life. The advice, in other words, is that people should not get too interested in their health or wealth (to take just two examples), because such goods are precarious, and when they are deprived of them depression and anger may be the result. Then they may start making claims against others, getting into the adversarial trend and ultimately falling away from pursuit of the Good. On the other hand, there is a less radical approach which permits the enjoyment of goods like health and wealth, but is willing to let these goods go without a struggle rather than get involved in 'sinful' conflict.

'HARM' AND THE FAITHFUL PERSON

It is at this stage that I can introduce a clearly theological note. In my opinion, the philosophical discussion of the possibility of limiting the concept of harm to moral harm, the harm to moral character, has marked Christian echoes, beginning in the early church and appearing again and again throughout Christian tradition.[46]

Many of the New Testament writings reveal the struggles of a small, powerless and persecuted group. The earliest strands of the literature, especially the letters to the Thessalonians and Corinthians, are marked by strong eschatological expectations which colour the moral outlook of the early community.[47] There is an air of detachment from worldly goods in Paul's advice to the Corinthians on adopting a state of life, such as marriage (1 Cor. 7.26,31). Some Christians took detachment to an extreme and decided to abstain from working, and Paul had to warn against this in his Second Letter to the Thessalonians (2 Thess. 3.6–12).

Clearly, New Testament morality, like Old Testament morality before it, emphasises community as opposed to individualism. Speaking of Pauline morality, John Ferguson comments on this communitarian emphasis:

The keyword is here *koinonia*, which is variously rendered fellowship, communion, contribution, distribution, partnership, sharing and other terms in such a way as to obscure the fact that it is a common thread running through the New Testament. The word comes in *Acts*, of the *common* life of the church (2, 42) and of the *sharing* of material resources (4, 32). Both passages are to be seen in the light of the immediately preceding gift of the Holy Spirit.[48]

No wonder, then, that Paul takes the Corinthians to task for the disputes which undermine the peace of the community. In fact, some of these disputes between Christians were brought out into the open in the pagan courts, to Paul's evident disgust. 'To have lawsuits at all with one another is defeat for you. Why not rather suffer wrong? Why not rather be defrauded? But you yourself wrong and defraud, and that even your own brethren.' (1. Cor. 6.7–8, RSV.). These words appear to be a critique of individual selfishness in claiming against others, when individual sacrifices ought to be made for the sake of the good of the community. Moreover, there is a hint of the view that a good man cannot be harmed ultimately, since the apostle counsels allowing oneself to be wronged rather than doing wrong. This is not to say that Paul failed to see such sacrifices as harmful to some extent, only that such suffering was ultimately worthwhile in the light of God's fidelity to his promises. For instance, one should keep in mind the eschatological perspective of the Christian community seen as joining in the judgement of the world when the End at last comes.[49]

One further scriptural example which is related to the safety of the good man comes from the First Letter of Peter. On the subject of the various duties which the Christian must undertake, the writer refers to the duties of servants to their masters (1 Pet. 2.18ff.). The duty of service is not just to the good and kindly but also to those who are harsh. There is no merit in suffering when one is being punished justly. However, there may be merit in suffering injustice patiently when this is understood as an aspect of the Disciple's imitation of the suffering Christ. Christ's redemptive suffering has brought humanity, seen as straying sheep, back to the shepherd of their souls. In the midst of suffering there is still a sense of safety in the hands of God. Commenting on the admonition to suffer humbly in this epistle, R. Schnackenburg gives the opinion that this 'is not an ethical admonition making a virtue out of necessity, but springs from the religious insight, that God alone can change the ultimate darkness of this world era, that only he can "exalt you in the time of visitation"' (1 Pet. 5.6).[50]

The objection may now be presented which argues that there is little sense in protesting against injustice, and claiming one's rights, when one is part of a tiny persecuted sect in a backwater of the Roman Empire. Surely the early Christian subordination to the ruling powers was simply a sign of the wise policy of 'keeping one's head down' and 'not making waves'. And, one might add, when Christianity became more sophisticated it soon found its voice in claiming what it thought was its due. This objection may well be partly valid, but it can easily enough be countered with the claim that the Church was merely following its Lord's advice to be 'as wise as serpents and as simple as doves' (Mtt. 10.16). However, I think there is more theologically to the examples mentioned above than a concerted attempt to close ranks and provide a respectable front for Jews and pagans alike.

I regard the New Testament doctrine on the essential safety of those who love God and do good as a valuable critique of efforts to brand all kinds of suffering as harmful, which, arguably, has been partly responsible for the bewildering proliferation of rights in modern times. For one thing, the suffering that Christians must bear does not come to an end when the crudest of persecutions are over. The rejection of immoderate personal claims is not merely a feature of the time when the Church expected an imminent *Parousia*. In every age the call goes out to Christians to embrace 'the fellowship of Christ's sufferings'.

In his article, 'The Fellowship of his Sufferings', Barnabas Ahern situates this conception in the life and teaching of St Paul:

Through conversion St. Paul gained a new spiritual life. On the road to Damascus he received from the risen Christ the messianic gift of the Holy Spirit who ever after inspired and ruled his activity as that of a true son of God. For the Apostle this meant, in the expressive phrase of Philippians 3:10, that he had come to know Christ, 'in the power of his resurrection.' But that was not all. He affirms in the same breath that, through conversion, he came to know also 'the fellowship of his sufferings.' This significant addition is in accord with the polarity of all Pauline thought which joins death and resurrection as two inseparable aspects of the same salvific mystery, whether in the life of Christ or in the lives of Christians.[51]

It would be a serious mistake, however, to think that the call to fellowship in the sufferings of Christ is limited to the group of apostles or to a certain period of time at the start of the Church's history. This call to fellowship in the sufferings of Christ and through these sufferings to the glory of the resurrection, is the basis of the Christian reality of baptism into Christ. For all the baptised there is a call to follow the Master through suffering and death into new life. There is no other way for the Christian to be saved. Ahern remarks on this striking feature of Paul's doctrine on Baptism:

For him sacramental death marks the point of departure for an altogether new life, in which the Christian ever remains 'dead to sin, but alive to God' (Rom. 6:11). This is possible only because, in Baptism, the Christian shares the very Spirit of Christ which endures forever in the body-person to which the new member is united.[52]

This sacramental death must not be unduly 'spiritualised', as if no struggle is involved in accepting Baptism in the first place, and afterwards in living out the implications of the new life in the Spirit. Consider, for instance, the doctrine in Galatians where Christians are said to have 'crucified their flesh with its passions and desires' (Gal. 5.24). On this, Ahern warns that 'The word "crucified" is not a mere figure. Baptism gives a share in the death which loving fidelity to God's will produced in Christ, so that Paul could write, "With Christ I have been nailed to the cross" (Gal. 2:19)' (p. 108). There is a real personal struggle in passing from the life of the flesh to the life of the Spirit, and walking in the Spirit itself is a constant challenge. Thus there is a constant tension in the Christian life between what has already happened to the individual in his or her calling and what needs to be achieved. Ahern puts it well,

Christian life, therefore, involves an enduring paradox. The Christian, on the one hand, lives on an eschatological plane, sharing the risen life of the Savior and His love for the Father. Paul writes in the name of every Christian, 'I live, now not I, but Christ lives in me' (Gal. 2:20). On the other hand, the activity of the Holy Spirit has not yet transformed the whole of man, nor the whole of the world around him. (p. 109).

In the Pauline doctrine discussed so far, then, there is a sense of realism about the suffering that must be endured by Christians, and, at the same time, a sense of confidence in the possession of the believer by God's Spirit. This is particularly clear in Romans where Paul describes the *terminus* of Christian experience, 'If we are sons, we are heirs also: heirs indeed of God and joint heirs with Christ, since we suffer with him that we may also be glorified with him. For I reckon that the sufferings of this present time are not worthy to be compared with the glory to come to be revealed in us' (Rom. (8.) 17–18).

With regard to the language of rights the Christian perspective on being involved in the fellowship of Christ's suffering tends to undermine what I regard to be one of the main pillars of the ethos of claiming rights. This ethos assumes that suffering and pain are always harmful, have no redeeming features, and must always be the object of claims for relief. The Christian tradition, as I have outlined it, is not willing to accept such an assumption about the sufferings of this world.[53] Some sufferings are inevitable and represent a vital aspect of the Christian way of life.[54] Baptism is both a 'tomb and a womb', the Christian must die in order to live, and the painful death to self, to all that opposes God's will, continues throughout one's earthly life. The claiming of rights, on the other hand, tends to become linked with strenuous efforts to avoid all suffering. This form of language is associated with individual autonomy and power over one's life, whereas Christianity tends towards a recognition of the necessity of human weakness, service of others rather than developing personal power and autonomy, and a total dependence on the grace and will of God. There is even the temptation presented by the language of rights of becoming like the pharisee of the Gospel, marching to the front of God's house and claiming against Him.

The Christian way offers a theology of suffering which relativises the concept of 'harm'. Clearly, the most serious harm that can occur to the believer is alienation from God through sin. Earlier I mentioned that this New Testament view of 'harm' has been echoed down through the ages in the Christian tradition. Before offering some criticism of this stand in relation to the language of rights, I want to discuss briefly two examples from the Christian tradition which attempt to remain faithful to the theology discussed above.

THE FRANCISCAN TRADITION

The fact that Francesco Bernardone remains one of the most popular saints of the Christian Church and has such a wide appeal even today, suggests that his interpretation of, and living out of, the Christian faith should be taken seriously. Unfortunately, the attractiveness of St Francis for many is based on a superficial and sentimental understanding of his life and teaching. If there is one thing that St Francis was not, it was the caricature of a nature loving hippy that is sometimes presented for public consumption. He was above all a man who took the imitation of Christ seriously, an almost literal imitation which concentrated on the poverty and obedience of Jesus. The question of poverty has always been a controversial one in the Franciscan tradition, often narrowly focussing on a material interpretation of this evangelical virtue.[55] More important than this, however, is a more profound interpretation of poverty, as mentioned in the following quotation from Simon Tugwell:

In the later Franciscan tradition it is precisely material poverty which is regarded as crucial, and this in turn comes to mean little more than legal poverty; but for Francis himself the essential poverty is seen in the abandonment of rights, in the abandonment of one's own will. In one of his *Admonitions* he is quite explicit: 'Who is it who abandons everything he possesses? It is the person who yields himself totally to obedience in the hands of his superior' (Admonition 3:3).[56]

Of course, Francis would not have expressed his vocation in terms of the language of rights, since that form of language was unknown in his day, but Tugwell is wise to use this language to describe and explore Francis' basic attitude. Consider again the language used earlier to elucidate the rights concept – claims, entitlements, powers and liberties – and it has to be said that Francis turned these on their head. The 'Poor Man of Assisi' called his followers *fratres minores* or lesser brothers. This means in the words of Tugwell:

Francis wants his friars to be *minores* precisely in the sense that they are never to be in a position to control things, they are to be at the mercy of whatever happens. (p. 129)

But control over things and avoidance of being at the mercy
of whatever happens is the basic rationale of rights language,
the very opposite of the Franciscan spirit, which is sometimes
said to be a recovery of the true spirit of the Gospel. Francis did
not seek security and protection for himself or his followers. This
is a position founded on a particular understanding of divine
providence. As Tugwell expresses it, 'If this is God's world,
ruled by his providence, we ought not to have to protect
ourselves against it. Whatever happens is God's gift to us' (*ibid.*,
p. 130). Tugwell sees this whole stress on 'radical unprotectedness' as based on a Christological foundation. Francis wished
to imitate the unprotectedness of Christ. This is the true
background to Francis' love of nature, a love which was far from
sentimental:

The exposure to nature which is a genuine part of Franciscan tradition
is not primarily a matter of fresh air and fun, it is most typically a
sharing in Christ's exposure to maltreatment and rejection. Francis
was no romantic, sentimentalising and idealising the raw life of
nature; he knew very well what happens to people who strip off the
customary ways we have devised of insulating ourselves against the
world outside: they get crucified. But it is only on the basis of a
readiness to be crucified that redemption can operate. (*ibid.*, pp. 132–
3)

It is reasoning of this kind that explains the sense in which
Francis of Assisi must have experienced what Wittgenstein was
trying to express in the position that the good man may feel safe,
though suffering harm in the ordinary sense of that word. In
Francis' case, the feeling of being absolutely safe is based on
nothing else but a profound faith in the working of a loving
divine providence. He was a firm believer in the phrase of St
Paul, 'All things work for the good of those who love God'
(Rom. 8.28), and this means *all* things, even the painful things.

This radical life project of the early Franciscan tradition was
as 'scandalous' to people in the Church in the twelfth century
as it is today. Many of his advisers urged Francis to adopt the
rule of some already existing order which would not be so severe
and demanding, but he refused to consider such a step. Pope
Innocent gave verbal approval to the original rule of St Francis

around 1209, and was probably wise to withhold written approbation until Francis showed that this seemingly impossible life could be lived over time, and without falling into the unorthodoxies of his predecessors, such as Peter Waldo. The example of the Franciscan Order down through the centuries often gives the impression that the radical approach of its founder needs to be 'adapted' for the sake of lesser men and women than the '*Poverello*'. Still, the possibility of a simple Gospel style of life without the distractions which lead one into concern for one's rights against others maintains a certain attractiveness.

CHRISTIAN PACIFISM

In the contemporary world, even within the Christian tradition, radical pacifism is likely to be a strictly minority position. The 'right' to self-defence and the doctrine of the 'just war' are widely accepted as a more realistic approach to the violence of humankind. However, there are some voices that sound out in favour of the pacifist stance.

Take Stanley Hauerwas, for example. In *The Peaceable Kingdom*, he shows a clear hostility to much of the rights-language currently in vogue, especially when a right to violence for the sake of justice is in question:

Therefore Christians cannot seek justice from the barrel of a gun; and we must be suspicious of that justice that relies on manipulation of our less than worthy motives, for God does not rule creation through coercion, but through a cross.[57]

Hauerwas is very much in line with the Franciscan critique of Christians trying to get into positions of control; this is not the strategy of the peaceable kingdom. In fact, as eschatological people, according to this theologian, there is a very real sense in which Christians must be out of control: 'Living out of control' is part of the virtues of patience and hope. And he goes on to say:

For the irony is that no one is more controlled than those who assume they are in control or desire to be in control. It is the rich above all whose wealth gives them the illusion of independence, separateness, of being in control. But all of us in one way or another willingly submit to the illusion that we can rid our world of chance and surprise. Yet when we do that our world becomes diminished as we try to live securely rather than well. (p. 105)

This seems to me to be an admirable repetition of what Tugwell has portrayed as the theology of St Francis. If the language of rights is used as an instrument of control in the sense that Hauerwas has described, then moral scepticism about this form of language is to be taken very seriously indeed. The reference above to living 'securely rather than well' is a recognition of the risks of discomfort arising from pursuit of the Good.

Indeed, Hauerwas becomes even more explicit in his reservations about rights-language in his criticism of a 'natural law' ethic:

For example, natural law is often expressed today in the language of universal rights – the right to be free, to worship, to speak, to choose one's vocation, etc. Such language, at least in principle, seems to embody the highest human ideals. But it also facilitates the assumption that since anyone who denies such rights is morally obtuse and should be "forced" to recognise the error of his ways. Indeed, we overlook too easily how the language of 'rights', in spite of its potential for good, contains within its logic a powerful justification for violence (p. 61).

When it comes to the Christian strategy for facing aggression, Hauerwas discusses the argument between the Niebuhr brothers, Richard and Reinhold, from the pages of *The Christian Century* in 1932. This concerned the proper Christian response to the Japanese invasion of Manchuria. Hauerwas tends to side with the pacifism of Richard Niebuhr, who felt that there was a way of 'doing nothing' which is still theologically significant.[58] Christian in-activity, for Richard Niebuhr and for Hauerwas, is the type founded on a belief in a force in history that will ultimately create a different kind of world from the one currently experienced. Moreover, the Christian way of doing nothing entails an attitude of humility, the recognition that man's righteous indignation is far from being actually righteous. Christians must wait for God to act, and, in the meantime, stand aloof from movements such as nationalism and capitalism, uniting in a higher loyalty and preparing in this way for the future. Either way, human life on earth seems touched by tragedy. For Reinhold Niebuhr this stems from the imperfect, even sinful, response of Christians to violence, which is still a necessary one. For his brother Richard and for Stanley Hauerwas, on the other hand, tragedy stems from refusing to respond to violence with violence and thus running the risk of being abused by violent men. The pacifist tends to believe that it is better to suffer evil than to do evil. Those who refuse to take such a radical stance are forced to speak of necessary evil in a just war, or the lesser of two evils, or they attempt to glorify retaliatory violence as righteous indignation.

One of the major influences on the theology of Hauerwas is the thought of John Howard Yoder. Many of the themes brought out above concerning the radicalism of Christian responses to suffering and evil find parallels in his work, especially in his *The Politics of Jesus*. He tends to be critical of the mendicant tradition in its attempt to justify a literal imitation of Christ's life by reference to the Gospel story.[59] The early Christians were not concerned with imitating the poverty of Christ, or the fact that he was a carpenter. Paul's advice on remaining unmarried does not refer to the example of Jesus, though tradition holds he remained single. The only area of the earthly life of Jesus which is set before Christians for their imitation is, according to Yoder, the carrying of the cross.

With regard to this concept of sharing in Christ's cross, the fellowship of his sufferings, Yoder is quite specific:

The cross of Calvary was not a difficult family situation, not a frustration of visions of personal fulfilment, a crushing debt or a nagging in-law; it was the political, legally to be expected result of a moral clash with the powers ruling his society. Already the early Christians had to be warned against claiming merit for any and all suffering; only if their suffering be innocent, and a result of the evil will of their adversaries, may it be understood as meaningful before God (1 Pet. 2:18–21; 3:14–18; 4:1, 13–16; 5:9; James 4:10).[60]

Interestingly, Yoder cites the case from the Letter of Peter where servants are required to be subordinate even to harsh and unjust masters. Note, too, that this kind of suffering is 'meaningful before God' in Yoder's opinion. Once again, I am not claiming that Yoder denies that pacifism brings harm to individuals. It is simply the case that harm of one type has to be embraced to avoid a more ultimate kind of harm – eternal death.

Finally, on this question of pacifism, what is most interesting in Yoder's work is his insistence on the realism of a pacifist ethic. In his fifth chapter he instances ways of non-violent resistance used successfully by the Jews against the Romans, and he entitles another, later chapter 'Revolutionary Subordination' (*ibid.*, pp. 90–3; 163–92). This is important as a critique of the assumption that violent resistance to evil is practically always necessary. It can also be used to question the need to claim rights in situations of conflict. Yoder and Hauerwas thus encourage Christians in particular to expend more energy in the area of ethical imagination before, and often instead of, getting involved in violent adversarial positions.

ANSWERING SCEPTICISM

I wish now to respond to the preceding sections which centre on moral philosophical and theological scepticism concerning the concept of 'harm' which underlies so much of human rights-claims.

First, I want to admit the strength of what has been said, especially from the Christian point of view, as a support for the position that rights-language needs to be severely moderated if it is to be morally valuable. In particular, the approach argued above rightly attacks the view that one can have an automatic right against any and all harm (in the ordinary sense of the word) that might touch one's life. There can be an obsessive fear of any suffering or deprivation which paralyses people from getting on with life, and this fear may be expressed in part by the urge to claim rights against others.[61] In the light of this trend, the world needs to hear the words of Christ blessing humanity's negative feelings. Moreover, I believe there is some sense to the position that moral harm is one of the most serious kinds of harm to be guarded against in life.

Having admitted the value of the objections to some extent, I must still voice some reservations about the details of the objections. For instance, some care must be taken in accepting an anti-naturalistic position. There is a danger in making a rigid distinction between pre-moral and moral values, such that the latter come to be transported into a mysterious world of their own, entry into which is by private intuitions alone.

Without getting too deeply immersed in the argument over ethical naturalism, I shall mention what I regard to be the main features of the controversy. In her article 'Moral Beliefs', Philippa Foot answered the question 'Why be Moral?' by saying that the virtues can only be recommended if they constitute a good to the virtuous man.[62] In other words, the reason for being moral is that it pays to be moral in the ordinary sense in which people live in peace and harmony and enjoy the good things of life. Foot believed that immoral people may prosper for a while, but in the long term will be unhappy.[63] Foot's original position was an attempt to revive a form of ethical naturalism in reaction to the metaethical theories – emotivism and prescriptivism – in vogue at the time. Hare's prescriptivism, in particular, tended to create a wide gap indeed between facts and values, and left the discernment of values at a highly subjective, almost arbitrary level.

In reply to Mrs Foot, the philosophers D. Z. Phillips and H. O. Mounce argued that morality cannot be reduced to prudential factors in this way.[64] In fact, they argued that people can remain prosperous and relatively happy (in the sense meant by Foot) by adopting an evil life-style. If a person is powerful enough and cares little for public opinion a life of crime certainly does pay.

So, according to Phillips and Mounce, a person can only be moral for moral reasons. The good person does not reduce morality to prospering or faring well in an everyday sense, though no doubt he or she will want to fare well so long as that is possible without doing wrong. For the anti-naturalist position, to prosper or to fare well must be understood morally in the first place; there is something irrational in claiming that an evil person can 'prosper' since prosperity is so intimately linked with goodness. But is not this an example of a stipulative definition, deciding to link prosperity and happiness with moral goodness? There is indeed a sense in which this definition appears as stipulative, but I feel that it may still have wide appeal, so much so that it takes on the quality of a discovery or revelation. One may seem to be forcing a definition on others, whereas in fact one is appealing to others to recognise a common enough experience. In the case of being morally good, it is quite a respectable position, I think, to hold that this is such an important human value that its absence must entail some unhappiness. The major problem, however, in speaking in this way is that 'happiness' is generally understood in a psychologically subjective way. Thus, it is difficult to convince the person who enjoys the effects of wrong actions that he must be unhappy 'deep down' or 'subconsciously'.

The main drawback I find with the position of Winch, and Phillips and Mounce, is that it makes too much of the conflict between maintaining one's moral character and participating in what I have called pre-moral values. Usually, moral goodness involves the harmonious arrangement of these values by the individual moral agent. Note that reference to health and life as being pre-moral values does not imply that such values are unimportant, or indeed that they are unrelated to moral life. As used in recent Roman Catholic ethics, the category of the pre-moral relates to values important to human beings seen in an abstract way, before being chosen by individuals in particular circumstances.[65] It is only when these values are taken in a personal sense, when they become the object of individual choices, and even claims, that they become truly 'moral' values.

Thus, personal moral character does depend on the attitude one has towards 'pre-moral' values, and the ways in which one seeks to participate in them together with others. Indeed, there may be occasions when the basic values of human living have to be sacrificed for the sake of moral character and moral goodness, for instance, martyrs give up the possibility of enjoying many goods, rather than act directly against a basic good or value. But the point is that personal moral goodness always involves a positive respect for pre-moral goods or values. For the most part, then, moral agents can maintain their moral goodness and prosper in the ordinary sense of enjoying pre-moral values. In fact, moral goodness is based on respect for such values.

The second drawback in concentrating on personal moral goodness or character at the expense of all other values is that it may be self-defeating. In avoiding moral harm one can be willing to sacrifice the good of others too easily. In order to avoid the adversarial objection, one may avoid making claims for others in the cause of one's own moral rectitude. The aim of moral goodness seems to be like the aim of happiness – neither should be sought directly; they come by concentrating on something else, especially the welfare of others. The New Testament insistence on living according to the Spirit and avoiding the things of the flesh is not supposed to lead to personal navel-gazing and obsessive concern with one's own spiritual and moral progress. By concentrating on the teaching and example of Christ one comes to live an altruistic, loving way of life. At a later stage of Christian history, when the mendicant orders began to appear, some members of the older monastic orders were shocked at the notion of 'religious' moving about outside of the cloister, but the good of others was regarded by the friars as a justification for making the world their cloister, even at the cost of committing some 'unavoidable sins'.[66]

It is extremely difficult to avoid the scope of rights-language, even in radical moral and religious systems such as Franciscanism and pacifism. For if a vision such as these is deemed central to life, how can one let it go without a struggle? Although Francis wanted to live a precarious and unprotected life, he still had to consider the right to follow conscience, to say yes to the revelation he felt came from God. This is why Francis so stubbornly refused to adopt any other existing rule of life. He was driven by the message of God, as he saw it, and in this case the least one can say is that the right to live according to the Gospel followed from the duty to live it. The claims of Francis seem odd in contemporary terms; who today wishes to live insecurely? But for those enchanted by the Christian Gospel, poverty was paradoxically the greatest treasure.

With regard to pacifism, something similar can be said. A

radical right is being claimed, a right of conscience, not to be forced into forms of self-defence regarded as immoral and unChristian. It involves the claim to be a conscientious objector in wartime, and perhaps the claim against other Christians as well as against non-believers to consider pacifism as a legitimate response to violence.

Ultimately, there must be at least one right that can be claimed, namely, the right to be morally good, to follow one's conscience.[67] The problem remains as to how wide the scope of this right really is. If one takes ethical naturalism seriously and underlines the importance of pre-moral values, then rights to participation in these cannot be excluded, though they may need to be moderated when conflict arises.

CONCLUSION

In a recent book review, David Little states that, 'At present, it is difficult both to live with and without "rights-talk".'[68] I hope that the last three chapters have illustrated the truth of this statement. In particular, this chapter has underlined the drawbacks and disadvantages of rights-language from a moral point of view. Yes, the language of rights can be a cover for individual and group selfishness, for instance, when human rights remain at an abstract level, and when the equality built into the basic concept is not cashed in practical terms. I argued that the virtue of fraternity is needed to save human rights from abstraction and self-centredness.

In response to the criticism that the language of rights leads to an adversarial approach to human conflict, the answer must be 'Yes and No'. 'Yes' in the sense that the 'limited intelligence' and 'limited sympathies' of humanity can lead to situations where justice can only be achieved by making claims against those reluctant to accept their duties. 'No' in the sense that not all rights-claims demand such an adversarial background; in some cases arbitration and negotiation can proceed on a civilised basis, which avoids a major part of the bitterness arising from personal conflict. It remains the case that humanity needs at times to stand up for rights rather than acting as a doormat for unscrupulous elements.

This last remark is also partly the answer to the critique related to the question 'Can the good/faithful man be harmed?'. In so far as being morally good demands participation in certain basic pre-moral values, then claims to such participation in my own life and in the lives of others must be taken seriously. Of course such claims can multiply to an extent that scandalises many, and which may damage the respectability of rights-language in general. For instance, the obsessive desire to rid humanity of all pain and deprivation is not a good basis for developing a set of realistic rights-claims. (In fact, one might say that the distinction between claims and liberties mentioned in chapter 2, is a sign that people cannot expect to escape all harm in their relations with others.)

From the Christian perspective it is equally clear that suffering and pain are not the unmitigated disaster they are sometimes made out to be. They can be part of God's providence in general, and part of the Christian vocation to share in the fellowship of Christ's sufferings in particular. There remains a sense in which the greatest harm that can befall a faithful person is moral harm, and avoidance of this can call for the sacrifice of pre-moral values. However, for the most part human flourishing consists of harmonious participation in a set of pre-moral goods. And such participation requires the ability to claim as well as the ability to waive claims when the circumstances are apt.

CHAPTER 5

Imagination, metaethics and rights

The second half of our initial discussion of definition took as its base the wider notion of connotation mentioned by Hospers.[1] This centred on the power of various terms to affect people who hear or see them in different ways. Pictorial and poetic meanings are among the chief examples offered by Hospers. Emotive meaning is another example. It was suggested that such understandings are not mere subjective reactions to a term, not just an instance of the 'pragmatics' of a term, but also part of the 'semantics' of a term or concept. This approach led us to consider in an introductory manner the possibility of an imaginative analysis of terms, recognising that images may often be richer in terms of meaning than the concepts which attempt to pin them down. As Sallie McFague suggested, concepts may discipline images, but images also feed concepts. A concept may become so widely accepted that we forget its limitations in bringing out the full meaning of an image.[2] Returning to the connection between image and concept we may see the value of criticising a particular conceptualisation, replacing it with one or more new concepts which represent the image in a more satisfactory way.

In the following pages I hope to bring out the importance of imagination in elucidating the meaning of rights, and thus the importance of imagination in metaethics as well as in normative ethics. Beginning with some initial points on the importance of imagination in general I want to pass on as quickly as possible to consider the value of metaphors and models. My suggestion will be that some of the terms we have already been using to define rights, especially 'freedom' and 'power' may be under-

stood as models by which a richer understanding of the nature
and value of rights-language can be gained.

The important role of imagination in human knowing and
being in the world has at last been widely recognised across the
boundaries of various disciplines. Where once the value of
imagination was largely restricted to the category of art and
literature, it has now escaped such limits, and finds a home in
philosophy, science and theology. Imagination has come of age.
Like the language of rights it has become respectable, even
indispensable.

James Mackey, for instance, speaks of the necessity 'to rescue
imagination from its imprisonment in the age-old prejudice that
it is the faculty of the childish and the fanciful, wilful, wild, and
at times demoniacally destructive'.[3] And he goes on to show
how contemporary philosophers such as Mary Warnock have
shown the essential need for imagination in epistemology,
especially in relation to perception.[4] Philip Keane looks to the
history of epistemology and sees room for imagination in the
thought of Aristotle (placing more emphasis on sense experience
than Plato), Aquinas (with his concept of imagination as an
internal sense and the *vis cogitativa*, 'which evaluates the sense
data in an instinctual as opposed to a reflective manner') and
Newman (with his informal inference involving the 'illative
sense').[5]

Keane stresses as well the importance of contemporary
philosophical movements in unfolding the value of imagination.
There is, for instance, the whole area of hermeneutics, the
history of which he summarises from Schleiermacher to Ricoeur.
This involves a number of philosophical movements, including
Husserl's phenomenology, with its deep influence (especially on
Ricoeur), and Heidegger's wedding between ontology and
hermeneutics, with its equally profound influence on Gadamer,
notably in his *Truth and Method*.[6] The work of Ricoeur on the
interpretation of texts is especially significant and influential, in
particular concepts such as 'distantiation',[7] the 'polysemic'

aspect of many words, and above all the paradigmatic textual reality of metaphor, bring out the need for creativity in the interpreter as well as recognising the creativity of the original writer. And creativity, of course, is practically synonymous with imagination.[8]

In science, too, imagination has found a secure home.[9] We recognise in first place the role of creative imagination in the process of discovering new insights and the history of human inventiveness. Before discussing the value of creative imagination in ethics, Daniel Maguire,[10] gives us some insights into scientific discoveries. For instance, he cites examples from J. Bronowski[11] and Arthur Koestler.[12] There is the famous discovery of Newton's where he sees the connection between gravity on earth – the apple falling – and gravity beyond our atmosphere applying to the orbiting planets. Or take Guten-berg's invention of the printing press after watching grapes being crushed in a wine-press. In cases such as these imagination involves the discovery of hidden likenesses, relating two realities which up to then had seemed so dissimilar. Inventiveness, then, is an act of liberation, 'the defeat of habit by originality'.[13]

In second place, science employs imagination in its use of models to understand complex phenomena. There are many kinds of models used in science. The following types are mentioned by Max Black: scale models, analogue models, mathematical models and theoretical models.[14] Interestingly, Black understands the use of models in science as akin to the use of metaphor, where models are sustained and systematic meta-phors. He goes on to say:

A memorable metaphor has the power to bring two separate domains into cognitive and emotional relation by using language directly appropriate to the one as a lens for seeing the other; the implications, suggestions and supporting values entwined with the literal use of the metaphorical expression enable us to see a new subject matter in a new way.[15]

In this way scientific models begin with a reality that is relatively well known, using this to throw light on something which is less well known. In other words, the scientist is engaged in finding similarities, likenesses between things which are dissimilar or unalike. As Black expresses it:

They... bring about a wedding of disparate subjects, by a distinctive operation of transfer of the *implications* of relatively well-organised cognitive fields. And as with other weddings, their outcomes are unpredictable. Use of a particular model may amount to nothing more than a strained and artificial description of a domain sufficiently known otherwise. But it may also help us to notice what otherwise would be overlooked, to shift the relative emphasis attached to details – in short, to *see new connections*.[16]

The role of models in theology and science has received much attention from Ian Barbour. He informs us that:

Broadly speaking, a model is a symbolic representation of selected aspects of the behaviour of a complex system for particular purposes. It is an imaginative tool for ordering experience, rather than a description of the world.[17]

Models and metaphors are neither literal pictures of reality nor useful fictions, says Barbour. A metaphor, for instance:

proposes analogies between the normal context of a word and a new context into which it is introduced. Some, but not all, of the familiar connotations of the word are transferred. 'The Lion is King of the beasts', but it has only some of the attributes of royalty. 'Love is a fire', but we do not expect it to cook a meal. There is a tension between affirmation and negation, for in analogy there are both similarities and differences.[18]

So a metaphor is not literally true. No one expects someone to get out the scales when a friend says that his heart is heavy, yet this mode of speech is not merely decorative or rhetorical. Barbour insists that such remarks have cognitive content. Metaphorical forms of speech are open ended, or we might say they have open-texture, not allowing for replacement or perfect paraphrase.

MODELS AND METAPHORS

Already we have seen a connection established between metaphors and models. Max Black treats of them together regarding models as sustained and systematic metaphors, with models being more complex, and ultimately more useful in developing knowledge than metaphors. To quote him once again:

Metaphor and model-making, reveal new relationships; both are attempts to pour new content into old bottles. But a metaphor operates largely with *commonplace* implications. You need only proverbial knowledge, as it were, to have your metaphor understood; but the maker of a scientific model must have prior control of a well-knit scientific theory if he is to do more than hang an attractive picture on an algebraic formula. Systematic complexity of the source of the model and capacity for analogical development are of the essence.[19]

Immediately following these words Black in turn cites Stephen Toulmin, who remarks:

It is in fact a great virtue of a good model that it does suggest further questions, taking us beyond the phenomena from which we began, and tempts us to formulate hypotheses which turn out to be experimentally fertile... Certainly it is this suggestiveness, and systematic deployability, that makes a good model something more than a simple metaphor.[20]

Barbour thinks that metaphors are used only momentarily, on the spur of the moment as it were, 'for the sake of an immediate impression or insight'. Symbols, on the other hand, he feels are more permanent, especially religious symbols which 'become part of the language of a religious community in its scripture and liturgy and in its continuing life and thought'.[21] I am not sure that such a distinction is wholly persuasive. For one thing, we have to distinguish between momentary metaphors and metaphors that become established or dominant,[22] and then further distinguish between dominant metaphors which have a richness of structure that enable us to develop them into models. Part of the problem here may be a confusion in the use of the terms 'metaphor' and 'symbol'. Sometimes they are not distinguished at all and used interchangeably.[23] On other occasions one term takes over the meaning of the other, with the latter then being abandoned or ignored. For instance, John Macquarrie practically ignores metaphors, saying that our response to them is mainly aesthetic.[24] Their cognitive value is not discussed. Instead he focuses on symbols and analogues. The main difference between these, according to Macquarrie, is that symbols are more obscure and in need of careful interpretation, while analogues are almost self-interpreting.[25] Also an analogue tends to stress the element of likeness between itself and that for which it stands. Thus, Macquarrie considers our use of the term 'Father' for God as involving the employment of an analogue. The believer wishes to establish some intrinsic likeness between the parent-child relation and the relation of God to his creatures. Such an image is almost self-interpreting and is based on a universally known reality.

Sallie McFague, on the other hand, would reject the application of the terms 'symbol' and 'analogue' to the father image precisely because the emphasis in using these words seems to be on the likeness between the image and the reality it supposedly stands for. She prefers to see the characterisation of God as father as involving the use of metaphor, since metaphor lays the emphasis on the tension between the image and the reality. Metaphor is iconoclastic and sceptical; it underlines the 'is and is not' nature of our imagery. Therefore, to suggest that God is our father, is a metaphorical form of speech which expresses a paradox: God is a father and is not a father. And a further consequence of such an approach insists on the value of different metaphors correcting and complementing one another. For instance, McFague develops in some detail towards the end of her work another metaphor for God, that of 'friend',[26] but this too is a tensive image which must not be given absolute status, since to do so would be a form of idolatry.

While writers like McFague make much of the distinction between symbol and metaphor, one wonders if this distinction amounts to much, once one takes into account the tensive nature of our imagery, be it metaphorical or symbolic. Even McFague has to recognise that those who employ a different terminology from herself may mean practically the same thing. David Tracy, for instance, is praised by McFague for his work on the analogical imagination; she admits that his views are 'in many ways identical with my understanding of the analogical sensibility'.[27] For Tracy the analogical imagination is metaphorical. It allows the systematic theologian 'to note the profound similarities-in-difference in all reality'.[28] Instead of labouring the distinction any further I intend to follow the usage of writers like McFague and use the language of metaphor rather than the language of symbol.[29]

Metaphor is the foundation for models. Whether a model develops from a metaphor depends on the potential richness and complexity of the metaphor, but also on the subjective interests of the user. A metaphor such as the fatherhood of God can be a dominant or root metaphor and yet may remain unchosen for model status, even though it has a certain complexity, a certain structure of relationships which allow it to be chosen as a potential model for God. A believer may well recognise that to call God one's Father is not literally true while enshrining an important truth. He or she may not wish to develop the metaphor into a model. And yet there is great potential in the metaphor since the relationships between fathers and their children are relatively complex and rich so that a theological model could be constructed easily enough. Many forms of the Divine Command theory of moral obligation, for instance, function in terms of this model and its underlying metaphor.[30] If God is our father, then by analogy with earthly fathers and their children we have some duty to obey his commands. But God is not the same as any human father and the difference in attributes between God's fatherhood and human fatherhood may make quite a difference in terms of our moral theory. Once again the tensive quality of the metaphor must be taken into account.

Max Black argues that a metaphor provides a 'lens' through which we see something new in a certain subject matter. This point distinguishes metaphor from simile. One of his examples of a metaphor/model is the image of war as a chess game.[31] Now a simile would express the relationship in terms of likeness, comparing the two, but Black claims that a metaphor acts differently. Instead of saying, 'War is *like* a chess game', one says, 'War is a chess game', and the meaning of the two statements is different. The difference, according to Black, is like that between 'looking at a scene through blue spectacles' and 'comparing that scene with something else' (*ibid.*). The value of this metaphor cum model lies in holding together in permanent tension two active ideas with their associated commonplaces. And a further interesting feature of this example is that each idea can be useful in elucidating features of the other. Not only does chess act as a lens or grid for looking at war, but war can act in a similar way in relation to chess – consider some very highly competitive chess games where the opponents display great mutual animosity. The overall emphasis which distinguishes metaphor from other forms of imagery is that it brings together very different subjects, and through their interaction light is thrown on each. Usually, however, the metaphor or the modifier, as it is sometimes called, is relatively familiar, and it is employed to elucidate the less familiar subject matter. It is precisely because metaphors involve such a fundamental dissimilarity between subjects that they often have a shock effect when juxtaposed, and also present difficulties in explaining how it is that the modifier clarifies the subject.[32]

Before going on to summarise the basic features of models and metaphors, it will be useful to give some further examples of models from different areas of life. The following cases come from Sallie McFague's *Metaphorical Theology*.[33]

Various historical periods are characterised by specific models, examples being: 'the Dark Ages,' 'the Renaissance,' 'the age of Aquarius'. Such metaphors have rich connotations, positive and negative, but obviously cannot be taken literally. Consider a recent model of the modern city, portrayed as 'the concrete jungle'. Note the bringing together of seemingly disparate subjects with shocking, yet telling, effect. Society has often been regarded metaphorically as an organism and McFague reveals how such a model is fleshed out or developed culturally. In the United States during the 1950s (the McCarthy era) communism could be seen as a type of 'germ' infecting an otherwise healthy organism. The metaphor presents danger to society in the form of a disease coming from outside. But the same basic metaphor of society as an organism can change with time, so that the danger to society comes to be seen as originating from within and is now called a 'cancer'. Still another modern metaphor is the description of our contemporary society as 'the computer age'. This model is especially apt for inversion. On one hand, we model the computer on the human brain, and on the other hand we have begun to model the human brain on the computer. Which is the case? Are we like computers or are they like us? The choice of model matters a great deal to the ways in which we imagine ourselves and also to the ways in which we treat each other.

MAIN CHARACTERISTICS OF MODELS

Let us try to summarise some of the central features of metaphorical thinking. We should keep in mind that some of these features may be defining characteristics, while others are merely accompanying characteristics, ones which are not necessarily criteria for the application of the terms 'metaphor' or 'model'.

Models give us some understanding of a relatively unfamiliar object by means of language associated with, and taken from, a more familiar object. 'This' is seen as 'that'. But the connection is made out in a structured and comprehensive manner. This distinguishes models from metaphors.

The two objects at the heart of the model are always disparate but share some relevant features to some extent. Thus the relationship between the objects is tensive. Although 'this' is seen as 'that', 'that' is not a literal description of 'this'. Models and metaphors as imaginative forms see threads of similarity in dissimilar objects or ideas, and maintain the tension between the similarity and dissimilarity.

Because models bring together disparate objects in relation, they often have a shocking effect. Parables seen as extended metaphors and as potential models are a clear example of such an effect.[34]

Models do not function as pictures of objects but stress 'the basic processes, relations and structures' that govern phenomena.[35]

Models, according to Barbour, are imaginative tools for ordering and interpreting experience rather than describing it.[36]

Models inhabit a position midway between the language of imagery and conceptual language and participate in each category. A mixed type of language is involved.[37]

Because the model cannot give a comprehensive understanding of its object, it may require the use of alternative models either in tandem with, or instead of, itself to elucidate the object. Thus all models are limited and provisional in terms of their cognitive value.[38]

'A promising model is one with implications rich enough to suggest novel hypotheses and speculations in the primary field of investigation.'[39] Some features of the model which may have been ignored – sometimes called 'neutral analogy' ('aspects of a model that have not yet been identified as either positive or negative, as either applying or not applying')[40] – turn out to have relevance in bringing out new connections. Barbour speaks of the 'extensible' characteristic of models, i.e. their openness to be used again and again to help interpret new patterns of experience.[41]

The most effective models are specific and common, such as 'body' and 'machine' applied to society.[42] They also participate in the dialectic between simplicity and complexity. Simplicity, McFague tells us, copes with the chaotic; complexity guards against over-simplification.

Models tend to affect our attitudes and behaviour, though often in a subliminal way. Powerful models have strong emotional associations attached to them. McFague puts it well in saying that 'we live within our models as fish live in the sea'.[43]

MODELS: POSSIBLE ABUSES AND DANGERS

Having presented various characteristics associated with models, it is necessary to state some of the pitfalls attending the use of metaphorical language. According to McFague the main pitfalls follow on directly from ignoring or playing down some of the characteristics mentioned above.

One major danger, for instance, would involve 'assimilation' – 'the shocking, powerful metaphor becomes trite and accepted' (*ibid.*, p. 41). From the sphere of religion the example of

Christ's words 'This is my body' has become so familiar that its metaphorical significance is forgotten. Douglas Berggren puts it well: 'It is the familiar, or inherited or submerged metaphor which is the most dangerous.'[44] As well as familiarity and habit, which are enemies of novelty, blinding one to the possibility of new connections, there is the related danger of literalising our metaphors. In the case of the eucharistic words above there is the danger of an exaggerated sacramental realism which ignores the 'is and is not' dimension of those words. The tensive aspect of metaphor disappears from sight.

Another danger stressed by McFague in particular concerns the temptation to treat a particular model as absolute. In terms of religious models this may lead to idolatry, especially when one model of God is underlined to the exclusion of others. And another implication of concentrating on a single model is that such a model may be seen as irrelevant by many people. This is a general problem with religious language where images lose their meaning and application over time. And, of course, the example to which McFague returns again and again is that of patriarchal images of God, which are fast becoming more and more irrelevant to many women. Mary Hesse warns against any attempt to find 'a perfect metaphor' to explain everything.[45] Multiple models and metaphors are to be encouraged instead of canonising a single imaginative approach.

Related to the profound influence models and metaphors have on our attitudes, linked with the fact that such influence is often subconscious or subliminal, we should be wary of using metaphorical forms of expression without being aware of their power to mould our understandings and our behaviour in negative directions. Alastair Campbell illustrates how problems arise from this point of view in relation to medical treatment. One approach to such treatment employs, presumably in an unconscious way, a military metaphor. 'Campaigns' are mounted against diseases, which are said to 'invade' the body and must be 'combatted' (often 'aggressively') and 'wiped out' or 'defeated'. Campbell then mentions one important effect of this model, namely, the presentation of an image which makes the patient 'into an inert battlefield across which the rival forces

of treatment and disease relentlessly march'.[46] A metaphor
suggesting such an approach to medical treatment may be
criticised heavily in terms of its stress on the patient's passivity,
and the model may need to be adapted or complemented or
replaced with the help of other models.

So far I have dealt with the list of features characterising
metaphorical language as if it were clearcut and uncontroversial. This impression, however, is quite misleading, and in
fact each point could do with further examination, qualification
and criticism. For instance, many of the characteristics listed
come from an approach to models which concentrates on a
scientific paradigm (and a natural science paradigm to boot),
and we have paid little critical attention to the formulation of
models in other fields such as the human sciences, ethics and
religion. To give her her due McFague recognises these issues
and devotes some time to their discussion, but we cannot afford
to get bogged down totally at this level. Nevertheless, we must
take these problems into account both now, and later on when
we apply metaphorical thinking to theological approaches to
rights analysis.

At this point let me just mention one or two critical issues
arising from some of the features of models so baldly presented
in the last few pages.

McFague puts great emphasis again and again in her work on
the shocking effect of metaphor. At times she gives the
impression that this feature is essential for the proper functioning
of the term. But it is difficult to see how this can be so for all
models and all types of models. Mary Hesse disagrees on this
point, saying that, while scientific models may be unexpected,
their principle aim is not to shock.[47] McFague's stress on this
effect is, as we saw, connected with her fear that metaphors can
become literalised, lose their novelty, and that similarity rather
than dissimilarity comes to the fore in our minds. Thus, shock is
a sign that metaphor is recognised precisely as metaphor, and
the absence of such a reaction is equally a sign that the
metaphor is dying or has died. But is a psychological effect of
this kind essential for respecting metaphors and models? I
cannot help feeling that the shock factor is an accompanying

characteristic of metaphorical language and not a defining characteristic. Surely it is possible to avoid literalism, to see dissimilarity between an object and its modifier, without gasping and bringing on an apoplectic fit. To use Black's example here, can we not see the difference between war and a chess game without experiencing any emotional reaction?

Very much related to the shocking effect of metaphor is the insistence on the disparity between the object and the model or metaphor. Wars and chess games, atoms and waves, computers and brains, God and human fathers, God's Kingdom and a fishing net are all quite odd combinations which preclude us from identifying one with the other in any simple way. Still the question comes to mind, how different do objects have to be from each other for one to act as a model or metaphor for the other? If one concentrates on the importance of difference alone one may be led to recognize only the most bizarre situations as metaphorical, forgetting that similarity in some respects is essential to metaphor as well as dissimilarity. My suggestion is that different metaphors and models may lie along a spectrum, with the most bizarre and shocking examples at one end and relatively familiar and generally accepted examples at the other. The spectrum is the line which stretches from literal language to metaphorical language, and as one moves from one end to the other the tension between similarity and dissimilarity increases or decreases. Where the tension between the object and its modifier is weak we come close to the boundary between the metaphorical and the literal use of language. The border, however, is imprecise. Thus it is possible that some metaphors and models may be borderline cases drawing close to literal attribution.[48]

From the point of view of normative ethics, if we use models care must be shown to construct ones which challenge us to face up to our obligations and which help us to see moral reality as it really is. The issue here is somewhat related to the recognition of the effect metaphorical thinking has on our attitudes, and thus on our behaviour. Metaphors can be helpful but they can also hinder our moral development. For example, if metaphors and models are like grids or lenses through which we see reality in a deeper way, we must be aware of how lenses and grids can screen out certain features which may make us uncomfortable.[49] Black's trusty example of war as a chess game comes to mind yet again. A chess-game model of war brings out useful features of socially organised aggression. There are the opposing players who, like generals, move their men/pieces around the board/ battleground. Pawns, like individual soldiers, are sacrificed for the sake of ultimate victory, and so on. But the game is a game, not a war. It can be enjoyed as a leisure activity. Nothing much depends on it; you can stop or start at whim, and, above all, there is no blood, no loss of life, no suffering. A chess game screens out the messy aspects of war. In fact, such a model can be used to criticise military leaders who move men to their deaths from their comfortable positions far to the rear. (One is reminded of the poetry of Sassoon). Metaphor becomes satire. In this case our anger flares up because there are some who are willing to treat war as a game, who treat the metaphor as literally true and miss out on the shocking differences between the two.

While on the subject of models in ethics, it may be argued that their function need not be limited merely to the ordering of moral experience or its interpretation. Another function may be to help in the justification (and critique) of moral terms and moral positions. We should recall the point made in the opening chapter, that meaning and justification of moral terms often go hand in hand.

One final point on the basic features of models: it is said that metaphorical thinking takes the relatively unfamiliar object and throws some light on it by means of another more familiar object. Obviously we are more familiar with human fathers than with God, and with the behaviour of waves and particles more than the behaviour of atoms, so it makes sense to use these familiar models. However, the validity of this general assertion should not lead us to the illicit conclusion that the familiar area must necessarily be simple or easy to grasp. As Max Black states,

It has been said that the model must belong to a more 'familiar' realm than the system to which it is applied. This is true enough, if familiarity is taken to mean belonging to a well-established and thoroughly explored realm. But the model need not belong to a realm of common experience. It may be as recondite as we please, provided we know how to use it.[50]

Now familiarity is a relative concept. An expert in a particular area may of course take for granted what a layman may find abstruse. Thus one view of models sees them as illustrative devices for the novice or learner in a particular field. C. S. Lewis demonstrates this point. From the point of view of the teacher or master the metaphor or model is a teaching aid which he himself does not need because of his direct grasp of the subject. But from the angle of the pupil or disciple the metaphor is absolutely essential, for without it he has no way of understanding the subject. Perhaps at a later date the pupil will, like his teacher, feel at home with the subject and no longer need the model or metaphor.[51] However, this example should not blind us to the existence of situations where a model is familiar to one user and obscure to another, and situations where the object being modelled is more familiar to some than the model itself. This issue is of some importance when we attempt to use terms like 'freedom' and 'power' as models for rights. In an absolute sense none of these terms or images is simpler or more familiar than the others. Still, this problem may turn out to be to our advantage in so far as each term may act as a metaphor for the others, depending on our familiarity with each term.

TWO INITIAL METAPHORS FOR RIGHTS

It is time we began to apply our analysis of metaphors and models to the concept of having a right. As a first tentative step I have picked two simple metaphors which may have model potential.

The chain metaphor

In his book, *Rights and Persons*, A. I. Melden, chooses to use the image of a chain as a metaphor for rights.[52] In his fifth chapter he reflects on the relationship between rights and goods, and the chain metaphor appears in the context of a response to the moral philosophy of H. A. Prichard where that philosopher is

accused of reifying obligation. But to understand obligations
and rights properly, Melden suggests, we must see them in
relational terms, hence the chain metaphor or model. A right is
like a chain between two persons. Sometimes it is pulled taut,
but often it can be afforded some slack in accordance with
changes in the relationship. Thus a right may be waived,
relinquished, forfeited, infringed, exercised, enjoyed. The chain
metaphor seems to cover some of the area mentioned in an
earlier chapter when we discussed the Choice Theory of rights
advocated by Hart and by Wellman. One's rights give one the
freedom to decide whether to hold another person strictly to his
or her obligations – pulling the chain taut – and the freedom to
waive one's claim in certain circumstances, thus releasing
another from fulfilling an obligation – allowing the chain to
slacken.

In this case we are certainly dealing with a metaphor,
according to the criteria discussed earlier in this chapter. A
chain is a relatively simple and familiar object which brings out
a key feature of the relatively unfamiliar and certainly more
complex object of rights – the 'binding' nature of the normative
relationship between claims and obligations. Obviously, chains
and rights are quite different from each other and are unlikely
to be identified or treated as synonymous. The image of a chain
also has some emotive significance, and is bound to affect our
attitudes to some extent. It is an open question, I think, whether
one should say that the metaphor is shocking or even very odd.
Whether it has much potential for development to the status of
model is also questionable. In my opinion it lacks the depth of
structure which would allow it to bring out the richness and
complexity of rights language. It has limited application,
underlining the distinction between enforcing one's claims and
waiving them, and perhaps it could be pushed a step or two
further. For instance, relinquishing a right has the right-holder
unchaining himself from another and allowing more freedom to
a person usually under obligation. It even brings out to some
extent the burden rights can be for the right-holder, since he too
is tied to the bearers of correlative obligations, in the sense that
he must put thought into the question whether or not he should

make a claim. So-called mandatory rights, for instance, mean that a person with a right to do something also has an obligation to do it. But does this mean that another chain must link persons? Concerning human rights does every person have chains tying them to millions of others? Where a right is violated or infringed what happens to the chain? If you claim on behalf of another how does the metaphor apply? Obviously then the chain metaphor has its limitations. We might consider it a relatively low-level model or auxiliary model. Or we may wish to leave it at the level of mere metaphor.

The net metaphor

John Hardwig has written an essay, 'Should Women Think in Terms of Rights?', in which his main argument is

that thinking in terms of rights is not the way to understand what is going on in close personal relationships, that the category of rights is not an appropriate ethical category for healthy personal relationships, and that it is not the basis for an appropriate ideal for personal relationships.[53]

And it is in this context that he presents the net metaphor:

... rights are like the net underneath the tightrope act. The net keeps people and their lives from being ruined if they fall off the wire. But the act is ruined if the net actually comes into play. (p. 453)

This ingenious image participates in the main features of metaphorical thinking. A net is not literally identifiable with rights, so the tensive nature of metaphors is maintained. There is some important thread of similarity between two diverse objects, and the modifier (net) is more familiar than the object it modifies. It is also relatively simple and easy to handle, since the features of safety nets are well known to us. One may well argue that this metaphor has much potential for development into a model of rights, or at least a model of some central feature of rights. It directs our attention to both positive and negative features of their use. Rights give fundamental protection to persons who possess them. Without the possibility of claiming rights lives could be ruined; in some cases lives can be lost, just as the circus artist can break his neck if he falls in the absence of a net. Yet, as Hardwig points out, if the net is actually used, while a life may be saved, the circus act or performance is ruined. People do not come to the circus to see trapeze artists falling into safety nets. The presumption is that professionals have such expertise as to make the net practically redundant. So it is, and so it should be, regarding the exercise of rights in personal relationships. When rights are used in these circumstances something has gone radically wrong. The love and affection that once guided the relationship no longer function and the process of living together has become fraught with difficulties, frustrations and pain.

Hardwig mixes his metaphors to some extent. As well as the safety net he also uses the image of the warning light. Once we begin to think in terms of rights in personal relationships it is as if a warning light begins to flash, telling us that our relationships are no longer as healthy as they once were. Perhaps the safety net metaphor takes us a stage further in the breakdown of relationships to the stage when we are actually claiming rights in an adversarial manner. We have, so to speak, fallen off the wire, and now flounder in a humiliating way in the net, no doubt happy that our life has been spared, but at the same time perhaps ashamed and guilty at having had to use the net.

Of course the model has its limitations. From the start it was suggested as an interpretation of the relationship between rights and personal relationships, showing the tension between the two. But it would be difficult to apply the model as it is to other special rights, such as ones arising from contracts between relative strangers, and more difficult still to apply to human rights. The problem is that, while rights of all types are a bit like safety nets, claiming or exercising them explicitly is not always harmful to human relationships, since many of these are impersonal and somewhat distant. It is probably unrealistic to expect all relationships to emulate intimate personal ones and to hope for a society in which claiming rights becomes a redundant exercise. One final limitation comes to mind. Hardwig's safety net metaphor sees the use of the net as a necessary evil at times. Falling into the net spoils the performance; claiming rights in a family situation says little for the quality of life within that intimate group. But Hardwig fails to see how the claiming of rights can become a skilled performance of its own. Standing up for one's rights may call for great subtlety and diplomacy. As we shall see below, claiming rights is sometimes an expression of dignity, which gains us respect, not opprobrium. Thus, the use of the safety net does not necessarily leave us floundering in humiliation, but gives us a fresh opportunity to improve our performance. We live to fight another day.

The two metaphors or models we have discussed are relatively uncontroversial and simple tools which help us to interpret the meaning of rights. They are not particularly rich or comprehensive however, and hardly merit the status of dominant metaphors or paradigmatic models. Their value lies in their particular focus: the chain stresses the way rights work through the correlativity of claims and duties, allowing for a diversity of relationships between these normative realities in different circumstances;[54] the net stresses the function of rights in protecting basic values, while warning us of the (often steep) price to be paid for using them, especially in personal contexts. I would now like to introduce two familiar concepts 'freedom' and 'power' with the suggestion that these may be considered as metaphors and potential models to elucidate our terminology of rights.

FREEDOM AND POWER AS METAPHORICAL

I must admit from the outset that reference to 'freedom' and 'power' as metaphors is a controversial move on my part. For one thing, am I not guilty of inconsistency in terms of my earlier approach to definition in which these terms turned up as equivalent words? In other words, I cannot define rights in terms of freedom and power and then turn around and say that these terms are really metaphors, the reason being simply that a metaphor or model is not a literal description of an object. Freedom and power, unlike chains and nets, seem too close to the definition of rights to be useful as metaphors.

In reply to this objection, I would argue that, while the

second chapter concentrated to a large extent on definition, I
made no claim that each word suggested as an equivalent term
for rights was equally important from the point of view of formal
definition. In addition I never claimed that formal definition
was the be-all and end-all of analysis. In fact my position in
these chapters is that metaethics involves an analysis of terms
which must include some aspect of definition and a further
aspect of imaginative analysis depending on metaphors and
models. In my opinion, terms like 'claim' and 'entitlement' are
more or less definitional in relation to rights, while terms like
'freedom' and 'power' are not definitional but metaphorical
with regard to rights. And since metaphors emphasise the
tension between similarity and dissimilarity, the 'is and is not',
I can see no reason why at times metaphors cannot be brought
into the work of analysis at a secondary level. Naturally, great
vigilance must be shown lest the tensive dimension of metaphor
is lost in this process. Remember too the qualification I
introduced in relation to metaphorical thinkers' insistence on
diversity between objects and their modifiers. This diversity
may vary along a spectrum from the literal to the metaphorical,
so that some metaphors and models can in fact come close to
literal forms of speech. It remains to be seen where 'freedom'
and 'power' feature along this spectrum.

On the positive side, talk of 'freedom' and 'power' appear to
be extremely rich metaphors, while also being rather familiar.
So much has been written on these subjects drawing out many
subtle distinctions, that there must be a great deal of potential
in treating these terms as models. Again, we must remember
that familiarity is relative, and that discussions of freedom and
power are rarely simple. However, the familiar complexities of
these subjects augurs well for us if we decide to treat them as
models for rights. 'Freedom' and 'power' are also terms with
emotive effect, and as metaphors they are likely to have a strong
influence on attitudes and behaviour. Furthermore, there are
certain connections between these terms and rights (especially
human rights) which have a possible shock effect on us, though
familiarity with these connections can undermine this effect so
that the metaphor loses its biting edge.

RIGHTS AND FREEDOM

With the aid of Joel Feinberg's essay on 'The Idea of a Free Man'[55] I shall present some of the main features of what we mean when we say that a person is free.

Usually we think of two aspects, sometimes called negative and positive freedom, but which Feinberg describes as simply freedom from impediments and freedom to do (or omit, or be, or have).[56] Frequently individuals are clearer on one or other area in their life. For instance, a person may know what he wants to do while not realising the impediments or constraints which may be lying in wait for him. Or, more commonly, a person may recognise the constraints from which she wishes to be free, while having little clear idea of what she wishes to use her freedom for (for example a person looking for a divorce, but with no immediate future plans). These are not two different types of freedom, according to Feinberg, just two different sides of the same coin. Positive freedom or 'freedom for' always depends to some extent on negative freedom or 'freedom from', i.e. absence of constraint. In so far as rights involve at a basic level freedom from constraint, freedom seems to be part of the analysis of rights. However, we must not jump to this conclusion too hastily, before taking a closer look at different types of constraint.

Feinberg distinguishes four categories of constraints, giving practical examples of each.[57] There are 'internal positive' constraints as when people suffer from headaches, obsessive thoughts and compulsive desires, all of which impede that person from carrying out ambitions, achieving ends, even if these are only a restful night or a moment of peace. Then there are 'internal negative' constraints: ignorance, weakness, various deficiencies in skill or talent. There is an absence of something essential which is a necessary means to one's ends. There are also 'external' constraints of a 'positive' kind; here we think of barred windows, locked doors and fixed bayonets, which prevent one from acting freely. And, finally, the 'external negative' category, examples of which include lack of money, transportation or weapons. So a constraint is defined simply as 'something – anything – that prevents one from doing something. Therefore, if nothing prevents me from doing x, I am free to do x'.

If rights are identified with freedom in the sense of absence of constraints, they would appear to give us only a limited freedom when exercised. In fact, the constraints our rights might be most appropriate in overcoming are mainly the external categories (negative and positive). Under the heading external positive constraints, for instance, it makes sense to argue for rights against false imprisonment and threats of physical violence. And regarding external negative constraints we may argue for a right to a basic wage and a public transport system. (These may, in some countries, amount to manifesto rights and thus are controversial.) Rights against internal constraints, on the other hand, present greater problems in terms of meaning and justification. The positive internal category is exemplified by headaches, obsessive thoughts and compulsive desires, but it is difficult to see how one could have a right not to have a headache or to be free from neurosis. Granted, one may have a right to medical treatment, but this does not amount to a right to be healed (though the growing practice of litigation in medical practice tends to ignore this distinction in practice). The negative internal constraints included ignorance and weakness as well as deficiencies in skill and talent. The problem with this category is that it combines lack of opportunity and lack of ability. In some cases rights can overcome the former, as when education (a typical human right) dispenses with ignorance and can help develop skills. But rights are not helpful in overcoming lack of talent. If you have no talent for playing a musical instrument, you are unlikely to have a right to become a concert pianist.

When thinking of rights in terms of freedom understood as absence of constraint, we may be tempted to forget that our claims are not only claims to something, but also against someone. In the examples given in the last paragraph, for instance, it is clear that we have no rights against ignorance or disease or poverty. If we have rights to be free of constraints, these must be rights against people who either impose these constraints on us or who are able to free us from them and have some reason to do so. Thus the language of rights must be limited to the freedom from constraint which comes to us through certain kinds of relationships. The important issues regarding rights as freedom from constraint include the ability of others (morally, physically, psychologically) to help us overcome impediments to fruitful living, and whether others have good reason to limit their own freedom or to constrain themselves for our benefit. Thus, there can be no simple identification of rights and freedom from constraint, since there are potentially many constraints which others are in no position to free us from, and concerning which they have no obligation towards us.

Rights against others, then, function best in the sphere of external constraints, and have limited application to the internal sphere of personal freedom. But it is clear that moral freedom depends to a great extent on internal factors. Feinberg insists upon this point in his article. One could be free from all types of external constraints and many internal ones too and yet live a life characterised by *anomie* or normlessness. One's inner life could be anarchic because one has no organised set of aims or ends, no hierarchy of values. Feinberg likens such a person to a road system without any rules, traffic signs, police, etc.[58] All one's rights might be respected, but one has little freedom, for which one has only oneself to blame.

Although the anarchic personality may have his rights protected and respected, due perhaps to a combination of the benevolence of others and good luck, a person in this condition has little capacity to claim his rights. This argument is put forward by Michael Meyer in an interesting article on the connection between dignity, rights and self-control.[59] Responding to Feinberg's general argument that the capacity to claim rights is an essential aspect of human dignity, Meyer points out that a person without self-control cannot claim rights and therefore can suffer a loss of dignity. This is the case, he says, because rights imply some order and moral direction. And he goes on to declare, concerning human rights, that their value 'relies fundamentally on our own ability to make these rights serve our own ends'.[60] The key point here is that humans must already show signs of a basic freedom in terms of absence of constraint – the internal constraint of *anomie* – in order to participate in a meaningful way in the further freedom from constraint that rights do imply. And this basic aspect of self-control or organisation is not a right against others; it is something we must do ourselves or not do at all. One might say that this is the basic meaning of autonomy, the ability to organise our inner life of values and purposes, intentions and dispositions. Usually this feature of human life is taken for granted and is assumed as a necessary background to claiming rights. Where self-control and self-legislation are absent and normlessness reigns, some form of claiming may take place, but it is difficult to see how it can be taken seriously either by the claimant himself or by those to whom such claims are addressed.

So far we have reduced the link between rights and freedom to the area where constraints are in some sense due to the influence of other people on our life. However, there is a further sense in which even the absence of these constraints would not necessarily be a sign of rights being respected by others. The freedom involved in having and claiming rights involves a special kind of absence of constraint, one which is due to us as a key element of our status as free persons. Feinberg brings out this issue in his reference to the use of the word 'free' as a legal status word (and we can extend this to the moral status of persons). Historically, Feinberg reminds us, '... to call a man "free" was simply to describe his legal rights and contrast them with those of a slave'. And regarding the connection between rights and constraints he goes on to say on the same page:

The statuses of slave and freeman, however, were not defined by the presence or absence of *de facto* or *de iure* constraints, but rather by the possession or non-possession of *rights*, which is quite another matter.[61]

It is quite another matter because we can imagine situations where a slave had a benevolent, kindly master who allowed him a fair measure of freedom, both in the sense of absence of constraint and opportunities for the accomplishment of certain ends. If the master was a wealthy man as well as a kindly one, his slaves might well be better off from the point of view of absence of constraint and opportunity to act than poor freemen. But, according to Feinberg, there is a crucial difference between the *de jure* liberties of the freeman and those 'permitted' to the slave:

The freeman enjoys some of his legal liberties as a matter of right: no one else is permitted to nullify or withdraw them. When they are slow to be acknowledged, or where they appear to be withheld, he may lay claim to them and demand them as his due ... The liberties permitted the slave, on the other hand, are granted at the mere pleasure of his owner and may also be withdrawn at his mere displeasure. He owes his slave nothing and has no legal duty to 'permit' him any 'liberties' at all.[62]

Two senses of freedom seem to be involved here represented by the two phrases '*de facto*' and '*de jure*'. *De facto* freedom refers to absence of constraint and the opportunity to act without reference to its origin and justification. *De jure* freedom also involves similar 'freedom from' and 'freedom for', but with the origin and justification built in. In the example of the slave, his *de facto* freedom originates in the gift of his master, and the absence of constraint he enjoys is not something he can claim or justifiably demand, given the acceptance of the legitimacy of this institution. *De jure* freedom, on the other hand, may in some cases involve more constraints than are suffered by those with *de facto* freedom, but it is typically claimable. One is justified in demanding not to be constrained.

Underlying each concept is a different view of human worth and dignity. The slave has no freedom to claim because of his essentially inferior status in relation to his master, an inferiority which is of a 'natural' kind as opposed to a kind based on psychological traits or gifts and talents. By this is meant that a slave's very humanity is in question, while the humanity of a poor workman is accepted even though his social status is regarded as inferior. One is reminded of the feudal system where peasants were strictly controlled by their place in the social structure, but who, in spite of their poverty and hardship had (ideally at least) the freedom which is at the heart of rights. The freeman's capacity to claim is a clear sign of a basic equality of worth and dignity expressed in the fact that duties can be imposed on others which one can insist on or waive. The freedom which lies at the heart of rights then is justified in terms of a basic equality of dignity or worth. Since the slave is regarded as less than human he is not in a position to claim the goods or benefits which are the objects of human rights, nor can he be in a position to enjoy special rights against his owner because of the essential lack of equality in this relationship.

To have a right is to be in a position to claim some benefit against someone. Being in such a position is part of the concept of freedom. As I mentioned in the preliminary discussion of this concept in the last chapter we often connect freedom with the objects of our claims, freedom of conscience, freedom of speech, and the like. We talk of civil liberties to which we have a claim. But in the discussion above our focus has been on a different and more fundamental aspect of the connection between freedom and rights, namely, the manner in which claiming rights, insisting on a correlativity between our claims and duties on the part of others, is a vital form of freedom, quite apart from the actual achievement of our objectives. Thus, even in the case of controversial 'manifesto rights', although the claims of starving Africans to food cannot at present be respected in a satisfactory way, the ability to claim against the citizens of developed countries is an important reminder of the worth and value of our earth's poorer inhabitants. Though they are hampered by the constraints of starvation, ill-health and in other ways, the fact that their claim is liable to make conscientious persons feel guilty and uneasy is an important sign of their freedom. Only a free person is in a position to claim what is due. If we were in a position to take away every constraint and suffering from such people on the condition that they accept this action as a pure gift, and in turn exact a strict promise from them never to make claims against us again, we would be giving one type of freedom with one hand and taking another type away with the other. Again this brings us back to the original contrast between the slave and the freeman, *de facto* and *de jure* freedom. The slave may enjoy greater freedom from constraint, but the constrained freeman enjoys a greater dignity because what little freedom from constraint he has is strictly due to him. The free man caught in a poverty trap can have a pride which is not open to the slave.[63] Having rights is a necessary condition for such justified pride.

The argument so far has been that the concept of freedom is a useful model for elucidating the concept of rights. Freedom is a familiar enough concept, with a sufficient complexity and depth combined with practical applications to act as a lens or grid for understanding the less familiar concept of rights. Freedom is a metaphor or model for rights because there can be no literal identification between the two ideas. Even if one limits oneself to speaking of rights in terms of moral freedom, there is still no absolute identity between the terms; for instance, we saw that a basic aspect of this freedom is so personal – self-control and developing a hierarchy of values – that the language of rights has no application at this level. At the wider level, the analysis of different kinds of constraints which have a bearing on moral life often have ambiguous contacts with rights. Yet there is at least one vital point of contact where there seems to be a strong link between rights, freedom and equality of basic worth and dignity. This is the area of similarity in the midst of difference which I have dwelt upon in particular. Here we see that it is a particular form of absence of constraint which concerns us in using the terminology of rights; that rights bring out in a clear way the relational aspects of freedom; and that the connection between rights and freedom consists of elements of justification, as well as semantic content.

Much more could be said about rights and freedom, but I hope that these few arguments suffice to give some idea of what I mean when I claim that freedom can act as a model for rights. In the next chapter we shall say some more about the freedom model from a theological perspective. At this stage I shall mention one last point related to the claim that models and metaphors tend to be shocking due to their bringing together diverse objects in tensive relationship. Is it possible to see something shocking in the relationship between rights and freedom? At first sight such a suggestion seems far-fetched. Both concepts seem to fit together rather well. However, from the perspective of history, the notion of rights entails a radical critique of inequality and an affirmation of a fundamental worth or value possessed by all humans equally. The notion that basic freedom is due to all persons, and that all persons having rights entails recognition of an obligation to respect this basic freedom, must have been shocking for our ancestors in the age of slavery.

Henri Bergson attributes this basic insight to the Christian religion: 'Humanity had to wait till Christianity for the idea of universal brotherhood, with its implication of equality of rights and the sanctity of the person, to become operative.'[64] However Bergson recognises that Christianity did not live up to the creative implications of its own foundations. It took hundreds of years for the rights of man to be declared in a political context in the American and French Revolutions. The notion of a human right, then, is not obvious, but requires the creative, ethical imagination which sees the similarity of basic worth and dignity in all people underlying the more obvious dissimilarities which characterise different cultures, races and individuals. Bergson suggests that it is the idea of universal brotherhood which implies equality of rights, and the connection is indeed revolutionary. Even today there is something shocking in the implications arising from our rather glib references to human rights. The challenge presented in this form of language means that we are normatively related to other people, to millions of others in fact. Could it be that we have millions of brothers and sisters who are in some sense free to claim from us? No wonder the concept of human rights is watered down to the level of rhetoric. The freedom implied by rights is a costly freedom. The correlative obligations are to some extent burdensome or constraining. We can just about manage to pay the price in relation to our special rights. The rights of our blood relations, of friends and business associates are widely recognised and respected, but extending such respect on a world-wide scale means extending our concept of family, friend and associate in a shocking yet creative way. It is not at all clear that there is general acceptance of the costly implications of using rights-language consistently. Metaphorical language can be to our advantage in such situations by revealing new connections and their full implications.

Like freedom the concept of power is a familiar feature of our daily speech. It is also a very rich and complex subject with many diverse connotations. The concept has many nuances depending on whether one is studying it from the point of view of politics or psychology or physics or religion. So we will not expect some simple straightforward connection between rights and power, anymore than we encountered such a connection between rights and freedom. Rights and power have the typically tensive relationship associated with metaphor. Rights are, and are not, powers. There are points of contact and points of divergence. Certainly, if we accept the term power as a metaphor for rights, we will also be likely to accept its model status due to its rich open-texture and wide relationships. In fact, one of the primary advantages of this image is its relational quality which fits it for acting as a lens for seeing rights.

We begin by trying to show the complexity of the concept of power and its related terms from the point of view of political science. The ideas of Peter Bachrach and Morton Baratz will be a useful starting point. These authors make helpful distinctions between 'power' as such and related terms such as 'force', 'influence' and 'authority'.[65]

First, 'power' is defined as essentially relational as opposed to substantive or possessive. Three relational characteristics are mentioned. For power relationships to exist there must be a conflict of interests or values between two or more persons or groups. A power relationship exists only if one person or group bows to the wishes of someone else. And power relationships depend on the ability of a party to threaten another with sanctions if they do not change their position. These sanctions must be known to the party who is threatened. They must be rational and give the other a choice whether to comply or not. Furthermore, the sanction must be regarded as a deprivation, and as no idle threat (*ibid.*, pp. 21–3). To have power, then, is to be able to change another person's behaviour by means of threatened sanctions.

Second, Bachrach and Baratz, treat of the concept of 'force'. They deny that force is simply power exercised. Force does involve using threatened sanctions, but this is a failure of power, not its exercise. Power only succeeds when people act as you wish without actually having to use sanctions. The concept of force implies that the deterrent has become a reality. Force is non-rational, for the party who suffers has at this stage no choice whether or not to comply. Sometimes, force is non-relational, as when a person is shot in the back. The use of force is often an admission of defeat on the part of the would be wielder of power, but sometimes its use may actually help a person in the future exercise of power, since others see that threatened sanctions will be applied. Then again the successful exercise of power over time can actually reduce its effect because threatened sanctions are never applied in practice. 'Making an example of someone' can be useful at times. On the other hand, constant use of force can stiffen resistance and thus exclude the exercise of power (*ibid.*, pp. 27–30).

Third, our authors examine the concept of 'influence'. An influential person is one who can change others, winning them over to his own values and forms of behaviour, without reference to sanctions. People whom we admire and respect can have this ability. Influence is rational and relational. It does not involve manipulation.[66]

Finally, there is the important concept of 'authority'. This is sometimes seen in political science as formal or institutionalised power, but Bachrach and Baratz reject this definition.[67] Their emphasis lies on the relationship where one regards a communication from another as authoritative in terms of reasonableness of command in relation to one's own values. Thus authority is closer to influence than to power. Authority does not depend on sanctions, but on the attractiveness of rational argument. An exercise of authority respects people more than the use of power or force does, because it takes into account their value systems and respects their better nature. It tries to achieve a rational consensus rather than forcing through a particular point of view.

Authority can be genuine or false; for example, if a policeman enters your home giving the impression that he has a search warrant when in fact he has none, he oversteps his authority. Authority can degenerate into the use of power when those in positions of authority act unreasonably and subjects no longer accept their communications as authoritative. Civil disobedience may at times be a reaction to this process. Where authority is genuine, however, it can justify and limit both power and force. Sometimes, however, power can masquerade as authority, as in Orwell's 'Brave New World', where brainwashing not only commands obedience to the leaders, but encourages the subjects to actually love 'Big Brother'. In other words, those who wish to manipulate others often find that achieving a position of authority is the best way of moulding people in line with their programme (*ibid.*, pp. 32–6).

These political concepts help in the elucidation of rights-language because having and claiming rights is always a political reality, where politics is understood in the wider (and relatively crude) sense of the human experience of getting one's own way over others. The terms used above – 'power', 'force', 'influence' and 'authority' – all presuppose a potential conflict of interests between people in relationships and corresponding efforts on the part of all agents to change the way others act in line with their projects. And one could say that this view of life as basically political describes to some extent the meaning and function of rights.

We have set out to show that the notion of power can be used as a metaphor for rights. From what was said above in terms of the political science analysis of Bachrach and Baratz, we must recognise that there cannot be any simple literal identification of power and rights, though there are important points of contact between them. Again, this is a sign that power is a metaphor for, or model of, rights. There is a tension between these objects under discussion. Rights are, and are not, powers. In fact, this point is brought out very clearly in so far as the other related political concepts we mentioned also have points of contact with rights, though they are different from the term 'power'. It may be that here we have a number of different potential models of rights. For instance, we may end up preferring the use of the concept of 'authority', rather than 'power', as a lens for looking at rights.

Looking at the concept of power presented above, what connection is there between this concept and rights? For power-relationships to exist there is a necessary conflict of interests between persons or groups. Does this conflict necessarily exist as the context of rights? Not in all cases, surely, since people may have rights which are accepted by others without any sense of conflict. Where friends promise each other to perform some mutual service, the respective rights can be fulfilled without a murmur. One person may bow to another's wishes without complaint. Some rights can be respected without threat of sanction entering into the situation at all. Parents, for instance, usually respect their children's rights in a loving way without considering the possibility of punishment should they fail in their responsibilities.

Perhaps the connection between power and rights has more to do with claiming rights, rather than with simply having them. To have a right after all may mean a number of things, not all of which have a direct relation to power. For instance, one may have a right without knowing it, and if no one points its existence out to you it may never feature as a part of a power-relationship. One may realise that one has a right and decide not to claim it. A person may decide not to threaten sanctions against those who violate his rights, and the right might still remain in force.[68] So it looks as though it is the activity of claiming which often features in a power-relationship. When one claims something a threatened sanction is often implicit and sometimes explicit. And the fact that one has to claim some good may be a sign of some conflict of interests or values. Frequently the making of claims assumes that others either do not recognise the right, or that they recognise but fail to respect it. In the former case, claiming may not be a type of power, but simply informs others of some good that is due (for which knowledge they may be grateful) and a correlative obligation they may be quite willing to accept in terms of their own values. In the latter case, the claim is indeed a form of power since pressure is put on others to fulfil their recognised obligations.

Rights cannot be identified directly with the concept of force, even though the actual application of the threatened sanctions may be necessary at times to protect the exercise of our entitlements. As we saw in our earlier discussion of force, its use can enhance power in so far as people recognise that violation of rights will be punished. Bachrach and Baratz look upon the use of force as a sign of the failure of power, in the sense that force is a less satisfactory way of relating to others than the use of power. From the point of view of rights, however, we can argue that even power with its need for threat of sanctions is not the ideal method for achieving respect for them. Rights ought to be respected for their own sake, not because they carry some threat; and certainly not because they can sometimes act as a gun at our back!

Is the concept of influence at all helpful in relation to rights? I think it can be, because influence and authority differ from power and force in being able to change others without threat. Influence does imply an initial conflict of values between the person who influences and the person influenced, and we have seen that this is not necessarily the case in relation to all our claims against others. Yet rights can be influential. Like certain people who have influence over us due to our respect and admiration for them, the terminology of rights can have an almost awe-inspiring effect or influence, quite apart from our knowledge of sanctions attending our failure to respect them.

Finally there is the possibility of a useful connection between rights and authority. Authority has to do with a type of communication between persons characterised by its rational guiding force. Rights ideally ought to have such an authoritative status arising from their communicative role. Rights 'call out' to the reasonable man or woman to recognise their meaning, value and justification. Authority must take us further than influence in presenting the reasonable basis for the effect that rights-language sometimes has on us. Threats of sanctions and use of force are regarded as inappropriate or as a last resort as a means of gaining respect for rights, though the authority rights have can justify as well as limit the connection between them and the more robust forms of persuasion. As the use of force is a sign of the failure of power, so too is it a sign of the failure of authority, even more so in fact because authority, in the sense it is used here, has no direct connection with sanctions. While the use of force can enhance future uses of power, it plays no such role in relation to authority. The only force that can restore authority is the 'force' of reasonableness. Where rights lose their authority, what is required is not force but new insight and imagination.

In stressing the relational aspect of these political concepts Bachrach and Baratz enable us to see how power, force, influence and authority are experienced from two points of view – that of the person in the controlling position, and that of the person who is on the receiving end of some pressure to change. One point of view is not sufficient to understand the working of these concepts in everyday experience. To look at power from the angle of the person who wields it, ignores the fact that to wield power in practice there must be a positive response from the person or persons towards whom the exercise of power is directed. A powerful person is a person who, over time, has been successful in getting people to change their behaviour in line with his wishes. And the same conclusion applies regarding the other related concepts, especially influence and authority.

This twin perspective has obvious applications to our study of rights. If rights are related to the concepts at present under discussion then they would seem to depend for their existence on being recognised by others. But this raises the problem, already mentioned, that it is possible to have a right which is not recognised and not claimed by the holder of the right. Thus, it looks as if the relational aspect of power and its related concepts must be linked to the 'exercise' of rights and their being claimed, than to the wider notion of 'having' a claim or right. From the political point of view our interest is pragmatic; we want to change others, to bring them around to our way of thinking and behaving. Exercising rights falls into this category, especially when we have to insist on our rights against others.

Exercising a right can involve a power when we use our ability to claim as a threat to move others to fulfil their obligations, either towards ourselves or towards others. On occasion, the use of force may bring us the good or benefit we need or want, but on another level we are the poorer because forcing others to respect us has a contradictory aspect. To some extent this is also true of the link between rights and power, in view of the threat of sanctions. The concepts of influence and authority are more satisfactory in elucidating how rights are ideally exercised. Because sanctions are not the primary motivating force, and there is a greater emphasis on an appeal to reason in order to move people to recognise obligations correlative to rights, the exercise of rights takes on a certain dignity of its own. The notion of authority also has a closer connection with justification than has power, even though authority can masquerade as genuine when actually false or invalid. The lesson we learn is that respect for rights is not attained simply in the case that others give us what we want; what matters as well is the spirit in which that takes place, whether the relationship between the claimant and the bearer of the obligation is essentially conflictual or harmonious, strained or easy.

At this stage of our discussion the reader could object that I have in effect abandoned the initial suggestion that power is a helpful metaphor for rights in favour of a totally different concept and metaphor, authority. In my opinion, power and authority have different emphases, but they are not totally different. They are still relational concepts, and have some degree of rationality in common. It can be rational to change your position in response to the threat of sanctions even if this is not the more respected rationality of being convinced by the logic of another's argument. And we should allow room for the idea that failure to respect the reasonable approach of authority carries with it indirect, informal sanctions. Who, after all, wants to be stigmatised as irrational or unreasonable? It is also important to note that power and authority act as models for rights in different contexts. On one hand, the power model reflects the more pessimistic (or realistic, depending on your temperament) view of human life, regarding rights as always under threat, having to be fought for and enforced against reluctant fellow citizens. The authority model, on the other hand, tends towards optimism and idealism. It wants an approach to rights which stresses their inherent reasonableness. It says to us 'If only you could see the moral value of normative relationships of these kinds, there would be no need for threats and force.'

The concept of power has been defined by Bachrach and Baratz in a quite narrow sense as we have seen. This narrow focus has its usefulness as a stipulative definition, and applies to rights in certain cases. But it is too narrow to cover all situations where people have rights and go on to claim them. Therefore, we employ other concepts, as well as power, to draw out further implications of the normative relationships people enjoy or ought to enjoy. We have defined these also in relatively narrow terms, distinguishing in particular influence and authority from power and force. I can see no objection, however, to our saying that all of these concepts are intimately related and that all of them can be brought under the heading of power-relationships. This will demand a broadening of our focus and an acceptance of a wider definition and analysis of power which includes the other concepts of force, influence and authority. Having done this, we find ourselves with one rich model made up of diverse elements, each of which has some application to rights, and none of which alone is sufficient to pin down the meaning of our justified claims or entitlements.

CONCLUSION

In this chapter our concern has been to explore the possibility of developing an approach to metaethics which takes the im- agination into account in the analysis of ethical terms like 'rights'. We looked at the interest shown by many scholars across various disciplines in the value of metaphorical thinking, and applied this to the ethical sphere. The major characteristics of models as systematically developed metaphors were listed, and a number of metaphors and potential models of rights were

examined. Beginning with rather simple and limited examples
– chains and safety nets – we progressed to the more complex
and richer images of freedom and power. These metaphors are
easily developed into quite helpful models having both cognitive
and emotive aspects. As models these images point to selected
aspects of rights and act as an interpretation of our experience,
or as an ordering of experience, rather than as plain descriptions.
Thus, the language is both imagistic and conceptual.

None of the models used is sufficient on its own to bring out
the full meaning of rights, and multiple models are necessary to
increase our knowledge of this complex field. Because of the
particular depth of meaning associated with the terms 'freedom'
and 'power' they are particularly suitable to function as models,
for their implications and associations have potentially wide
applications. Furthermore, since metaphorical thinking involves a bifocal vision, not only does freedom and power
elucidate the meaning of rights, but there is also a sense in which
rights can elucidate the concepts of freedom and power. Having
the freedom and the power to claim, for instance, distinguishes
the legal and moral status of the free person from that of the
slave. Because models and metaphors maintain a tension
between similarity and dissimilarity of related objects, often the
ways in which objects differ are as instructive as the ways in
which they are alike. That rights involve a particular type of
freedom and have little or nothing to do with other types of
freedom is an important insight, just as insights into how rights
are related to power, force, influence and authority should not
be ignored.

Finally, I believe it would be foolish to ignore the role this
chapter plays in adding to our previous response to scepticism
about rights. In the previous two chapters we presented and
rebutted conceptual and normative scepticism using conceptual
and normative ethical tools. In this chapter, and in the following
chapters, as we develop the imaginative approach to metaethics,
scepticism concerning rights comes under attack from the moral
imagination. The images presented should have a certain 'feel'
about them which convinces us of the positive role rights play in
the moral life.

CHAPTER 6

Theological imagination and rights

In the last chapter we introduced the idea of the importance of imagination in science and philosophy, and hinted at its importance in theology as well. Theologians like McFague, Tracy, Mackey, and Campbell urge us to take imagination seriously in our study of the relationship between God and humanity. An initial effort was made to lay down some foundations on which we will build the ethical models of freedom and power. We saw the usefulness of Feinberg's analysis of freedom and learned from the political science analysis of power from the pens of Bachrach and Baratz. Each model goes some way towards helping us understand the meaning and value of the language of rights. At the same time we recognised the limitations of these models as they stand.

There is a need at this stage to begin to examine these models of rights from a Christian ethical perspective. In this chapter the focus will fall on the freedom model of rights. We will examine the views of theologians who have underlined the value of this topic in their writings. In particular I will stress the example of Jesus Christ whose radical stance in relation to freedom is said to be close to cynic radicalism. It will be pointed out that he functions as a model of autonomy, even though he was perfectly obedient to God, his Father. And there will be a lengthy discussion of the connections between rights and religious freedom, and between rights and fundamental equality. All in all an effort will be made to convey a religious vision of freedom which adds to the study of this model from the secular perspective in the last chapter.

As we continue to elucidate the notion of rights by means of the ethical imagination, let us consider some further advantages of employing a theological imagination to human experience.

John McIntyre is yet another theologian to advocate the advantage of an imaginative approach to theology. At the beginning of his book, *Faith, Theology and Imagination*,[1] he cites from another Scottish religious thinker, John Baillie, who once wrote:

I have long been of the opinion that the part played by the imagination in the soul's dealings with God, though it has always been understood by those skilled in the practice of the Christian cure of souls, has never been given proper place in Christian theology, which has been too much ruled by intellectualist preconceptions.[2]

McIntyre suggests that the imagination has been traditionally suspect in theological circles. In the Authorised Version of the Bible, for instance, the English translations of the three main words for imagination tended to be pejorative, 'uniformly implying that imagination is unacceptable to God in all its machinations, and therefore to be eliminated from the minds and thoughts of his servants'.[3] Although these translations are no longer generally accepted, the influence of nearly 350 years is to some extent still with us. Calvin was hostile to the use of images, especially in worship. He was an opponent of 'iconolatry', says McIntyre.[4] Thus, we have the iconoclastic tradition, even amounting to 'iconophobia'. There is also, according to McIntyre, a tradition of 'aniconastic' (sic) thought in theology, that is a tradition of imageless thought as a norm for theological reflection and articulation. Consider *The Cloud of Unknowing*[5] from mystical theology, and in modern times the process of demythologisation which moves in the direction of a highly sterilised theology devoid of all rich images.

On the positive side McIntyre insists on the great advantages of an imaginative theology. At the most basic level of theology imagination is said to be one of God's attributes, specifically related to his love and freedom. Thus, 'Imagination is the medium of God's loving penetration into the world of the sinner. It is the form which God's awareness takes of the condition of the other who stands over against him in rebellion and hatred.'[6]

McIntyre writes beautifully of God's imaginativeness in Creation and especially in the Incarnation. In the parable of the dishonest tenants (Mtt. 21.33–45) God is seen as acting with 'daring imaginativeness' by sending his own Son, after already sending the prophets throughout the Old Testament. The Incarnation is a shock. It is familiar to us, yet still hard to accept. Christmas is a special time, he suggests, because we have a chance to allow the shock of the Incarnation to grasp us imaginatively (p. 55). Later in the same chapter there is a discussion of the role of the Spirit and his imaginative action in the world. From the Acts of the Apostles to the modern Pentecostal Movement, God's Spirit continues to blow where he wills. As well as being influenced by John Baillie in the quotation already given above, McIntyre is impressed greatly by George MacDonald's essay entitled 'The Imagination: Its Function and Its Culture', from whom he borrows the notion that 'The imagination of man is made in the image of the imagination of God.'[7] For MacDonald, McIntyre tells us, imagination and faith are closely related since the former is a faculty which seeks out the unknown. Imagination is 'the form which faith takes in face of the unknown'. A similar point is hinted at by Daniel Maguire when he states that

Creative Imagination is the supreme faculty of moral man. Through it he breaks out of the bondage of the current state of things. Through it he perceives the possible that is latent in the actual but which would be unseen by any less exalted consciousness. Like God's Spirit in the Book of Genesis, creative imagination can find the possibilities of order in the 'formless void' and begin the rout of chaos.[8]

If this is true, it gives a massive boost to the respectability of imagination and once again acts as a critique of overly discursive approaches to religious reality. In fact, we could go further and argue that, for the believer, the use of imagination is not an optional extra in life, but involves a strict obligation to act in accordance with one's dignity as made in God's image.

In Christian theology the parables of the Gospels are a prime example of the application of the imagination to the interpretation of human life, including the moral life. Consider as an example the parables of the Kingdom of God.[9] The Kingdom of God is itself, according to Sallie McFague, a root metaphor in the teachings of Jesus, but the parables are in turn extended metaphors which shed light on the dominant Kingdom metaphor. McFague insists that

What is crucial in these stories is the *plot*; they are exemplars, not discrete poetic metaphors. As Ricoeur has said perceptively, the interactive partners in permanent tension in a parable are two ways of being in the world, one of which is conventional and the other, the way of the kingdom. A parable is a judgement or assertion of similarity and difference between two thoughts in permanent tension with one another: one is the ordinary way of being in the world and the other, the extraordinary way.[10]

The parables, then, bring together many of the themes we have explored as part of our analysis of imagination. They involve extended metaphors or models, connecting dissimilar realities and using the ordinary to explore the extraordinary. They involve an indirect grasp of reality, and are particularly appropriate as an introduction to mystery. Above all they are not simply productive of theoretical knowledge, but involve practical reason, leading us to see the world differently. Thus, parables reveal the unsettling and uncomfortable side of the imagination. As Daniel Maguire puts it, 'Creativity upsets the timid little order we have achieved, and makes the uncourageous cringe.'[11] The Brazilian philosopher Rubem Alves is quoted by Maguire as saying that 'creativity is a forbidden act. The organisation of our world is essentially sterile and hates anything that could be the seed of regeneration'.[12]

In *The Responsible Self*, H. Richard Niebuhr argues that contemporary men and women ask for general symbols which will help them to understand their status as moral agents. Niebuhr's own idea of 'responsibility' is itself a new root-metaphor which functions in this way.[13]

But there are other metaphors, similes and symbols which have guided our self-understanding in the history of Christian ethics as Niebuhr reminds us. In particular there is 'synecdoche', a way of apprehending the whole of our activity with the aid of one activity seen as representative of all. The whole, then, is like one of its parts. For instance, life is like a warfare (echoes of Campbell's military metaphor in relation to medical practice here).[14] We use various images from war to describe our moral life. Temptation has to be 'fought' or 'struggled' with and 'overcome'. We experience internal 'conflicts'. Our conscience 'attacks' us and so on. Or another image, mentioned by Niebuhr, is that of life as a pilgrimage or journey. People are said to 'travel' through life and we talk about the American or Christian 'way'. We remember the words of Christ when he contrasts the 'easy way' that leads to destruction and the 'narrow road' which leads to eternal life. For Christians, Jesus Christ is 'the way, the truth and the life'. And if life is a pilgrimage, then it has a religious dimension throughout, which is coloured by the destination.[15] Similes are taken from the world of commerce as when we speak of our 'indebtedness' to God and others, or when we employ the language of contracts and refer to what is 'due'.

For Niebuhr two of the greatest synecdoches in the Western World are given the labels 'homo faber' and 'homo politicus'. The first image underlines the aspect of craftsmanship in human life, the way in which humanity works towards goals or ends. The second image stresses the aspect of citizenship, the way in which humans participate in the state or society in which laws have to be made and obeyed. To these dominant historical symbols he now adds a third – 'homo dialogicus' (p. 160).

At the level of Christian ethics, Niebuhr insists on the importance of the person of Christ as a basic symbolic form for Christians (*ibid.*, p. 154) and later on refers to him as a fundamental and indispensable metaphor.[16] At the same time he recognises the limits of any single symbol or metaphor to capture the whole of moral reality. He asks, 'Is the Christ symbol the only or the wholly dominant and completely adequate form for Christians, or is it always associated with other symbols so that it is impossible for Christians to define themselves simply as Christians?' (p. 157). Theologians like Barth who try to work with one symbol, the Christ, find themselves using associated biblical symbols to complement the central image – Word of God, Servant, Lord, Covenant, etc. – and Niebuhr concludes:

The situation of Christians then seems to be this: they cannot understand themselves or direct their actions or give form to their conduct without the use of the symbol Jesus Christ, but with the aid of that symbol only they never succeed in understanding themselves and their values or in giving shape to their conduct (p. 158).

This approach to Christian ethics by way of symbol and metaphor is one of the keys to unlocking the value of imagination for that subject. Most important is the reminder of the need for different images to complement and criticise one another. We have stressed this point already from the work of Sallie McFague. Without a critical stance regarding metaphor, our traditional metaphors become conventional and border on idolatry.

Niebuhr's reference to Christ as *the* central symbol of Christianity runs parallel to McFague's reference to Christ as *the* 'parable of God', once we recall that parables are often extended metaphors and partake of the characteristics of metaphorical language. Parables are characterised by their 'indirection', since they do not speak directly of God's essence or attributes; by their 'extravagance', due to their surprising and shocking connections; and by their 'ordinariness' as seen in the subject matter taken from everyday experience. Applying these elements to the person of Christ, McFague insists that

These characteristics of indirection, extravagance and mundanity are epitomised in *the* parable of the New Testament, the story of Jesus. This 'metaphor' above all others in the New Testament is in many ways the most obvious one and at the same time the most difficult to grasp... because this 'parable' is a human life, the most complex and multidimensional of all metaphors, with unlimited possibilities for interpretation.[17]

But remember Niebuhr's qualification that, although the Christ symbol or metaphor is necessary for Christian self-understanding, it is not sufficient on its own, requiring further help from other religious images and also from metaphors which straddle the divide between belief and unbelief. In fact, the ordinariness of the parables reflected in the ordinariness of the humanity of Jesus is a reminder that the metaphors and models used to interpret religious experience are frequently very mundane. Thus, our approach to the analysis of rights has so far relied on ordinary human images and concepts, whereas it is now opportune to examine the specifically religious dimension of these images such as freedom and power. The suggestion is being made that Christian ethics makes a distinctive contribution to the analysis of rights by developing interpretations based on a theological understanding of our root-metaphors of freedom and power, as well as developing its own specific religious imagery, for example, that of covenant.

FREEDOM AND RIGHTS IN A CHRISTIAN CONTEXT

It would be extremely tedious to summarise here the voluminous theological literature on the subject of freedom, autonomy and liberation.[18] What I will do is to present some basic understandings of Christian freedom which will have some bearing on the analysis of rights. It is important again to note that there is no literal identification of freedom or liberation with respect for rights, any more than our philosophical study of freedom led to such an identification. Christian freedom is a much wider reality than having and claiming rights. However, our approach to freedom from a religious perspective does change our understanding of rights, and certainly must affect the ways in which we exercise them.

We noted in the last chapter that having rights and claiming them is not sufficient to show that a person is free in the moral sense. Certainly, having rights is a sign of freedom as a legal and moral status, but even in order to exercise them there must be a developed sense of autonomy in the etymological sense of being self-regulating, in charge of one's own inner life, having a consistent set of values which guide decisions and behaviour. Rights without self-control are sterile. In the Christian tradition the same point holds: self-control, inner discipline – even amounting to a relatively strict asceticism – is fundamental for freedom.[19] However, unlike the secular tradition which makes inner freedom a matter of human will-power, helped by our internalisation of social norms and encouraged by fear of human sanctions, the religious believer holds that this inner freedom derives from God's grace and the guidance of divine laws. But even this is not a deep enough analysis of freedom for the Christian.

Part of the tradition holds that freedom is an ultimate status established at creation when humanity was made in God's image. A further aspect of this tradition asserts that this image was somewhat tarnished by sin, an abuse of freedom, but is fully restored in Christ by his death and resurrection. The ultimate freedom for the Christian is given by God. It is the offer of a right relationship with one's creator and redeemer, accepted in faith and love, and experienced through forgiveness and conversion. Freedom comes to us without our having any right to it, since forgiveness can hardly be a right. Freedom reaches beyond this world in traditional Christianity; it has an eschatological dimension in so far as God's gift of forgiveness is said to open the gates of Heaven to the sinner, freeing one from eternal death.

The fundamental notion of freedom for the Christian stresses the initiative of God. From the human point of view the gift must be used appropriately. The believer must live out the implications of a radical freedom, a freedom which is supremely demanding, even 'threatening'.

F. GERALD DOWNING: FREEDOM AS A THREAT

In his book, *Jesus and the Threat of Freedom*, F. Gerald Downing argues that the teaching and example of Jesus and his first disciples had much in common with that of the Cynic philosophers of the Greek World.

On an errand to the market for some fish in a first-century east Mediterranean city, jostling with slaves and wives of workmen and children coming home from school and leisured gentlemen on their way to meet their friends at the baths, your attention is distracted by an eccentric character who doesn't seem to be buying or selling anything. Dressed in a simple cloak, leaning on a stick, looking as though he's not got a penny to his name, not even a change of shirt or a bag for food, he seems to be claiming to be some kind of physician.

'If you think you're in good health,' he shouts, 'don't bother to stop. I'm only here for the ones who are ready to admit they're a bit sickly. Or more than a bit'

We ourselves have very likely heard something of this before, perhaps from Matthew's gospel. But the man in the market place is not a Christian. He is a 'dogged philosopher', a follower of Diogenes, who was a native of Sinope on the Black Sea, but lived most of his adult life in Corinth, in the fourth century BCE. The speaker is a Cynic.[20]

Downing insists that the Cynics were like the early Christians in being heavily critical of the society in which they lived.[21] Both groups would have sounded 'political' to their hearers. 'It was popular preachers like our Cynic who did their best to free people to be more fully and richly human, in the time of Christ' (p. 4).

Most interesting from our point of view the Cynics sounded rather Christian in their references to the divine source of their free status – 'a free man under Father Zeus, afraid of none of the great lords'. Downing compares this with a Christian formulation of freedom: 'no longer a slave, but a son – and if you are a son, you're God's heir' (*ibid.*). Downing admits that at times it is not clear how the Cynics view God or the gods; sometimes their references may be 'no more than rhetorical flourishes'; on other occasions, under stoic influence, God may be understood as 'the impersonal though dynamic pattern' discerned in the universe. But there are references which appear to underline a more personal type of deity. There are parallels in cynic thought to the words of Jesus regarding the paternal care God shows for his children (Luke 11.11). For instance, Dio is cited:

In their dreams young children often reach out their arms to absent parents, filled with deeply and intensely felt longing ... in just the same way we humans love the Gods who do us good and are our kin, and we feel a deep desire to be with them and enjoy their company in every way possible.[22]

Or take this quotation from Epictetus:

God has not merely given us these abilities of ours so we may put up with whatever happens without being humiliated or broken by it; as a good king and most truly a father to us, he's given us these abilities without external constraints, unhampered. He's put them entirely into our hands, without reserving even for himself any power to hinder or restrain.[23]

Here we have a pre-Christian religious view of human autonomy combined with a personal view of God, using metaphors quite familiar to the Judaeo-Christian tradition. Epictetus is also quoted as saying, 'I am a free human being and a friend of God, so I must obey him of my own free will' (*ibid.*). Downing comments on this to the effect that, 'The nearest early Christian analogy is in Galatians 4.1–7 and Romans 8.14–17…We are adult children of a caring father; and if we submit, it is freely, under no compulsion. It is worth noting that we are far from any divine undergirding of an authoritarian or hierarchical view of society.' (*ibid.*)

The freedom advocated by both Cynics and Christians was of a practical kind, not an ivory tower, academic discussion of life's problems or preaching without practice. As such it was threatening to the established powers of society and to all those who were living an unexamined or mediocre existence. Downing mentions that the Roman imperial government didn't worry too much about 'wide-ranging discussions of political theory by intellectuals among themselves' (p. 58). But the Cynics were in a different category:

…a movement which stressed action, and pressed for a lifestyle different from that which maintained the even tenour and efficient running of things, was dangerous. 'Innovation' and 'rebellion' are almost synonymous. Energetic conservation of the old is fine. Critical discussion of it can be tolerated. Alternative life-styles put into practice are a threat.[24]

What is said of the Cynics is also true of the early Christians. Freedom for them meant something similar to the philosophy of the Cynics – 'the possibility of change, of adopting a new life-style not bound by conventional restrictions determining in advance the roles people must play out…It is this that constitutes the "repentance" John and Jesus are both said to have proclaimed.'[25]

The value of freedom, according to Christian tradition, lies in the possession of a particular status, which is relational –

expressed in terms of being a child of God, a brother or sister of Christ, God's friend, and so on. But this status brings with it certain rights and obligations to embark upon a life-style which is appropriate to one's relational identity. Such a life-style may well be disruptive of society, and the rights which are claimed may be very different from those sought by one's fellow citizens.

It is tempting to accuse Christian freedom of being a rather emaciated concept when compared with the ordinary human, non-religious concept. If freedom is given by God as a particular status and requires us to live according to divine commands, then how free are we in the ordinary sense of enjoying absence of constraint and having opportunities to follow out our own plans? In particular, when we look at the life-style of Jesus and his followers, as well as the life-style of the Cynics, we may feel that their interests in the material side of life are so limited that to call them free is a misuse of the term. Isaiah Berlin warns against an application of the term 'freedom' to the life-style commended by some forms of rationalist and idealistic philosophy, as well as some religions. He labels this general approach 'The retreat to the inner citadel'.

It is as if I had performed a strategic retreat into an inner citadel – my reason, my soul, my 'noumenal self' – which, do what they may, neither external blind force, nor human malice, can touch. I have withdrawn into myself; there, and there alone, I am secure... This is the traditional self-emancipation of ascetics and quietists, of stoics or Buddhist sages, men of various religions or none, who have fled the world, and escaped the yoke of society or public opinion, by some process of deliberate self-transformation that enables them to care no longer for any of its values, to remain, isolated and independent, on its edges, no longer vulnerable to its weapons.[26]

But this is not Christian freedom, even though certain strands of that religion tend in this direction. It certainly finds no support in biblical thought as Luise Schottroff reminds us.

In Seneca, for example (*De Beneficiis* III, 20,1) we find the concept of an inner liberty, attainable in spite of outward conditions. But this is not a biblical idea... The notion of an inner liberty, independent of whether people are in fact hungry, or enslaved, or it may be prosperous, belongs to the situation of a wealthy class which sees its opportunities for political action restricted (see Seneca). But the Bible speaks with the voice of people marked by the experiences of subjection.

Lack of freedom – like freedom – is always understood in the Bible *as a whole*. The New Testament word 'body' (*soma*) expresses this totality: servitude is bodily, psychological, social and religious reality. All sectors of human identity are affected – even hopes are destroyed (we only have to look at Rom. 6:12–14). The inner life and outward conditions are not separated, and the physical sufferings of bondage are exactly described.[27]

If freedom from a Christian perspective were divorced from the material realities of this world and relegated to some spiritual sphere, it is difficult to see how there would be any room for a Christian doctrine or justification for rights. However, our present wholistic approach to human life, together with an incarnational theology of the person, insists on this wedding between the material and the spiritual, so that the person who ignores the body is in danger of losing his soul. Thus, there is an important role for rights in the protection of the whole person. Let us now turn to a particular attempt to justify rights in terms of freedom understood in a Christian light.

DONAL MURRAY: HUMAN RIGHTS AND RELIGIOUS FREEDOM

In an article entitled, 'The Theological Basis for Human Rights', the Irish theologian, Donal Murray, begins in a relatively conventional way by stating that the foundation of rights is the dignity of the human person.[28] This is hardly controversial. However, the next step in fleshing out the notion of rights and dignity is more questionable. His basic position is as follows: 'In this reflection, I would like to suggest that it is indeed in the area of religious freedom that we can begin to tease out the meaning of human dignity and the manner in which human rights can be derived from it' (*ibid.*) Murray agrees that this contention is counterintuitive if it refers to the limited sphere of 'what one might call ecclesiastical activities'. In fact, the concept of religious freedom is wider and more basic. Religious freedom is, to quote Pope John Paul II, 'the most fundamental of rights functioning as the first of duties, which is the duty to move towards God in the light of truth, with that movement of the heart which is love.' (*ibid.*).

The ultimate and most basic freedom for the believer exists in the context of the relationship with God. In the quotation just cited above, rights are regarded as being in the service of the obligation to draw close to God.[29] Murray's analysis of freedom is a development from this starting point. The believer must recognise the limits of his freedom. It is not the same as God's omnipotence. Human freedom must be realistic concerning what can be achieved. It is a mixture of admiring consent to God's creation and an attitude of hope which recognises the limits of freedom, yet longs for total liberation. Paul Ricoeur is quoted at this point:

Admiration says: the world is good, it is the possible homeland of freedom: I am content. Hope says: the world is not the *definitive* homeland of freedom: I consent to the greatest possible extent, but I hope to be delivered from what is terrifying and, at the end of time, to possess a new body and a new nature in harmony with freedom.[30]

There is a tension, then, in the concept and experience of human freedom based on the believer's confidence in the power of God's unlimited freedom to transform existence, and his sad recognition of human limitation, including moral weakness or sin, which holds back the primary work of God in liberating humanity and its environment. There must be an attitude of humility which accepts that what freedom we have is mainly a result of God's gift, and what freedom we lack is mainly a matter of human sin (always keeping in mind that it is moral freedom that is in question).

The concept of religious freedom as essentially a duty to seek out God in truth and love seems to stress the activity of humanity. But what has been said already regarding God's freedom and grace, must lead Christians to insist on the fact that their free movement towards God is only possible because God enables them to make such a response. No one would dare to approach God in love if God had not first given a loving invitation. The core of freedom from the Christian perspective, then, implies that God has initiated a loving relationship with humanity in which his own absolute freedom is shared with us to some extent. The most basic aspect of this freedom for humanity is the choice they must make to respond either positively or negatively to God's revelation of himself. In turn, part of this response of human freedom to divine freedom must involve our relationships with fellow humans, and it is here that the doctrine of rights has its place in the Christian scheme.

Freedom, from the Christian point of view, is a gift of God. In creating the human race God gave a nature made in his own image. This is one traditional approach to grounding human dignity. Humans are in some sense like God. What exactly the image of God in men and women is has given rise to much discussion in theology.[31] In this work already we have noted McIntyre's view that the use of imagination is a sign of being made in God's image, and the approach just mentioned above concerning the freedom to enter into relationships with others is another possible approach to the theology of God's image. In fact, these two spheres taken together present us with a concrete ethical application of the image concept to daily living. McIntyre devotes a chapter of his book to the ethical dimension of imagination, in which he argues that this category helps overcome a whole series of basic tensions in Christian ethics. In particular McIntyre stresses the role imagination plays in the central principle of love, whereby it gives the moral agent 'a heightened perceptivity towards other persons which will discern in them qualities concealed from casual observers, as well as difficulties and sufferings that are affecting them, even to the attractiveness that underlies the superficial unattractive-ness'.[32] God acts towards humanity in free and imaginative patterns. Freely he initiates relationships and creatively main-tains and renews them.[33] That is a fundamental Christian belief. It follows that, to be made in the image of God, a human creature will, and should, display these characteristics to some extent. There is a calling built into one's very being to enter into relationships and to develop them creatively and imaginatively. If ethics is about anything, surely it is about this fundamental feature of human existence. It follows, too, I think, that the

basic rights of humankind are precisely the valid claims we
possess to be ourselves, to live out our destiny as relational
beings, growing more like God all our days. And not only do we
have rights to remain true to our identity as made in God's
image, but more fundamentally rights are indicative of that
identity. In other words we can often actually express our
freedom and creative imagination when claiming rights for
ourselves and others.

This analysis of freedom from a Christian perspective has
something fundamental in common with the earlier philosophical analysis of this concept. One of Feinberg's insights into
freedom concerns the use of the term as a legal or moral status
word, distinguishing the freeman from the slave. And he pointed
out the connection between freedom, equality and rights in the
context of that distinction. The free person is different from the
slave in having rights. The slave is not allowed to 'be himself',
the person God created him to be. His freedom to be creative in
relating to others is severely curtailed. Even though the slave
may have a kind master and thus live with comparative absence
of constraint, because he has no right to this situation he is not
free in the important sense we have been elucidating.

From the beginning of his reflection on human rights Murray
brings together the notions of freedom and equality. He cites the
position of the Roman Catholic International Theological
Commission that equality rather than religious freedom is the
most fundamental human right (p. 81). He also notes that '... it
has commonly been suggested that the basis [of human rights]
is to be found in the triad of freedom, equality and participation'.[34] His approach is simply to use freedom as a key to
understanding all three concepts 'in a full and balanced way'.
Equality is part of the 'internal logic' of freedom and the notion
of freedom 'implies reciprocity and equality' (p. 85). At the
same time Murray is critical of reducing the analysis of human
rights to equality for fear of individualism. Thus he states that:

Over-emphasis on laws and rights can lead to individualism. After all,
if the other is only my equal, why should I allow his interests to take
precedence over mine? In particular, why should I ever think of going
beyond his or her strict rights? To put it another way, the demands

made on me by the rights of others do not seem to be adequately expressed in terms of equality. (p. 89)

Murray answers the problem in this way:

The Christian revelation provides the most fundamental reason why one must go beyond legal rules, not just in relation to God but also in relation to one's neighbour. Equality is no longer an adequate model for interpersonal relations. In respecting the freedom of another person one is respecting something which is a dialogue with the Infinite. (p. 92)

Freedom is then seen in a Trinitarian setting:

I respect another person not just because he or she is like me. I respect every other person because Jesus Christ, the Son of God, has united himself to that person to set him or her free (Gal. 5:1); the Spirit, whose presence gives freedom (2 Cor. 3:17) is within them; the Father, the source and goal of freedom, has loved them first. The freedom which we respect is not only an 'exceptional sign of the image of God in the human being', it is a sign of his presence; its deepest meaning lies in his friendship.

This is the ultimate reason why human rights are unconditional and inalienable. To respect them is to respond not just to one's equals but to God. (p. 92)

One must not make too much of this contrast between human equality and the intimate human relationship with God as the foundation of human rights.[35] Equality is not demoted; its meaning is deepened, as is the concept of our being made in the image of God, by the further qualification that all humans are essentially equal due to the loving attitude of God towards them. This love is already implicit in the creation of human creatures and in the establishment of the Old Testament covenants, but it is revealed in its deepest form in the mission of Jesus Christ and in his new covenant. Relying on the notion of the image of God alone raises questions as to whether this has not been ruined by sin, as well as questions about God's ongoing relationship with humanity; for instance, God could be seen in a deistic light, creating humans in his own image and then more or less forgetting them, whereas in the religious tradition of Christianity God constantly reiterates his commitment to creation in salvation history.

Basing freedom and rights on the notion of relational status presents further problems, especially when the relationships in question are highly specific, for example from family life. The relationship between children and parents involves forms of freedom which do not apply in the case of strangers. Likewise, specific relationships between, say, brothers and sisters or between friends have associated rights and duties which are well recognised and widely accepted as normative. However, these relationships are of such a personal and specific kind that we may well wonder how they can be used to ground the most general claims or entitlements such as human rights. Human rights are by definition the valid claims persons can make on the basis of their essential humanity, usually judged in terms of fundamental needs. It would be odd in the light of this understanding to claim a human right on the basis of being a son or daughter of a named individual. Such a claim could justify certain special moral rights, but nothing more than that. To ground rights on the idea of being a child of God, or a friend of Christ, or even on a covenant relationship, may cause us more problems than we imagine, unless we interpret these relationships as having universal application. This move helps us to realise that references to relationships within the 'family of God' are strictly metaphorical and analogical (as are secular counterparts of the 'family' or 'brotherhood' of man). All sorts of qualifications need to be made in using this relational terminology. For instance, if we are children of God we are not so in the same way as Jesus was and is a son – we are 'adopted'. And, again the problem arises of deciding if God as father has rights and duties.

The concept of image of God is on the face of it more appropriate as a basis for speaking about the more general human rights and freedom, precisely because of its generality, because it is so widely accepted in the Christian tradition that every person, believer and non-believer alike, is somehow a reflection of God. Whereas the notion of a family relationship generally presupposes intimate knowledge between members, the image of God concept seems to permit relationships of respect at a distance between comparative and absolute strangers. There is also the problem of specifying exactly what qualities of human life reflect God's life. If it is rational or intellectual qualities alone that count, then the image of God concept is quite different from the concept of intimate relationships, and the two notions fit very uncomfortably in this religious tradition, giving us a rather confused basis for freedom and rights. If the image of God idea is interpreted differently as a relational concept and in a less rationalistic, but imaginative, way, then it comes close to the relational metaphors of family, friends, disciples, with which we are so familiar.

The position taken in this discussion so far has implied a refusal to separate these two approaches to the religious grounding of freedom and rights. To be made in the image of God is to share in God's personal–relational nature. From creation humanity is called in freedom to be members of God's people, to be his family. Christianity knows no impersonal basis for justifying respect for human rights and human freedom. A reading of the notion of image of God in terms of specific human qualities taken in the abstract, such as rationality and all it implies, seems to be far from the minds of the biblical writers. To take an approach of that sort would be like a mother reasoning that she should respect her children because they have certain clear indicators of humanhood such as a reasonable IQ.[36] Christianity's fundamental problem in this field is that of imitating God whose supreme power allows him to love all humanity equally. When believers attempt to translate this into moral terms as a guide for human behaviour by means of a concept like human rights, according to which we encourage the ideal of seeing all people as one family under heaven, there would appear to be a failure of nerve. We gag at the notion. Of course this reaction is almost a typical response to metaphorical thinking, where the metaphor is so shocking that it is sometimes rejected and more often paid a degree of lip-service, while in reality its implications are ignored.

Murray is correct, I think, in saying that an overemphasis on rights can lead to individualism. He is also justified in stating that all of morality can hardly be reduced to respect for rights; the example of forgiveness he presents to illustrate this is a good one. Morality transcends both rights and obligations in the sphere of supererogation. However, his questions concerning the limits of equality are puzzling, when he asks 'if the other is only my equal, why should I allow his interests to take precedence over mine?' and, secondly, 'why should I ever think of going beyond his or her strict rights?'.

In reply to the first question, when equality is discussed what we are talking about is an equal fundamental dignity and worth, not about giving everyone's interests equal weight from moment to moment. The answer to the question depends on the interests involved: if my interests in a particular case are of relatively low value, and the interests of another are more fundamental, then my belief in human equality is a good reason for giving way to the needs of another, and I can expect the same treatment from others if the situation is reversed. If equally fundamental interests are in conflict, then the goods may be shared between equals, or else some kind of 'toss up' may be demanded of the kind used to solve moral dilemmas where, for instance, not everyone in a lifeboat can survive, and the occupants draw lots to see who will be saved.[37]

Regarding the second question, we can make a distinction between equality and equity. Though everyone living has equal dignity or value, in fact not everyone has enjoyed an equal share in the world's goods. Some, indeed, have been discriminated against and should now be the object of reverse discrimination[38] to bring them up to the level of the more privileged members of society – hence the notion of a 'preferential option for the poor'. But, since helping the poor is often regarded as an imperfect obligation and not a strict right, the poor cannot claim help as a right. Yet I may have some obligation to go beyond respect for strict rights precisely because of my belief in equal dignity or worth.

Thus, I find myself dissenting from Murray's declaration that 'the demands made on me by the rights of others do not seem to be adequately expressed in terms of equality', as well as from his view that we must go further and invoke the claims of God as the rationale for respecting such rights. It is quite sufficient to say that our equality is God-given and has a special status to provide a solid ground for a Christian understanding of the normative value of rights. And this is just as good a reason for speaking about 'the absolute source' of the demands made on us by the rights of others as any reference to these demands as God's rights. I shall have more to say about God's rights later, largely of a critical nature. At this juncture I am simply claiming that Murray is not convincing in his argument for basing human rights on the claims of God. Certainly it does not follow that we need to refer to God's claims to solve our problems when the interests of equals are in conflict. For how would appealing to God's rights tell me whether I should sacrifice my interests for another, or that I should accept another equal's sacrifice on my behalf in these situations?

So far we have been examining Christian notions of freedom which stress the particular status freedom gives each and every human person. Because of the gift of God all of humanity is basically free and equal from the point of view of their essential worth and dignity. There are, as we have hinted, some problems in interpreting the origins of this gift. For instance, does dignity and equal freedom come at creation, so that freedom is essentially static, given once and for all by God's unchanging decree? Or does freedom come in degrees as part of a dynamic changing set of relationships between God and humanity? The term 'liberation' might be regarded as a better expression of the religious believer's understanding of his tradition on this point precisely because of its dynamic connotation. Is not God seen throughout scripture as a liberator, constantly freeing his people from various situations of slavery? Is not Jesus the paradigm of liberation in his saving activity? My impression is that freedom is indeed best interpreted as liberation because of the changing relationship between men, women and God. There is an essential freedom which, as God's gift, remains unchanged, but in view of humanity's limited response has to be offered afresh by God and accepted anew by weak-willed creatures.

Much attention has been given in this section to the exploration of a Christian structure of (equal) freedom in the hope that this concept will act as a useful metaphor or model for our understanding of rights in a Christian context. It has been stated again and again that metaphorical thought lives within the tension of similarity and difference, 'is' and 'is not', and at this point it certainly looks as though freedom and rights are quite distinct in terms of traditional religious belief. Claiming rights from the secular, philosophical point of view is an expression of our free and equal status, without which we lose our freedom and undermine our dignity. But the Christian viewpoint of freedom is different from the secular approach, so perhaps we can expect a different attitude towards rights. For instance, a non-religious approach to freedom, if it is not sceptical concerning freedom's very existence, will probably accept it as a 'given' in the sense of being a brute fact – freedom is just there. Christianity claims that freedom is 'given' in a personal sense; it is granted to us by an absolute being. Furthermore, the tradition of Christianity gives the impression that the ongoing work of liberation is primarily God's work, not ours. Murray mentions the threefold liberation which has come through the death and resurrection of Christ: freedom from law, freedom from death and freedom from sin (pp. 91–6). In each of these the initiative is taken by God and the power to further each is God's. Human rights appear to have no place here.

Freedom from law, according to Murray, involves a liberation from legalistic pharisaism, and, above all, a change in motive to a loving response to God's offer of friendship. Talk of rights in this context seems to contradict this new orientation. Claiming seems the opposite of loving obedience, and is often accused of encouraging a minimalistic approach to morality. Freedom from death in the sense of eternal salvation is surely God's doing and has little or nothing to do with claiming entitlements. Lastly, freedom from sin is again fundamentally the action of God in granting forgiveness, a gift which Murray insists cannot be a right.

Where then does the doctrine of rights fit into the theological concept of freedom? It seems that theology has such an interest in stressing God's initiative against various forms of pelagianism that freedom is almost taken out of human hands. In fact, the move to base all rights on God's rights, as Murray suggests, is a symptom of this attitude. All human claims are strictly subordinate to God's freedom and God's rights, and if we are not careful, human freedom is swallowed up or melts away in the light of such an emphasis.

Clearly, the idea of rights comes into play when we are discussing that aspect of human freedom which drives humanity to respond to God. This was Murray's initial point in underlining the right to religious freedom. However, he does not develop this notion in any great depth. He obviously believes that human rights are a form of 'mandatory' right, as when he quotes the present pope on the subject of religious freedom, which is, 'the most fundamental of rights functioning as the first of duties, which is the duty to move towards God in the light of truth'.[39] For the Christian, then, human rights are not discretionary, they are at the service of our duty towards God. To fail to respect human rights is to abuse the gift of freedom written into one's very nature. Treating other people badly is to insult God in whose image they are made. Wronging another person can also harm those who love him because they share in his suffering. Since God is said to love men and women infinitely and to identify with their suffering – 'what you do to the least of these you to do to me' – it is arguable that God is wronged by the violation of human rights.

The Christian tradition tends then to associate human rights with God's rights, so that respect for the former is a key element in our proper use of God's gift of freedom. Rights become subordinate to obligation in every case. Regarding my own rights I must claim them in order to fulfil my duties towards God. And the rights of others must be respected for the same reason; after all, everyone shares the same dignity and freedom.

Much of this argument makes sense and can hardly be denied if one wishes to accept the mainstream Christian tradition regarding the relationship between God and humans, but some elements in this approach do have an odd ring and need further elucidation.

COLIN GUNTON: RIGHTS, HETERONOMY AND AUTONOMY

Is there not a contradiction in stressing freedom and rights so much and then reducing these to obligation? For most people having obligations, being obliged to do things, is a far cry from being free. To put this point in another way, does this emphasis on God's rights and our obligations not smack of heteronomy rather than autonomy? Even slaves have the right to do what they are obliged to do, have they not?

In his discussion of freedom Colin Gunton reminds us that for many of the thinkers of the Enlightenment religion was a source of alienation in the way in which it demanded obedience in a passive way to external authority. Autonomy was displaced by heteronomy. But Gunton argues that it is a mistake 'to oppose heteronomy and autonomy, authority and freedom, the passive reception of law and its free creation, obedience and free will'.[40]

It is true, Gunton admits, that right action can seem to be burdensome and heteronomous at times. Consider the temptations of Christ in the Gospels of Matthew and Luke. The context is the calling and empowerment of Jesus by his Father 'to enter upon a particular kind of career and to perform it humanly' (p. 93). The temptations are to a kind of 'autonomy' – for Jesus to act as a powerful and charismatic individual. However, Jesus rejects this option in favour of a kind of 'heteronomy'. 'The Son of God, the chosen and inspired one, is, as such, the one who is obedient.' The 'law of his being' leads to the cross, as Luke suggests in his report that the tempter will return at that time (Luke 23.37). And Gunton goes on, 'But the obedience was free. To describe it as a heteronomy is to mistake the character of all that the Gospels show us about the kind of human being that Jesus was' (*ibid.*, p. 93). In John's Gospel too we find the paradox of Jesus seemingly passive in the hands of his captors, yet actually in charge of the situation. And, above all, Jesus is subordinate to the Father: 'The Son can do nothing of his own accord' (Jn. 5.19). Thus Gunton can say about Jesus that 'From his obedience derives a freedom that is often seen as the mark of his behaviour: free from messianic stereotypes and free to enter into relationship with all who would allow it.'[41]

Gunton develops his argument with great conviction. The example of Christ presents us 'with a view of the relation between obedience and freedom, heteronomy and autonomy, that can be used to illuminate the human–divine relationship in general' (p. 95). According to Gunton, it is important not to divide Jesus up into divine and human aspects, saying that his obedience was a feature of his humanity alone. Remember that Jesus in Luke's Gospel is tempted as the Son of God. So this author concludes:

Jesus's behaviour is a demonstration in action of what it is to be Godlike. He is not only obedient to the father, but is also a way of God's action in and towards the world.

Here we reach the very heart of the matter. The fact that we talk of grace means not that God demands obedience from outside, but that he came alongside us in a particular human life. The very obedience and freedom of Jesus as a man is also and at the same time the freedom and self-giving of God to human existence. (p. 99)

This line of thinking, Gunton admits, is influenced by modern continental thinking, especially by those like Moltmann who speak of the 'Crucified God'.[42] Thus, 'The God who upholds the moral order does not do so heteronomously, from outside, but from within, by himself taking responsibility for our condition.'[43]

I find this Christological approach of Gunton's quite compelling and certainly more enriching than the few words written by Murray on 'freedom in Christ', followed by the somewhat abstract references to freedom from law, death and sin. It is the personal example of the God–Man, Jesus Christ, which provides a convincing model of moral and religious freedom. However the question still remains how this analysis of freedom relates to rights. Does this interpretation of the obedience of Jesus as true autonomy and freedom not legitimise the position of Murray and many others that obligation is the primary moral concept rather than rights? Gunton, in his argument, refers also to Paul's contrast of Adam and Jesus in the second chapter of the Letter to the Philippians. Jesus, unlike Adam, does not snatch at equality with God, but is characterised by self-emptying obedience. We might even say that Jesus did not claim his right to be regarded as God's equal. And the moral of this example is that we should have the same mind as Christ.

I think it would be a mistake to establish a great divide between the language of rights and the language of obligation, favouring one to the exclusion of the other. What our discussion of freedom leads us to surely is a recognition that this concept is the primary ethical one, and that both rights and obligations derive their value equally from their relationship to human freedom. Thus, freedom is a model for both rights and obligations. This assertion makes sense in view of Gunton's refusal to see obligation as necessarily heteronomous along with commonly held intuitions that rights are necessarily protective of autonomy. Both rights and obligations can be heteronomous; obligations, when we are too lazy to 'own them' rationally, and rights when we 'make claims' without 'having a claim', or when we claim inappropriately. And both rights and obligations are aspects of autonomy when they serve true human freedom. Even though we can distinguish rights from duties and obligations the doctrine of correlativity forbids a strict separation of these normative concepts either from each other or from their basis in freedom. What links all three concepts is the idea of 'what is due to the human person'. Because of the quality of human freedom based on God's gift of creation and redemption respect is due to each person, a respect which involves justified claims and correlative obligations.

Interestingly, Murray and Gunton between them attempt to raise both rights and duties to the divine level in their reflections on freedom. Murray, as we saw, feels that equality is not sufficient as a ground for human rights – they must be raised to the status of claims made by God. Thus my human rights are ultimately God's rights. When I claim justly I have God's authority to do so, and violation of my rights is deep down not just any mere moral fault, but sacrilege and blasphemy. Gunton, on the other hand, raises the moral quality of obedience and obligation to the transcendent level by stressing the obedience of Christ as Son of God, not simply as the Carpenter's son. Now God has rights and he also has obligations, while remaining perfectly free and perfectly himself. It then remains open to argue that being made in the image and likeness of God involves a sharing in his freedom by sharing in the rights and duties of God.

I have already indicated that I have reservations about depending on the concept of 'God's rights', though I can understand the temptation to speak in this way. In general, too, we should be wary of speaking about 'God's obligations'. It is sufficient that God establishes the value of rights and obligations, and commands men and women to enter into and respect the normative relationships they involve. There are safer ways of expressing the transcendent element in the language of rights and obligations than a simple transfer of these notions to God. The main method is the way we have gone in this section, stressing the special dignity of humanity in terms of a fundamental freedom which is possessed equally by all, a freedom expressed particularly by the concepts of being made in God's image and being called into an intimate relationship with him.

Rights and duties play an important role in protecting equal freedom. Duties or obligations towards others remind us, in the process of fulfilling them, that those we serve have no more and no less dignity and basic freedom than we have ourselves, and that we have the justification to claim the same treatment, the performance of the same obligations, other things being equal, from others. From the point of view of the right-holder the same attitude is required. If human rights are protective of the claimant's freedom and that freedom is possessed by all equally, then the claimant has obligations to respect the rights of others in the same way as he claims rights against others. An important implication of this argument is that having rights is not the only way Christians can speak of human freedom and dignity – having duties can be revelatory of these fundamental values as well.

Earlier, I asked a rhetorical question concerning the rights of slaves to fulfil their obligations. Since they are obliged to act in certain ways, surely they have rights to act without constraint? But this does not make sense. Where a slave is a mere chattel or possession of another, he or she has no rights at all within that

institution, unjust as it is. But neither has the slave obligations in
the sense that the freeman has. Note that the slave may be
obliged to work as his master sees fit, but 'being obliged' is not
the same as having an obligation.[44] Being obliged to act does not
necessarily imply freedom in the moral sense; quite the opposite,
in fact – the slave is forced to act – he does not choose freely to
respect the rights of another. The freeman's rights can only be
respected by the freely accepted obligations of another freeman.
The slave is an animated tool. If he had obligations it would be
a sign of a capacity that only a freeman has. To allow that a
slave has obligations correlative to the rights of another would
be to recognise in him a dignity and freedom which would make
him in turn a candidate for possessing rights. Rights are always
claimed against other people, never against animals or
machines. Once the slave-owner thinks of himself as having
rights against his slaves, then he must logically admit that they
have obligations, and if they have obligations then there must
be some relationship of equality, some aspect of freedom which
bridges the gap between master and slave.

According to this way of thinking, the dignity of the freeman
lies not only in his having rights, but also in his having
obligations. The evil of slavery lies not just in denying certain
persons their capacity to make valid claims, but also in denying
them their capacity to freely perform their duties or obligations.
The latter as well as the former speaks to us of the equal dignity
of all who participate in normative relationships involving
human rights and duties/obligations.[45] Since human rights are
held against other humans, to have an obligation to respect such
a right is a sign of one's own humanity, with the corollary that
one has an equal claim to the performance of a similar obligatory
action on the part of another. No one can have a human right
alone, for against whom could one claim it? But once one claims
a right one implicitly recognises the existence of someone who
can make a similar claim in similar circumstances.

The protection of freedom appears to demand that attention
be paid both to rights and to duties or obligations. Where
obligations are a condition of freedom we have a right to
attempt to be faithful to them. Likewise, where rights are a

condition of freedom, we have an obligation to claim them for ourselves and to respect them in the lives of others. If we reduce freedom to the right to perform obligations or to act in line with duty, the danger is that slavery returns under the guise of a moral rationale. It is a clever ploy indeed which convinces a slave that he is really free because of the dignity of his service. He remains a slave until those he serves are willing to serve him in return. In so far as we fail to claim our rights and the rights of others we allow certain individuals and groups to ignore their obligation to respect the equal dignity and freedom of all.

It should be noted at this stage in our analysis of Christian notions of freedom and rights that the particular rights given emphasis here are 'human rights', where the objects are such basic interests of men and women that we seem to have little or no moral freedom to choose not to promote them. But this is slightly misleading since, even in the case of human rights, claimants have at times the power to waive their claims for their own sake and for the sake of others. For instance, the right to life need not be exercised in every circumstance, and patients have the right to reject certain medical treatment which would be regarded as exceptionally burdensome (sometimes called 'extraordinary means'). In some cases, a person might waive his right to self-defence, allowing another person to injure him rather than injuring the aggressor. Important too are the special moral rights we have discussed earlier. They allow us a wide element of discretion or freedom, especially with regard to the initiation of relationships and the taking on of specific roles which establish certain rights and duties. Some of our rights are claims to be allowed to perform acts of imperfect obligations or supererogation in which we help others in ways 'beyond the call of duty', if we so wish. These points bring out the complexity of the relationship between rights and freedom. They urge us to reject any simplistic view to the effect that all rights are in the service of obligation, as well as the view that all obligations necessarily serve rights.

CONCLUSION

In our examination of the specifically Christian interpretation of freedom as a model for the understanding of rights, we began with the assertion that freedom is a wider concept than rights, from both the philosophical and theological perspectives.

Theologically, the basis of freedom is the creation of humankind by God. Freedom appears to be an essential element in the elucidation of the concept of the image of God as it is expressed in human experience. Specifically, it was stated that the freedom in question was relational, since from the beginning men and women were given the gift of being able to respond to God's revelation of himself, as well as entering into social relationships with one another. The language of covenant reflects this reality, and thus rightly claims to be a central religious image or metaphor. And yet this freedom falls precisely into the category of gift. It is not a right we can claim, but is in the ordinary sense of the word a 'privilege'. No one has the right to be created, much less to be created in God's image. Nor has humanity any claim to enter into covenant with God or to be redeemed by the Messiah, and thus liberated from the slavery of sin.

Rights come into play when, in the light of the free status bestowed on men and women by God, they live out that status in a particular manner. Human rights are rights to adopt a certain life-style which because of its radical, even revolutionary, quality can meet much opposition from those who disagree with it. But living up to one's status as a child of God, made in his image, and imitating his imaginative fidelity to others, requires the possibility of claiming rights, often under the title of 'religious freedom'. Such a freedom is, we recall, not simply an internal spiritual reality, the retreat to a hidden citadel, but involves the whole person, including material needs.

A fundamental aspect of Christian freedom is its connection with equality. Every person has an equal dignity in the eyes of God, and the believer holds that this is an ultimate, if not the ultimate, truth about humankind. In Christian ethics the ideal is to see others with the eyes of God, an impossible task, but a constant challenge nevertheless. Being in a position to claim rights is an important aspect of this ideal. Having rights one can claim as a free child of God, made in his image, is literally a 'status symbol' which one can hardly do without. To stand up and say 'I have a right not to be constrained in this way. I am justified in being free to do this action because of my religious identity', is a reminder to all of the special respect due to each person, and ultimately to God himself.

Having and claiming rights brings out the more dynamic aspect of Christian freedom. We have a free status, but in co-operation with the grace of God we become more free – we are liberated throughout life by our moral and religious decisions. According to Feinberg, freedom is, as well as being a legal status word, a 'status associated virtue word'. By this he means that freedom consists in 'a set of virtues of character, namely, those taken to be especially becoming to a man of free status'.[46] Since character is constructed by means of human choice we have to ensure that we maintain our freedom by standing up for ourselves. As Feinberg expresses the point: 'a free man, having nothing to fear, is dignified and deliberate, and can look any man in the eye'. (*ibid.*) Having rights is a sign of freedom, and claiming them is often necessary to remind ourselves and others of this special status.

Freedom is the basic underlying moral concept which gives meaning to both rights and duties or obligations. Human dignity does not depend on having rights alone, as if rights were the only sign of freedom and autonomy. Because of the intimate connection between rights and duties or obligations, this whole set of normative concepts together reflects the nature of human autonomy. Having an obligation to another person is not a form of heteronomy, I argued, but often the opposite, namely an indication of real autonomy. A person who is never expected to take on or fulfil obligations would have little part to play in the moral community. Someone who has obligations, say, to respect a human right of another, is by that very fact a candidate for having the same right.

Finally, this section on Christian freedom stressed the personal example of Christ as the paradigm case, revealing the character of freedom. Again the relational aspect is to the fore, with the Father–Son relationship acting as a model of autonomy-in-obedience. God does not impose himself heteronomously on anyone. Rather does he draw or attract his children to make a free choice of commitment to himself and to others. As early as Epictetus, humans have recognised that the only god worthy of worship is one who treats them as adult children with a basic autonomy of their own. The Father of Jesus is that God.

CHAPTER 7

Rights, power and covenant

Having examined the freedom model of rights from the Christian ethical perspective in the last chapter, we now move on to consider the power model of rights from the same perspective. Again we build our model on insights taken from some key theological writings, as well as from a humanistic psychological approach to power which contributes to our Christian understanding of that subject. This psychological approach complements the political science analysis studied in the last chapter, especially in the link between 'authority' and what is called 'integrative power' or 'power with' others.

The most challenging aspect of this religious analysis of power will derive from our examination of recent ideas on the 'power' of God and of his Son, Jesus. In particular we will encounter the notion of power-in-weakness and the aspect of power as seen in the experience of patient waiting for the response of others to rights-claims.

Finally, a major part of this chapter will be devoted to the introduction and development of a further model of rights, a covenant model, which straddles the divide between secular and religious morality. The rich distinctions found in the biblical theology of covenant provide a promising model of rights, which has added value in being closely related to the models of freedom and power.

Theologians, like philosophers, tend to recognise the ambiguity of the term 'power'. Not only are there different kinds of power, from the impersonal electric current to the spiritual 'power' of prayer, but the word has definite pejorative meanings or negative associations, especially when we think of political life. In fact, the metaphor of power starts off with more negative associations than freedom, although, as we shall see, the two images are closely related.

Paul Tillich explains the predominance of the pejorative meaning of power with the suggestion that the concept has been separated from two other associated concepts of love and justice, and has been identified too easily with compulsion.[1] Spiritual power, he claims, is the greatest power of all, but has nothing to do with compulsion (*ibid.*). Love and power are often thought to be opposites: that love implies a resignation of power and power is a denial of love, is a common position according to Tillich. But he rejects this approach: 'One could say that constructive social ethics are impossible as long as power is looked at with distrust and love is reduced to its emotional or ethical quality.'[2]

Such an approach would mean a separation of religion from politics, which Tillich will not countenance. There must be love, he insists, in structures of power, and without power 'love becomes chaotic surrender'. An ontological analysis is necessary to bring out the true relationship between the concepts of love, justice and power. Thus, from the ontological perspective the will-to-power is 'a designation of the dynamic self-affirmation of life' (p. 36). Power is always over something – over non-being, the negativities of finite existence. 'That which is conquered by the power of being is non-being' (p. 37). All our everyday encounters with others involve one centre of power reacting against another. Tillich cites Sartre from *Being and Nothingness* on this point. Power is experienced relationally in many situations from 'the accidental look of a man at another' to the most complex of love relations.

Power does have some relation to compulsion, Tillich admits: 'Power actualises itself through force and compulsion. But power is neither the one nor the other. It is being, actualising itself over against the threat of non-being.'

Karl Rahner defines power as

a certain self-assertion and resistance proper to a given being and hence as its innate possibility of acting spontaneously, without the previous consent of another, to interfere with and change the actual constitution of that other.[3]

In this general sense, according to Rahner, every existing being has some power, the nature of which changes according to the specific nature of the being in question, according to the region and dimension where it is possible to bring about change and the means used. We can speak then of the 'power' of knowledge, doctrine, faith, love, courage and prayer, since each affects the situation of others previous to his consent and changes that situation to some degree.[4]

Rahner holds that some uses of power are 'sublimer' than others – for example, the power of prayer or the courage to act morally is on a higher level or degree of being, 'of higher moral and ontological rank than for instance the power due to the possession of the atomic bomb' (*ibid.*). Above all, however, power is best predicated of God alone, who in the Creed is said to be almighty. All human power pales into insignificance when put beside the omnipotence of God. '[W]e remember that power ceases to be itself if it is fundamentally only partially powerful, half powerless and not able to claim to be alone all-powerful' (p. 391). Thus, for Rahner, the concept of power is certainly not a univocal one.

Much of Rahner's essay treats of the more negative aspect of power relations, namely the element of force, from a theological perspective. Thus, his first theological thesis concerning force asserts that 'In the actual order of salvation, as it is, and as it was originally willed by God, it stems from sin' (*ibid.*, p. 393). He explains this in terms of the traditional concept of concupiscence. Man's freedom is limited by powers and forces from outside which cut across his free decisions. In paradise power would still exist, Rahner thinks, as a capacity to act, but it 'would address itself to the free decision in an appeal to insight and love' (*ibid.*). Power then would no longer have the sinful connotation of bypassing the consent of another.

We notice here the important connection between power and freedom. Authentic power respects human freedom, whereas force fails in this regard with its connotation of bypassing consent. In effect what Rahner refers to as the ideal use of power is what we spoke of in an earlier chapter as 'authority'. Authority does not depend on sanctions, either threatened or actually employed, to affect change in another. It appeals to reason, or to what Rahner has called above 'insight and love'. Having said this, one would imagine that force would be eliminated from Christian choice entirely. But Rahner does not take this line. His second thesis states that 'Power, including physical force, is (although stemming from sin, manifesting it and tempting to it) not itself sin, but a gift of God, an expression of his power' (*ibid.*, p. 395).

Power is one of the 'existentials' of man's life on earth. It is seen by Rahner as 'the space of freedom', the condition of the possibility of freedom. No one can act freely without interfering in the freedom of others, without doing 'violence' to another 'in a metaphysical but very real sense' (p. 396). He asserts that 'power and freedom are mutually and dialectically inter-dependent' (p. 399), and even goes on to speak about the 'rights of freedom' and the 'rights of power' being in conflict, yet co-existing. From the context he is clearly thinking about political decisions and the imposition of government policy, for he accepts that political leaders may have to impose solutions without the consent of the citizens, with the result that some suffer. He concludes that 'Power, which on principle always had to wait on the consent of those affected by it, would not be power at all.' To hold such a view would be 'a utopian caricature of democracy' (p. 401).

Rahner's final theological thesis concerning power understood as force is as follows: 'In the actual order of things, its exercise – at least on the whole – is not irrelevant to salvation: it is a process of salvation or perdition' (p. 402). In a way such a declaration is uncontroversial from the Christian point of view, once one accepts that the use of power is a basic aspect of existence and has an important role to play in moral life. We would expect the believer to accept the advice of Rahner that such a fundamental reality 'must be used with the grace of Christ, with faith and love'. Likewise his position that it is our human task 'to attempt to move from lower to higher exercise of power and thus to greater exercise of freedom' (*ibid.*, p. 405) must be widely acceptable to both believer and non-believer alike.

The arguments of theologians like Tillich and Rahner echo very much the sense of ambivalence felt by moral philosophers and political scientists regarding the analysis of power-relations. There seems to be a common feeling that some forms of the exercise of power are downright sinful (where justice and love are excluded; others are necessary evils (as when we act paternalistically, overriding the need for the consent of others); and others still, quite respectable and beneficent uses, in cases where power is authoritative. In relation to rights, we have already noted in the second chapter that justified claims or entitlements are moral (or legal) powers in so far as they give us some control over the behaviour of others by the imposition of an obligation or duty. They can, and often do, involve the threat of sanction. Sometimes we have to enforce our claims against stern opposition, while on other occasions rights are respected because of their rational basis as part of a normative ethical system. It is on these latter occasions that the power which lies at the heart of rights is closest to the experience of freedom. The proper exercise of rights involves a relatively 'high exercise' of power for the sake of freedom. For instance, when we invoke human rights, not only do we assert our own dignity as free beings in making these claims, but we equally assert the dignity of those who have the correlative obligations, since only free men and women can have the capacity or power to respond to the freedom and dignity of others.

Another theologian who sees value in a closer analysis of power, and especially in the relationship between power and rights, is Alan Falconer. In his opinion the matrix out of which the struggle for human rights arises is provided by the phenomenon of conflict or alienation.[5] Looking deeper into the nature of conflict he examines the individual's need for self-affirmation and self-assertion. It is the 'courage to be' to use Tillich's phrase. The psychological dimension of this basic need of humanity is then studied with the help of ideas borrowed from Rollo May's work, *Power and Innocence.*[6]

ROLLO MAY AND THE PSYCHOLOGY OF POWER

May's theory is that human dignity requires of people that they exercise a certain personal power, a form of self-assertion. In his Preface, he shares a personal experience of this principle. When he was in his early thirties he contracted Tuberculosis. He attributes his condition at that time to his 'innocence', which became, he says, a passivity, an aversion to power. The TB bacilli took advantage, as it were, of his innocence as he waited passively for his monthly x-ray to see whether he was getting better or not. Later in his psychiatric practice, he encountered again and again the same problem in his patients – their powerlessness.

One of his patients was a young musician, Priscilla. She had 'one foot in schizophrenia', says May, 'and the other on a banana peel'. Interestingly, May states that she had 'considerable dignity' and 'a sense of humour' (p. 24)' 'But she could never get angry.' Her self-esteem was almost non-existent. (This is surprising in view of his assertion that she had an aura of dignity.) Her interaction with others was disastrous:

When she was exploited, as she often was, sexually and financially, she had no defenses, no way of drawing a line beyond which she could firmly say 'no,' no anger to support her...

Along with her inability to get angry, there went, as a necessary corollary, a deep experience of powerlessness and an almost complete lack of capacity to influence or affect other people in interpersonal relations. (pp. 24–5)

Yet Priscilla had an active dream life, 'as violent as her conscious life was docile'. And at times her unconscious would overflow into open violence, an inappropriate use of power which May interprets as an attempt to assert her own significance. Priscilla's powerlessness was not admirable. There is no virtue in such docility. It is not the meekness of the beatitude, which inherits the earth. It is a corruption, as May argues, quoting Edgar Z. Friedenberg who says that 'All weakness tends to corrupt and impotence corrupts absolutely.'[7] What people like Priscilla need is the realisation of their basic rights. Rights, as the justified moral power to claim some good or benefit, are the essential antidote to the fearful life-style of those who downgrade themselves and refuse to accept their dignity as free men and women. The slavery of earlier centuries was arguably less constraining than the psychological slavery of May's patients suffering from such low self-esteem.

The power Rollo May is centrally interested in is inter-personal: it means 'the ability to affect, to influence, and to change other persons' (p. 100). A purely personal power is called 'strength'. His description of the various kinds of power is once again helpful in our process of using power as a model for rights. Taken from the psychological perspective it supports and complements our earlier political-science analysis of Bachrach and Baratz.

There are two kinds of power which are essentially destructive and morally wrong. These are exploitative and manipulative modes of behaviour. Slavery and the use of raw force are examples of the exploitative type. May suggests that exploitative power is often used by those who have experiences of radical rejection and have no other way of relating to people. Always violence is involved, i.e. behaviour which ultimately violates the rights of others. Manipulation has close connections with exploitation, but the former is not so obvious as the latter, the difference between the two being like that between a 'gun-man' and a 'con-man'. Manipulation is often subtler and more covert than exploitation, but it still does violence to another.

A third type of power mentioned by May is called 'com-petitive' and is morally ambivalent. It is seen in practice on those occasions when we rejoice because others enjoy a lower status or level of achievement than we do. Found in various situations from university and business to the relationships between siblings and between friends, this type of power can be constructive or destructive. Competition can give zest and vitality to human relations, argues May. To gain something too easily can be frustrating, and as long as one does not take delight in the bad performance of another, competitive power can be a healthy feature of personal relationships. It can drain off some of the tension which might lead to worse conflict. However, competitive power may tend towards exploitation and manipulation and can easily give rise to negative dispositions of envy and jealousy (*ibid.*, p. 108).

In a fourth category, there is what May calls 'nutrient' power, exemplified in the care shown normally by parents towards their children, but also found in teaching roles and even in politics – for instance, where the president/king is seen as a national father figure. Again one can imagine different occasions when use of this power is either constructive or destructive. There is a justified and an unjustified paternalism, times when authority figures do have the right and the duty to regulate the lives of those in their charge, and times when this right and duty gives way to a growing autonomy on the part of children or pupils or citizens.

Finally, we have the category of 'integrative' power as May labels it. This type is found typically in co-operative behaviour between equals or near equals. According to May it occurs when 'My power abets my neighbour's power' (p. 110). One of the examples given of this exercise of power is the simple criticism of ideas that might take place at the end of a lecture which would help the speaker to refine his ideas. May also includes the example of non-violent civil rights campaigners like Martin Luther King under this heading. The power of non-violence can have the effect of disarming an opponent by challenging his values and working on his or her conscience.[8] I said that co-operation is the central theme of integrative power, but May is quick to point out that sometimes this type of power has to be pushed on another in the hope that he or she will ultimately see its constructive value. Obviously, correction and criticism may be welcome or unwelcome, while in itself being objectively valid and actually needed in a situation. Integrative power may at times look like nutrient power or even competitive power (when those criticised feel they are being belittled), whereas its ultimate rationale is different from these other types. It also seems to be the closest of May's categories to the category of authority we discussed earlier. Threats and sanctions are not used, but rather rational argument and the offer of respectful co-operation is depended on to achieve a harmony of purposes.

The kind of power involved in this integrative category is called 'power with' another person. This differs from exploitative/ manipulative 'power over' another; also from competitive 'power against' another; as well as from nutrient 'power for' another.

Now we mentioned that exploitative and manipulative power is actually detrimental to the cause of rights as the moral use of power. The other uses of power appear to have some positive relation to rights. Competitive power has been mentioned indirectly in our earlier discussion of economic competition and the role of liberty-rights. Nutrient power definitely directs our attention to the important rights possessed by the guardians of the young and the incompetent, but it is noteworthy that such power is usually destined to give way to integrative power, when children grow into adults and pupils become teachers (even in some cases collaborating with their own teachers). The ideal type of power, then, is the ideal type of right, involving a sharing of power or, as we mentioned above, a 'power with' another. Such power tends to explicitly recognise the equal dignity and freedom of others.

Rights in general, whether 'human' or 'special' are open to analysis in terms of integrative power or 'power with', for reasons already given. First, to enjoy a particular benefit one has to claim against others, and such a claim is a vital form of self-assertion. As we stressed in our discussion of freedom, to be in a position to claim a right is to distinguish one as a free person as opposed to a slave, no matter how well treated the slave is by his master. Second, we may ask, 'But isn't a claim really an example of "power over and against" another?' No, not really, it is rather a 'power with' another person, by means of the correlative obligation which one requires another human to perform. The performance of the obligation is itself a form of power on the part of another which the right-holder needs for his welfare.[9] Thus right-holders and the bearers of obligation wield power together, the former in claiming and the latter in responding to the claim. Claiming a human right is a good example of integrative power, which at one moment benefits the present claimant, but at the next moment may benefit the bearer of the obligation who changes sides and becomes a claimant in turn – that after all is the implication of the equality built into the meaning of the phrase 'human right'. (With relevant adaptations, special moral rights are also examples of integrative power, in so far as they usually include mutual exchange of claims and obligations.)

Third, the concept of integrative power or power with another is extremely important in the context of claiming rights for others or, better, enabling others to claim for themselves. Donal Murray emphasises this feature of our human responsibility, when he insists that:

The obtaining of freedom for others is a particularly challenging task. By definition, it excludes any element of paternalism. It cannot be an imposition; it cannot even be a gift, only an enablement. One does not obtain freedom for others by making them like oneself, but only by allowing them to become themselves. It is *their* personhood and *their* freedom which has to be fostered.[10]

Murray's remarks make sense with regard to human rights, the most basic rights of all. Although in the case of special moral rights we may 'give' some right to another, when it comes to human rights they are not within the power of humans to grant or to take away. Human rights are simply possessed by persons as persons, given their humanity. If they are given at all, then it can only be in the sense that they are a gift of God to each person when he or she is created. Murray's exclusion of 'any element of paternalism' in human rights also excludes nutrient power from being the key type of power in the exercise of rights. There is indeed a temptation to claim rights for others and to do so continuously, thus making another dependent on oneself. The idea of claiming rights for others is surely directed towards giving them a taste of what it is like to claim for themselves. Otherwise, the rights of others tend to become a subset of one's own rights. The concept of integrative power in this context implies a wish that other people recognise the innate or latent power they have in their possession of valid claims. It preaches a message of basic equality and freedom which is necessary if people are to work together, pooling their energies and their power. One cannot have 'power with' another, if that person has no confidence in himself or herself, no ability to stand up and be counted. Therefore, the first task of anyone interested in promoting integrative power must be to ensure that human rights are recognised in the first place by those in a position to claim them, that is, all human beings.

The emphasis on rights as a form of integrative power fits well with a number of things mentioned by Tillich and Rahner at the beginning of this chapter. Tillich, for instance, warned against our divorcing power from justice and love and linking it too closely with compulsion. Integrative power respects both justice and love, in refusing to impose itself except when absolutely necessary, by stressing the need we have for co-operation and the joy we can find in working with others. Alerting others to the power and freedom that they have as humans with reference to their basic rights is itself a work of justice and love. Enabling others to enter into positions where they can claim their entitlements for themselves is a prime example of a love which refuses to manipulate under the guise of morality. When Tillich says that there must be love in structures of power, one aspect of this truth applies to this responsibility we have to enable others to assert themselves legitimately. Rahner stressed that some forms of power are 'sublimer' than others and we have concluded that, indeed, integrative power is relatively sublime. The same point is at issue in his remark that we must move through life from the lower to the higher exercises of power, rejecting exploitation and manipulation, showing special care not to abuse competitive and nutrient forms, and encouraging the integrative use of power. The higher forms of power respect human freedom and dignity to a greater degree, and support Rahner's declaration that there can be no freedom without power.

THE POWER OF GOD

Rahner noted that power is perfectly predicated of God, who is traditionally held to be omnipotent. In his discussion of the relationship between power and love Rollo May brings in the notion of God's power. God is not only the God of love, but also of power, as we affirm in the Creed and also in the doxology concluding the Lord's Prayer – 'For thine is the Kingdom, the *Power*, and the Glory...' Just as power has to be guided by love, love has to be powerful to maintain its significance. It is even tempting to argue that human power is made in the image of God's power, just as human freedom images divine freedom, and to link this with our model of rights. Thus, it might be argued that human rights mirror God's rights as human power mirrors the power of God. Then we have a standard for judging human rights and the exercise of power on this earth.

A major problem arises here, however, due to the controversy in philosophy and theology concerning the analysis of God's power. Just when we have arrived at a satisfactory moral understanding of power as integrative, 'power with' others, it looks as if we may have the ground cut from under us due to serious criticism of the notion of God having and exercising power.

There are, I think, two main issues requiring our attention. The first has to do with making sense of how an omnipotent God acts in this world in a loving way. There are difficulties in accounting for God's action from the point of view of his eternal nature when this is understood in terms of timelessness. How can a person who is outside time do anything in time?[11] And, secondly, even if this could be explained satisfactorily, it would still leave us with a God who would seem to act in an arbitrary manner. As Janet Martin Soskice puts it, 'Why, for example, should God intervene to wither a fig tree yet allow thousands to die in concentration camps?'[12] These problems puzzle many modern theologians, such as Maurice Wiles,[13] David Jenkins,[14] Gordon Kaufman,[15] and many others. For instance, as Soskice expresses the issue, there seems to be a contradiction 'between understanding the world as fully determined by natural causes, and allowing that God may on occasion break into that causal order like a rogue elephant' (p. 935).

There is a problem in making sense of the traditional doctrine of miracles which is one aspect of God's omnipotence, and there is a problem in making sense of the absence of miracles as when we confront the problem of evil. In the classical formulation of theodicy, if God is all-powerful and all-loving, why does he allow such evil to occur? Our rehabilitation of the concept of power stresses that power needs to be used morally by humanity, but does this not apply equally to God? Does God wield his power responsibly? Looking at the world around us this remains unproven for many.

If we say that God acts lovingly in the world, we encounter the additional problem which arises with the doctrine of divine impassibility and changelessness. Love seems to imply a mutual relationship where each partner affects the other, but according to the traditional attributes of God, while he is said to love us, he cannot be affected by us. Jurgen Moltmann asks, 'Can a person experience "himself" in his relationship to God as person if God is certainly supposed to mean everything to him, but if he is not supposed to mean anything to God?' We must be able to ask not only 'how do I experience God?' but 'how does God experience me?'[16] Thus, the traditional view of God's power seems to violate man's autonomy, while the love of God appears to be all one-sided.

Soskice, having pointed out some of the philosophical difficulties associated with the traditional understanding of God's attributes, warns of the dangers of making man in God's image. If impassibility is an aspect of God's perfection, then surely we have a justification for a Stoic ethics where we cut ourselves off from all the messy feelings, passions and sufferings of daily life. We return to the inner citadel, which Berlin warned us was not the true home of freedom. On the other hand, the view of God as the cause of all that happens and as the special 'fixer' of awkward situations by means of an occasional miracle, can justify an unrestrained activism. If God is constantly creative and never sleeps, then we who are made in his image must keep busy as God's good servants.

This is not the place to enter into a detailed reply to these questions, but I shall quickly mention Soskice's summary response to these issues. Her first move is to transfer attention from philosophical theology to scripture, leading us back to

Exodus 3.14 where we encounter God's 'metaphysical ul-
timacy'. Following the lead of Walter Kasper she suggests that

> to develop this passage in terms of metaphysical ultimacy alone is to
> miss the sense of the Hebrew verb *hayah* which means not so much 'to
> be' as to 'effect', 'to be effective'. In this passage of Exodus then God
> is revealed not so much as Absolute Being, but in a promise that God
> is with the people in an effective way. The being and the power of God
> to effect are held together.[17]

On the face of it this reference doesn't seem to get us much
further in solving the problem of God's power. How is God
effective after all? To use her own example, is a God who is
effective in withering a fig tree and not effective in stopping
torture all that impressive? It seems that what is important for
Soskice in her formulation above is the fidelity of God to his
people, the fact that he is always there accompanying them
through joys and sorrows. In this light his effectiveness has to be
read in a less active and more passive light.

THE STATURE OF WAITING

So our author's second move is to invoke the example of Christ
in his passion, this time using the interpretation of passion and
passivity popularised by W. H. Vanstone in *The Stature of
Waiting*.[18] Jesus begins to undergo his passion, according to
Vanstone, when he is 'handed over' by Judas to the Jewish and
Roman authorities. We should not be so distracted by traditional references to the betrayal of Jesus as to forget the basic
change that takes place when the Messiah is handed over,
namely his transition from an active life to a passive one. Before
he is handed over, the Gospels, especially Mark, portray Jesus as
the controller of each situation he enters. He is the subject of
many of the verbs. He leaves behind him a trail of transformed
scenes – fishermen no longer at their nets, storms stilled, the
handicapped whole again. If anyone approaches omnipotence
in their daily activity, it is Jesus at the beginning of his public
ministry. But this changes dramatically in the last week of his
life. He is still the centre of attention but now he is the object of

the verbs, no longer the subject. His passion means not so much his suffering in the modern sense, but suffering in the older sense of allowing something to happen.

Soskice makes this comment on Vanstone's central insight:

Jesus' true godliness is revealed in his rejection of this tinkering, manipulative power and in his choice instead of the contradictory power of his passion, the power of 'letting be'...True omnipotence eternally suffers, that is allows, the world to be in its own dependent autonomy.[19]

There is something very important, indeed prophetic, in this emphasis on the need for the recognition of the moral value of passivity instead of concentrating attention on activity. Effectiveness is to be found in the former as well as in the latter. Obviously, the undergoing of his passion by Jesus is regarded by Christians as supremely effective.[20] Vanstone points this out from the Gospels. Mark has the centurion say 'Truly, this man was the Son of God' (15.39) when Jesus is on the cross, but there is nothing in the behaviour of this dying man which would lead a non-believer to recognise anything special. A theological point is being made here, insists Vanstone: 'According to Mark, the passion of Jesus was not His human misfortune: it was the decisive manifestation of His divinity' (p. 72). In John's account of the passion, there is a similar transition from activity to passivity. A time comes when the 'works' of Jesus – his miracles and preaching – come to an end and he must become the object of others' activity. Yet on the cross, he shouts out that his mission is accomplished (Jn. 19.30). Thus, his mission and his works are not identical; an important aspect of his mission of saving humankind lies in his endurance of passivity.

According to Vanstone, the life of Jesus is a model to be followed, partly because of his combination of active and passive dimensions of human existence. Jesus embraces the whole of human life, the times when we are in control and able to accomplish a great deal, and also the times when we are laid low, dependent on others, and seemingly useless. By embracing each dimension Jesus gives dignity to passion as well as to action. His life challenges the modern philosophy of the consumer society which insinuates that only the active are worthwhile and that being passive or inactive is to be degraded. To see the Son of God spreadeagled on the cross unable to move a muscle, yet in that moment saving the world, involves an outlook on human life which relativises the value of activity in the usual sense of that term.

In the life of Jesus, then, as interpreted by theologians like Vanstone and Moltmann, we are presented not only with a model of humanity, but also of divinity. This model of God is rather different from the traditional impassive, yet supremely active, God of the mainstream Christian theological tradition. We are now faced with a God who shares in the negative aspects of our human condition. Christians are becoming that bit more comfortable speaking about the sufferings of God, and when talking about God's 'power' there is a greater tendency to qualify such judgements with paradoxical references to God's 'weakness'. There is a widespread feeling that the God we need is not one who reaches down from Heaven to put things right, but one who empties himself of power and comes close to humankind in order to share in the experience of weakness.

Such a theological approach does not look as if it could be a fitting background to the notion of rights as powers. If God is no longer seen as a God of power in the ordinary sense of the word, and if humanity is both made in God's image and has some obligation to imitate him, then our common notion of the value of human power must undergo some change. The way in which God wields power must be the standard by which the human use of power is judged. And if God is now seen as one who embraces human weakness and refuses to act regularly in miraculous ways to overcome human suffering, then surely our emphasis on claiming rights and on self-assertion is out of place. Perhaps the favoured strategy for the believer is now simply to share the life of the poor, to enter into solidarity with the oppressed, rather than fighting against oppressors and encouraging the sufferers from injustice to claim their rights.

The danger at this stage is that we move from one extreme to another, from an emphasis on power as activity to power as passivity, whereas in fact power combines both aspects at

different times. There is a time for being active and a time for
being passive, and each is effective in its own way. Martin
Hengel reminds us of the special power which Jesus wielded
against the political and religious powers of his own day. He
quotes Zechariah 4.6 as a possible heading over the whole work
of Jesus, 'Not by might, nor by power, but by my Spirit, says the
Lord of Hosts.'[21] Again and again Jesus shows a power which
is that of a charismatic authority to criticise the ruling powers of
his land. He attacks the rich in the Sermon on the Mount –
'You cannot serve both God and mammon' (Mtt. 6.24). He
revises the Torah in the light of the love commandment and
outrages the scribes and the pharisees. The temple is cleansed,
involving an attack on the priestly hierarchy and insulting them
with the accusation of allowing the holy place to be made into
a den of thieves. 'That fox, Herod' doesn't escape criticism
either; and even Caesar is put in his proper place, for God must
be served first. Hengel summarises by saying of Jesus that 'He
waged his battle with the ruling powers of his people – to use a
formulation in the Augsberg Confession – "sine vi humana, sed
verbo", "without human power, simply by the word" (*ibid.*,
p. 18).

We recall as well that the word of Jesus was sufficient to heal
the sick, forgive sins and cast out devils – all signs of the
breaking into this world of God's Kingdom. These examples do
not allow us to fall back on some simple picture of Jesus as
passively accepting the evils of his day. There is no weakness in
these examples, but neither is there any abuse of power, no
force, as Hengel insists. Jesus is no demagogue. He doesn't force
hearers into faith. He works by rational argument alone. The
exousia of Jesus is best translated by the term 'authority' (as we
have understood this above) instead of 'power'.[22]

F. Gerald Downing in his comparison between the teachings
and life-style of the Cynics and Jesus claims that both are
characterised by a boldness in criticism. 'Cynics were notorious
for their loud-mouthed uninhibited frankness, "*parressia*"'.[23]
One sign of this frankness is the tradition in speech of abusing
hearers as all kinds of animals. Jesus calls his opposition a
'brood of vipers' (Luke. 3.7; Mtt. 23.33), whilst Epictetus refers

to the man who has become a wolf or a snake or a wasp.[24] And these are just two examples of the general habit Cynics and Jesus had of castigating their hearers. Such behaviour is not symptomatic of passive people who refuse to 'rock the boat'. In fact, the capacity and the courage to criticise others openly is a sign of a belief in one's own dignity and one's equality with others, which is also part of the basis of having and exercising rights. The slave may complain about his condition and talk about his master behind his back, but he cannot criticise openly, precisely because of his unfree status. To criticise another openly is a sign of freedom and of power. On many occasions claiming one's rights involves implicit criticism of others in so far as those claimed against are clearly unjust in refusing to accept their obligations. Even ignorance fails to excuse on every occasion, since there may be negligence in informing oneself of the just claims or entitlements of others. Thus, the criticism implicit in claiming rights is another indication that power and rights are closely related.

In the life and teaching of Jesus, then, we encounter a power, in the sense of charismatic authority, which is so sensitive to what is right and fitting in human behaviour that it cannot but stand up in a combination of divine judgement and fraternal correction to insist on change for the better. I do not want to be anachronistic in saying that Jesus went around aware of his own rights and claiming rights for others in any explicit way, but his awareness of his own relationship to his Father, as well as the equal value of all people in that same Father's eyes, makes it possible for us to use the language of rights as one way of talking about the ethics of Jesus.

My argument so far has pointed to the active aspect of God's opposition to all that enslaves human beings. God's representative, Jesus of Nazareth, was never frightened of standing up for those whose dignity as God's children, made in his image, was being threatened. What then of the emphasis on the passivity and weakness of God which is also displayed in the life of Jesus? Does this approach not encourage a moral quietism in which all is left to God? Hengel appears to come close to such a position when he says, concerning the preaching of God's reign by Jesus, 'Since God alone is judge, people need no longer fight for their own rights, or despise and condemn their neighbours.'[25] Could it not be the case that God's judgement is to be found partly in the struggle for human rights?

WAITING FOR RIGHTS

If we look again at Vanstone's insights into the value of passivity, we may understand its role in the life of Jesus and also in our own life. Passivity, for Vanstone, is expressed most often in the human experience of waiting.[26] He shows that modern life, although it stresses the value of activity, is developing more and more in the direction of passivity, and that this is experienced in our waiting on others. In a world of increasing technology and specialisation, if anything goes wrong, the technicians or experts must be called in to solve the problem, and we must wait more or less helplessly for them to arrive. If we are ill we have to wait for medical staff to serve us. For some operations there is a 'waiting list'. When we grow old, we wait for our pension cheque and for our grown-up children to take us out for Christmas lunch. The list of occasions when we have to wait on others is constantly growing. Vanstone's point is that in spite of this we do not lose our dignity. Since God himself embraced our passivity, it is in a sense alright to be sick or old or unemployed or generally helpless. Of course this is not a justification for doing nothing or allowing social evils, such as unemployment, to continue on their merry way; the point is that human dignity is not diminished by these experiences, even though our subjective sense of that dignity may suffer.

Above all in his concentration on waiting Vanstone brings out its connection with the virtue of love. Lovers are frequently depicted in literature as waiting figures. There is the physical aspect of waiting beside a telephone, for letters to arrive, for the actual coming of a loved one at the airport or station. More significant, however, is the way in which love, as a moral and religious reality, has waiting as an essential aspect in so far as love for another must involve our waiting for that person to respond to our love. It is obvious that love must be a free gift and that freedom has to be respected. One shows love for another, one offers the gift of love, but there can be no forcing another to love back. Even God cannot force a free response to his love. Here is the ultimate example of weakness or powerlessness, which can be experienced by the most powerful and influential people. No matter how much we may want others to love us, we have to wait for their free response. And there is always the possibility that the response will be negative. Unrequited love is one of the most painful realities we encounter in our short life-span. Yet it must be said that respect for the free choice of others as we wait for their response is a perfect example of what is in effect power-in-weakness. To accept our limitations in this area, to recognise that there is little we can do to force the issue and that force is in fact counter-productive, is a form of power. We are powerful in such situations because we are conserving our energy rather than wasting it on futile attempts to override the freedom of others. We show power in our self-control, in our acceptance of the most basic of limitations – that we cannot make others love us. Above all we display a moral and spiritual power in our respect for others and their rights.

At the end of his life Jesus moves from a position of activity to one of passivity or one of waiting. It is not that Jesus is simply waiting for his death, according to Vanstone, but rather that he waits for the response of the people to his offer of love. His public ministry has made this offer of love clear, and now it is up to the people of Jerusalem and their leaders to either accept or reject him in a final way. The waiting of Jesus is especially poignant in the Garden of Gethsemane. The ultimatum has been presented in his triumphal entry into the Holy City, his cleansing of the temple, his preaching during that last week. He showed the Jewish leaders the extent of his support, the viability of his claim, and now all he can do is wait. How will they come – 'as disciples or as executioners?' (p. 85). He doesn't know for sure, but he guesses that their coming will be the stuff of tragedy. And so he goes through the anguish of waiting for Judas and the others to bring the response to his ultimatum. The man of power is now powerless as he waits on lesser men to decide on his future.

Yet his powerlessness is not the same as ordinary weakness. The weak man would not have deliberately put himself in this position in the first place, and if he found himself going in this direction he would have fled in the opposite direction, as rapidly as Jonah fled from Ninevah and God's command to preach there. Though powerless to influence the personal decisions of others in his regard, Jesus is strong enough to accept the negative response and its terrible consequences. This is why it is not possible to talk in any simple way about the power or weakness of Jesus, and why we have opted for the paradoxical 'power-in-weakness' concept.

The idea of power-in-weakness, which has Jesus as its exemplar, acts as an important qualification of our model of rights as power. The emphasis throughout this work has been on the active aspect of having rights. Human dignity, and the sense of being free and equal, demands very often that we exercise rights openly and that we claim rights in an active way if there is the least sign that they are in danger of being ignored. Justice demands this approach, but does love also demand it?

Vanstone's establishment of the connection between passivity, waiting on others, and love has something important to say to us about the ways in which we understand and exercise rights. First, with regard to the claims we make against others, there is moral value in standing up for ourselves as we have pointed out, but there is also value in the quality (or stature) of our waiting for the response of others to our claims. What I have in mind here especially is the major distinction made earlier between 'power' and 'authority'. 'Power' seeks to change others by threat of sanction, and assumes a conflictual view of human intercourse. 'Authority' differs from the use of power by appealing to common values and rational argument. Ideally, then, rights should be closer to authority than to power. When people have to be threatened in order to move them to respect rights, or actually forced to fulfil their basic obligations to others, then to a certain extent the cause of both justice and love is undermined. Using the metaphor of the safety net, life is preserved but the beauty of the performance is lost. In order for rights to be authoritative, then, there is need at times for a more passive approach to their exercise. After all, it may take time for rational arguments to be developed, and even longer for them to sink in. A whole process of moral education may be necessary to give claimants the expertise to communicate the rationale behind their claims and to prepare the population in general to see the value in respecting rights. In general it is more satisfactory if people respect our rights voluntarily instead of doing so reluctantly. So we may have to wait for others at times to respond to our just claims, and while we wait we suffer, like Jesus in Gethsemane, hoping that the response will be positive, but often guessing that power or force may have to be used to achieve a basic level of justice. Love is willing to wait for a free response, even enduring some injustice, until our claims are heard.

Second, we can apply Vanstone's insights to the concept of having and exercising rights as a form of integrative power. In stressing the value of 'power with' others, we argued that the claiming of rights is one example of this. This occurs in the context of the correlativity of rights and duties. The dignity and freedom of moral agents is promoted in part by the co-operative process of claiming entitlements and fulfilling obligations. Rather than seeing the right-obligation relationship as implying the domination of one person by another, we should see it as an incorporation of two different aspects of a joint enterprise, where both parties have their own roles which give each dignity, freedom and power. This is why it is often just as bad to obstruct people in the carrying out of their obligations and duties, as it is to fail to respond to their claims. Now, working with others is often a frustrating business, as Vanstone points out. He shares a topical example, the American Space Shuttle:

This technological triumph was made possible by a complex system through which experts in various disciplines could draw widely on, and be facilitated by, the research and resources of experts in parallel or subordinate disciplines – in which, one might say, a great pyramid of mutual facilitation was erected with the creation of the Shuttle as its apex and goal. The system worked and the goal was triumphantly achieved – achieved as it never could have been achieved by a single individual or by many individuals working in isolation. But it is extremely significant that subsequent reports of the operation of the system indicate that the experience of those who were engaged in it was, primarily, not of facilitation but of *frustration* – the frustration of constantly waiting upon, or being held up for, the outcome of the research of other specialists and the information provided by them. (pp. 48–9)

I think we can say that the right-obligation relationship can involve a similar frustration because of the inequality of capacities or abilities that can exist in it between the parties. A claimant may have to wait for the person with the corresponding obligation to be in a position to carry out the obligation. Consider the already mentioned vexed question about manifesto rights where the interests claimed are clearly pressing and necessary, but the nomination of those bearing the duty or obligation to provide them is problematic. Here there must be an acceptance of some degree of waiting before the situation is clarified. Even when the parties on both sides are clearly known, the person or persons with the obligation may simply not have the resources to comply with the rights of those making claims. Nor is the problem totally one-sided. It is tempting to say that it is easy to claim rights, but more difficult to fulfil obligations, and sometimes it is, but I have already pointed out that the activity of claiming is ideally an exercise in authoritative communication, where the claim is conveyed to others in a rationally attractive way. Thus there is an onus on the claimant to present his case in a manner which takes into account the limitations of his hearers as well as their dignity as rational subjects. There are people who are quite willing to respect others' rights and to perform their obligations once they see the authority behind the claim. As a person with certain potential obligations towards others I may have to endure the frustration of waiting for a cogent justification of others' rights.

Third, there is an aspect of loving waiting in the process of enabling others to claim rights for themselves. When humans are weak and incompetent in various ways – children, some of the elderly, the oppressed – there is the temptation to claim rights for others on the basis of a paternalistic justification. Sometimes there is little hope for growth into, or a return to, autonomy, whereby the subject can claim his or her own rights, and then paternalism should continue more or less as a necessary evil. But it is definitely wrong to continue to claim rights for those who are well able to do this for themselves. We can imagine the tensions that can exist here. In some cases claiming rights for others is perceived as a burdensome obligation, and one is tempted to take the lazy way out, saying to others that they should look after their own rights from now on, when they are clearly not yet mature enough to take on this responsibility. In other cases the temptation is to hold on to people, to keep them dependent, to tell them that they are not yet ready to claim their rights and to maintain the paternalistic relationship. There are no absolute rules for judging when people are mature enough and resourceful enough to handle the language of rights for themselves, but there comes a time when a decision to let go must be taken. Then we will no longer claim rights for others. It is a risky decision, since to recognise the freedom of others to make their own choices, including moral choices involving the language of rights, may lead to disaster. Jesus recognised the right of people of his day to abuse their freedom. He waited, caught between hope and despair, and his death on the cross was the ultimate sign of the consequence of a wrong decision. But it was also the sign of a love which respected the freedom, and hence the dignity, of those who rejected him, as well as of those who accepted him.

Drawing together the main themes of our analysis of power as a model for rights, we have concentrated mainly on two perspectives taken from the human sciences. From political science we distinguished between power, force, influence and authority, and from psychology we took Rollo May's categories of power: exploitative, manipulative, competitive, nutrient and integrative. Some of these forms of power are strictly discouraged, while others are used or applied depending on circumstances.

Since we live in an imperfect world characterised by limited intelligence and limited sympathies, we sometimes have to enforce rights by means of threatened sanctions and physical force. But our argument has been that such strategies should be regarded as a last resort. The first resort involves the use of power in the sense of authority and the employment of what we have called integrative power or 'power with' others. These concepts form a bridge between power and freedom. The higher or more sublime use of power is that which respects the freedom of others. Authority involves this type of power; it is a form of integrative power. Authority as 'power with' others attempts to change them without overriding their consent where possible.

To have a justified claim is to have authority based on a rational moral position. In so far as human rights make sense, everyone has this authority to constrain others, to limit their freedom in one sense. Whereas the emphasis in the use of the freedom model of rights was absence of constraint in order that certain opportunities might be embraced, the emphasis in the use of the power model is the ability to constrain others for the sake of these same opportunities. Thus, power and freedom appear to be opposite sides of the same coin, as it were. They are complementary models for the elucidation of rights. Of course, each model still involves some limitation of both freedom and power. In the case of human rights we are forced to recognise that others have a similar claim to enjoy absence of constraint and the ability to constrain others – including ourselves. But more important is the fact that the authority behind rights, which is ultimately the equal dignity of all humanity in the eyes of God, has a rationality which both binds and frees us. In a society where rational argument is accepted, participants in moral discussion are bound by the logic of their arguments, and are also freed from the arbitrariness of bias and prejudice. It is absurd to claim that being rational makes us less free.

The specific Christian contribution which makes of power a theological model for rights begins with a recognition of the ambiguity found in our talk of God's power. Since our position all along has stressed the ways in which God respects our autonomy, we don't expect God to set all things right without human co-operation. At the same time the Christian tradition tends to reject modern forms of deism which banishes God from acting in the world in any way.

As in our discussion of freedom, it makes sense to refer to the example of Jesus as a guide to the proper use of the language of power in relation to God. The self-emptying of God's Word in becoming man revolutionises our concept of God's power. It is not simply the case that God has become weak by taking on a limited existence in the life of Jesus of Nazareth; after all, there are many examples of powerful activity in the public ministry, and we also pointed to the vociferous criticism levelled against the ruling powers of his day. What must really impress us is the power-in-weakness that is revealed in the willingness of Jesus to wait for, and respect, the free response of his people. In his life he preaches by example that there is a time for activity and a time for passivity, and that both are expressions of love. In activity we reveal one side of love – the aspect of caring for the practical needs of others, the aspect of beneficence as this is commonly understood. But there is also the aspect of passivity, when we wait for others to respond to our love. Here too we reveal our care for practical need, the need for freedom of choice in choosing our relationships. Ironically, the power-in-weakness of God is seen more clearly in the Garden of Gethsemane than on the cross, because the stature of his waiting is displayed more eloquently on the former occasion.

This language of power-in-weakness has important implications for the practice of claiming rights. In particular it discourages us from an overly aggressive pursuit of justice. What is needed frequently is greater patience in waiting for the seeds of co-operation between claimants and bearers of obligations or duties to grow. It takes time for the rationality of respecting rights to take hold of the imagination. Sometimes the expertise in communicating this rationality is lacking. There are all sorts of frustrations which inhibit the process of sharing power with others in the right-obligation relationship. As Vanstone puts it 'One is frustrated not because the system constantly fails to deliver but because one must constantly wait for it to deliver', (p. 49). Often one has to wait for others to get into a position where co-operation and power with them becomes possible. And the temptation is to impatience, to run ahead of others, to force the issue, to act on one's own. When this happens, as it often does, rights get the bad name of being individualistic.

A COVENANT MODEL OF RIGHTS

The penultimate model we take in our attempt to elucidate rights from a religious perspective utilises the biblical covenant theme.[27] Already we have mentioned this concept in relation to the fundamental notion of human dignity and the image of God which all persons possess as a gift. Here we need to enter in a deeper way into the rich depths of the covenant concept and experience.

We begin with a very useful study by Joseph Allen, *Love and Conflict: A Covenantal Model of Christian Ethics*.[28] Allen is a firm believer in the value of theological models, especially in Christian ethics. Any model of the moral life, he claims, 'has to do with how moral selves *are* related, and not merely how they ought to be related' (p. 15). Models tell us what is going on. They are descriptive and explanatory. But they also go deep – to the ontological level, that is to the ultimate ground and meaning of moral living. In his book he argues in favour of a model 'in which all moral relationships are understood to be *covenant relationships*' (*ibid.*, p. 16).

Allen tells us that covenant is a central, though not necessarily *the* central, theme in the Bible.[29] The essential characteristics of covenant are then presented. They occur between persons of unequal status, for instance, between God and humanity. Covenant is initiated by God and is not negotiated, thus revealing grace and power on the part of the deity. And the people must freely decide on their response to the gracious offer of a relationship.

There are two major types of covenant in the Bible, according to Allen. One is the so-called 'Promisory Covenant' as revealed in the relationship between God and people like Noah (Gen. 9.8–17), Abraham (Gen. 15 and 17), and David (2 Sam. 7). This type of relationship is 'one in which God performs an act of self-limitation through a solemn promise, but in which there is no mention (or only marginal mention) of obligations upon the human parties to the covenant' (p. 19). The second type of covenant is represented by the relationship established at Mount Sinai-Horeb and is called a 'Law Covenant'. This makes demands on people and seems to put less emphasis upon God's promises. The laws which bind the people of Israel to God tend to be seen in the context of covenant, as in the giving of the decalogue (Exod. 19.5; Deut. 5.2). The God who commands is the God who has liberated his people from slavery and who has given law as a sign of his love to be welcomed joyfully. The 'Torah' is not understood as we often understand law today, a necessary evil which restricts our freedom and enjoyment of life; it is understood as instruction and loving guidance, something which other nations, not so blessed by God, lack.[30] The covenant theme is found all through the Bible, not just in the books of the law, but also in the prophets. The famous passage from Micah 6.8 which refers to justice, kindness and walking humbly before God, is made up of basic covenant ideas.

The covenant theme is not forgotten in the New Testament. For the authors of the New Testament Jesus is the fulfilment of the scriptures, and for them the scriptures are the Old Testament. Some of the Christological titles, 'Son of Abraham', 'Son of David', present Jesus as the one who as the Messiah, the Christ, is the fulfilment of the covenant promises. In the last supper scene, covenant language is used to express the ritual significance of the meal and the following death on the cross. Allen states that references to the blood of the new covenant turn our minds back to the example of Moses ratifying the covenant by throwing blood on the altar. The idea of covenant appears in Paul's writings. Consider 2 Cor. 3 where old and new covenants are contrasted. Also there is Gal. 3.16 where Jesus is referred to as Abraham's offspring. Above all there is the fact that the two main divisions of the Bible into old and new 'testaments' is testimony to the centrality of the notion of covenant, since 'testament' and 'covenant' are practically synonymous.

THE NATURE OF A COVENANT RELATIONSHIP

At its heart a covenant relationship comes about through the interactions of entrusting and accepting entrustment. Allen recognises the risk involved in such activity, since entering into covenant is not usually done on the condition that others are actually trustworthy. One hopes that they will be, but there is no guarantee that they will. Yet such activity is basic to life, as Allen points out, and we are always engaged in the process of putting ourselves in the hands of others – doctors, car mechanics, teachers, parents, etc. A simple illustrative example of this trusting relationship is that of picking up a hitch-hiker on the road. In taking on the hitch-hiker the driver undertakes to drive safely and the hitch-hiker in turn undertakes not to harm his host and benefactor.

Central here is the intention to enter the relationship, according to Allen, though the intention does not have to be formally verbalised, since the act of covenanting may involve an informal type of performative which may be implicit and non-verbal or explicit and verbal. Deciding to have a child and actually having one may be done without much formal discussion, yet it involves a covenant relationship. This is also a good example of a covenant initiated by the intention of one or two persons intimately involving the life of a third (the child) and yet not involving the consent of that third party. Later on the child is expected to freely respond to the covenant relationship initiated by its parents.

The covenant relationship is said to remain in place even if the actions of people within the covenant are deceitful and the goals of the covenant are not achieved. This is part of the traditional ideal of the marriage covenant, which does not depend on perfect behaviour for its survival.

The theologian William May argues that covenant always implies a sense of indebtedness, and that 'responsiveness to gift' characterises the relationship.[31] Allen is not sure if this is always the case in human covenants, though it is certainly true of the covenant between God and humanity. In human relationships what is most often conveyed is a sense of responsibility, not of gift, though this latter feature may still be present in the background. The examples already mentioned of the driver–hitch-hiker and parent–child relationships do have this emphasis on gift, though the latter pertains more to the religious understanding of 'pro-creation', where the child is seen as a gift of God.

Allen claims that, 'When two or more persons enter into a covenant relationship, they thereby create and enter into a new moral community' (p. 37). This creation involves a more basic moral implication, according to Allen, including 'a recognition by each that the other has worth, that each matters for his or her own sake, and not merely that each is useful'. (*ibid.*) Thus, covenant implies not only an obligation to do x for A, but a respect for A in himself as an end. Covenant appears to be a more profound moral reality than, say, a business contract which prescinds from such ontological judgements and concentrates instead on pragmatic considerations.

Finally, Allen mentions that parties to a covenant come to have enduring responsibility to one another, throughout the life of the covenant. Parents must care for their children day in day out. Ten miles down the road the driver still has responsibilities for his passenger.

TWO FURTHER TYPES OF COVENANT

From the Bible we already noted two types of covenant initiated by God: the promisory and the law covenants. Allen looks closer at the promisory covenant with Noah and finds in it an inclusive character which is of vital importance. He says that 'From a Christian standpoint the whole of humanity is to be understood as one covenant community' (p. 39). This follows from that covenant with Noah which includes care even for the natural world. However, the inclusive covenant in reality stems from God's initiative in creation, and is confirmed throughout salvation history, decisively so in the life and teaching of Christ. This inclusive covenant is a bit like the parent–child relationship mentioned above. At first the child does not understand the nature of the family relationship, but gradually grows into a position where he or she makes a personal response, accepting family responsibilities. 'In this sense, the inclusive covenant exists prior to human agreement. Yet in another sense it awaits human trust and loyalty before it is fully present' (p. 40).

A second type of covenant Allen labels a 'Special Covenant', arising out of some *special* historical transaction between members of society or religious believers, and not only from their participation in the inclusive covenant. A whole range of relationships may be involved at this level. The scope of the relationships may include from small, intimate, primary groups, such as family, friendship, to large relatively impersonal groups, such as a nation-state or a church. The covenant may be of long or short duration. It may involve free choice or a voluntary aspect, as when one decides to marry or to join a club. But there is also a non-voluntary type, as in the case of belonging to a family.

Allen warns against any attempt to separate these two covenants:

Although we can distinguish between the inclusive covenant and special covenants, we cannot separate them. We are always in both at once, and ordinarily in several types of special covenants at once. Furthermore, it is only through our participation in our various special covenants that we are able to express concretely our participation in the inclusive covenant. (p. 45)

It is in relation to this distinction between inclusive and special covenants that we can begin to see the connection between covenant and rights. There is a pretty obvious parallel between these two types of covenant and two types of right – human and special moral rights. The inclusive covenant includes every person created in God's image, and it is common enough in Christian ethics to state that human rights are held by every person simply in virtue of their human nature, a nature which is made in God's image. So the people in possession of human rights, and the people participating in the inclusive covenant, are exactly the same group of individuals. Allen explicitly recognises this in saying that the two types of covenant are partly distinguished in terms of the different types of rights to which they give rise – human and special rights. The covenants are also distinguished on the basis of their origin: inclusive – God's entrusting of humanity at creation; special – humanity's being chosen for, or choosing to enter, a particular set of historical relationships. Membership is another distinguishing feature: the inclusive type obviously involves all humans, while the special type is limited to a smaller number. On the other hand, these covenants have in common a shared emphasis on respect for others as ends in themselves; a concern for the needs of other members and the requirement of faithfulness over time, which Allen identifies as 'agape' love.

It is necessary to keep in mind how the inclusive covenant prepares the way for the special covenants so that the latter are a concrete expression of the former. The inclusive covenant is essentially a religious concept since it concentrates on the initiative of God in creating humankind in his own image. The very existence of human beings is at issue as well as the general features of their existence. God not only created human creatures, he gave them a nature which is specifically relational, capable of responding to himself and to others. This nature, made in God's image, is said to possess a special dignity. In this work we have tried to spell out some aspects of this dignity using terms like freedom and power, which have been treated as models for the language of rights.

Human rights are the most basic rights we can claim. These are claims we are justified in making simply as persons having certain general needs required for survival and flourishing, but without regard to specific features such as age, sex, religion, colour, social status. Presupposed in the possession of these rights is the idea of an equal dignity or personal worth which demands that certain basic goods of life be respected. These goods include life itself, health, intimacy, freedom of conscience, education, the opportunity to work; the list could go on and on. But the possession of these basic goods on their own does not exhaust what we might call the moral quality of human existence. Their possession is the basis for the making of more personal choices regarding the ways in which we will participate in such general goods. The fact that our physical life is free from fear of attack, that we can go to the doctor when we feel ill and get proper treatment, that we are free to marry or remain single, make friends or choose the life of a recluse, is of vital importance to nearly everyone, but it is only the basic framework within which we make something of our lives. These basic goods provide us with the opportunities to go further in developing particular projects which will include special covenants and special moral rights.[32]

Again I must repeat a point made in an earlier chapter: that the general goods protected by human rights, which are central to the inclusive covenant, and the specific goods protected by special moral rights, which are central to the special covenants, are not simply gifts bestowed on us by other humans, (though there is a gift element in every covenant), they are things we can claim against others as their equals, as people with a justified freedom and power of self-assertion. This does not mean that we can claim against God who initiated the first inclusive covenant, but that we can claim against those who share that covenant with us as members of God's people, sharing in his image. So before we can enter into special covenants with others we must first have the assurance that we are the kind of beings that have the essential human dignity which makes such covenants possible. Slaves (as such) are not in this position, their failure to have their human rights respected must also limit greatly their ability to have special moral rights respected. If slaves are not recognised as forming part of the inclusive covenant, then the special covenants open to them are few and far between.

There is a tendency to think of human rights as rather impersonal and abstract, and special rights as personal and concrete. If every individual in this world has human rights against everyone else, then millions of strangers have rights against me and I can claim against millions I shall never meet. Special rights are more satisfactory from this point of view, because the typical examples are from family life where relationships are quite close. Parallel impressions may arise regarding the inclusive covenant and special covenants respectively. But these impressions are false. For one thing, some special rights and special covenants, while not having a universal scope have still a very wide scope indeed, involving normative relationships between virtual strangers. If I belong to a large institution, such as a church or a state (imagine the Republic of China), the rights of a member or of a citizen, and the special covenant relationships that exist in these instances, are nearly as distant as in the case of human rights and the inclusive covenant. Thus, we have a similar problem with each category of covenant and rights, where the people supposed to be involved in the normative relationships are only marginally acquainted or are complete strangers whose lives are unlikely to touch.

COVENANT AND UNIVERSALISM

In the religious tradition of Judaism and Christianity, the same image can be used to cover both types of covenant and both main types of rights; it is the image of God's family or God's people. In other words, covenants and rights are recognised as involving inter-personal relationships from start to finish and are not based on abstract features of human nature. That is why the notion of image of God is best understood in the light of a covenant relationship, rather than in the light of a metaphysical discussion of our special endowment as rational animals.

T. W. Manson points to the emphasis on corporate solidarity in the Old Testament which brings together religious and political aspects of Jewish life. He says that contemporary men and women tend to think of themselves primarily as individuals and find it hard to understand the tribal way of thinking:

It is extremely hard to think ourselves to the point of view where everyone within the tribe or clan is part of 'one flesh'; where if one member of the tribe is wounded or killed the tribe says not 'So-and-so's blood has been spilt' but '*Our* blood has been spilt'. That intensity of feeling for corporate solidarity has to be kept in mind continually. It comes out in a very striking way in Romans 11.14 where Paul speaks of stirring up 'his flesh' to jealousy, and it is quite clear that 'his flesh' means his fellow-countrymen, the Jewish people. It underlies his whole teaching about the Body of Christ.[33]

The Israelites differ from the Greeks in not having any term corresponding to the notion of 'fellow-citizens', argues Manson. Instead two words are used to describe the relationship between Israelites:

The normal thing in Hebrew usage was to say 'neighbour' if the idea was uppermost of being members of the same nation by physical descent, 'brother' if the emphasis was on the sharing of a common religious faith and loyalty. 'Brother' is the term of relationship when you are thinking of the group in its religious capacity; 'neighbour' when you are thinking of it in its political and economic capacity.[34]

Thus the religious aspect of Jewish life was partly expressed in terms of family relationship. As brothers the Jews shared the same divine Father who gave them commands as well as promises. But it must be doubted that the members of God's family knew one another as well as members of an ordinary family group, and the other term 'neighbour' which applies to the same people (but from a different angle) corrects the idea that the relationship between co-religionists is necessarily warm and intimate.

Of course, it will be objected, this view of Jewish group life refers not to an inclusive covenant, but to the special covenant which is restricted to the chosen people. Family images then seem out of place when talking about inclusive covenant and human rights. There is something to this, as Birger Gerhardsson recognises in his discussion of the ethos of the Jewish theocracy. Regarding the command in Leviticus 19, to love one's neighbour as oneself, he suggests that 'What was intended was thus not a universal love for people in general but loyal acceptance of responsibility toward one's fellow Israelites.' References to love of 'strangers' imply obligations to the 'full proselyte' and 'in fact confirms that there were boundaries limiting the area within which such love was expected. The real stranger, the foreigner, is not intended.'[35]

Still Gerhardsson holds that in this ethos of Jewish theocracy there is an implicit universalism 'which needed only to be released'. He goes on:

One important prerequisite of universalistic views is the conviction that Yahweh is not only Israel's but the whole world's God, and that he has created everything. In this light, all creation assumes a unity when placed in relation to God; further, all humankind becomes one both in relation to the rest of creation and in relation to God. The creation narratives in Genesis 1–2, with the well-known formula that human beings are created in God's 'image' and 'likeness'...give expression to an outlook which would come to play a very important role in the advent of universalism and the recognition of human dignity; compare as well a text like Psalm 8. The idea that the God of heaven provides for all creation was also a factor tending to erase boundaries and broaden perspectives (cf. Psalms 104 and 145).[36]

Gerhardsson admits that the development of the idea of the covenant with an emphasis on the relationship between God and the chosen people had a negative influence on the development of this universalism.[37] We might say that the notion of a special covenant came to be interpreted in a narrow, exclusive way, and the inclusive covenant faded into the background, whereas God's intention was, and is, that there should be no strict separation of these two covenants. All humans are called to be children of God, and thus to be brothers and sisters. The special covenant between God and Israel was a step along the way to the achievement of God's ultimate aim, the unity of the human race in his Kingdom.

In turn, if these two types of covenant are models for two types of rights – human and special – it is legitimate to propose that it is equally God's intention that we do not try to make too much of a distinction between these rights. This is not to argue that everyone we meet is to be treated in exactly the same way as we treat the members of our intimate family grouping, either nuclear or extended. To refer to the human race as one family under God is to use a metaphor or model which is not literally true and yet not totally untrue either. There are points of correspondence between the more intimate form of the institution and the wider and more extended image, which are important in ethics, especially in religious ethics. Most important is the common emphasis on a parent (or parents) who provides the focus of unity for the relationships within the family. In a certain family group, the members are brothers and sisters to one another as a result of their common relationship to their father and mother. One cannot be a father or mother without children, and one's identity as a parent comes to some extent from the biological relationship one has with the result of one's effort to procreate. And the same is true analogically of the God–human relationship. According to basic Christian belief persons are brothers and sisters of the same heavenly Father, who has 'adopted' them as his children. And when acting in relation to others rights and obligations follow from that identity as family members. However, in terms of the wider human 'family' all members are limited in their possession and exercise of rights and duties by the lack of personal knowledge of the other members and their predicaments, and also obviously by the scarcity of resources required to come to the aid of those whose predicaments are relatively well known.[38]

One might recall at this stage that manifesto rights are not merely a problem at the wider level of human rights, for example when faced with issues like world starvation; they are also problematic in the case of special moral rights and special covenants. Consider the moral dilemmas which frequently arise in the matter of caring for elderly parents. It is widely accepted that parents do have some rights against their adult sons and daughters to care for them in their old age. Sometimes this simply entails frequent visits and being available if an emergency should arise. But in some cases aged parents need the daily presence of a relative to enable them to live in a dignified way. This may involve a son or daughter staying at home and making great sacrifices of personal freedom to do so. There are also married sons and daughters who may take their parents into their homes to care for them in their latter years, and we can easily imagine the strains and the tensions which can arise between the generations. The question that comes to mind at once here is whether strict rights and duties are involved in the relationship between parents and their adult progeny, and, more important perhaps, what is the extent of these rights and duties? Adults can hardly be expected to give up their autonomy totally to care for their parents when they grow old, and married adults who have entered into a new special covenant may find a conflict of rights between the new set of relationships (wife and children) and the old set of relationships (parents and siblings).

In the discussion of manifesto rights, the main controversial issue is the nomination of the bearer of the obligation, granted that a person has some right in need of respect. In the case under discussion, who has the obligation to look after elderly parents? Is it the adult son or daughter who has remained single? Or does the burden of care spread out more or less equally between all adult children, independent of their vocational status? These are not easy questions to answer, but I raise them here to underline the point that special covenants and special rights are not always characterised by a clear relationship of correlativity between claims and duties or obligations. Thus, the rights and duties applying within intimate family groups can be relatively controversial and untidy as much as the rights and duties of people within the overall human 'family'. Just as it may be impossible to give practical help to people at the other side of the world, so too it may be equally difficult to come to the aid of close relations. In both cases, aid may be a matter of supererogation rather than strict rights with corresponding duty or obligation.[39]

What we are trying to guard against here is the temptation to draw a sharp contrast between human rights and special rights, inclusive covenant and special covenant, with the conclusion that a realistic ethics must concentrate on special covenants and special rights, since these are so precise and tidy, and pushing to one side the rhetoric of a starry-eyed idealism which urges us to think of universal normative relationships. The fundamental universalism of the Judaeo-Christian tradition rejects this sharp distinction, and, while recognising in practice our limited sympathies for strangers and mere acquaintances, actually encourages us to overcome this tendency and to reject the assumption that the majority of our fellow human beings are moral strangers to us. What happened historically was that the original inclusive covenant was largely forgotten and morality came to be dominated by special covenants until, in this modern age, there has been a welcome return to the inclusive covenant – notably with the help of the concept of human rights. But something interesting has happened to this distinction between types of covenants and types of rights, namely that the language of special covenants and special rights, for example the language used to describe family relationships has become in turn a model for the elucidation of the language of the inclusive covenant and human rights, as when we talk about the 'brotherhood of man' or the 'human family'.

PROMISORY AND LAW COVENANTS

Having looked at the close relationship between the inclusive covenant and special covenants, and used this to relativise the distinction between human rights and special moral rights in Christian ethics, we can now explore the other distinction made above, between the promisory and law types of covenant. Joseph Allen placed the Old Testament covenants between God and Noah, Abraham and David in the promisory category and contrasted these with the law covenant made with Moses. The former, unlike the latter, did not demand a response from humans in terms of a set of obligations, but underlined God's promise of fidelity to his creation. The promisory type covenant seems to present a situation where God has the obligations (due to his promise) and creatures have the corresponding rights or claims. The law type covenant, on the other hand, would appear to stress the requirement of a moral response on the part of creatures, failure to observe which, releases God from his promise to regard the Israelites as his people and permits him to punish them for their infidelity. Which covenant corresponds to the appropriate model for rights?

The promisory covenant sounds rather pleasant. It is good to know that God promises happiness and prosperity without demanding anything in return. But isn't it really too good to be true, an example of cheap grace, when grace ought to be more 'costly'? The law covenant, on the other hand, smacks of legalism. It appears to over-emphasise the human contribution to the divine–human relationship and contradicts the Pauline theology of justification by grace alone. Basing covenant on law is like trusting in 'good works' for salvation. In fact, these pictures of the two types of covenant are, when we make too much of the distinction, misleading stereotypes which fail to fulfil our needs.[40]

The value of the promisory covenant lies in its stress on God's initiative, rather than on the absence of human obligation in response to that initiative. It underlines God's transcendence and the fact that he enters into a covenant relationship more for our benefit than for his own. Although it is fitting, given God's loving nature, that he enter into covenant with rational-relational creatures through creation, it is not strictly necessary that God act in this way. His sovereign freedom must be respected. Any obligations men and women have do not benefit God but one another, so human obligations are not highlighted for fear of undermining the transcendence of God. Likewise, any literal emphasis on God's obligations to us must be understood as analogical, lest his transcendence be misunderstood or compromised.

The promisory covenant does not encourage the view that grace is cheap or that God can be counted on to do everything. Although formally the relationship appears rather one-sided, and human obligations are not given pride of place, human response is required, often of a very radical type. Witness the call of Abraham to leave home and country and his willingness to sacrifice Isaac in obedience to God's command. If creation is the first promisory covenant, then the flood is God's response to human infidelity to that covenant. The punishment of David for his sin of adultery is still another example of implicit moral requirements, which, when ignored, damage the covenant relationship, even if the relationship is not wholly broken.

A covenant relationship initiated by God which does not impose the obligation of a moral response is not worthy of God and only undermines human dignity. Thus, the law covenant is another aspect of the promisory covenant which brings out more clearly the human dimension of the God–man relationship. According to the Jewish tradition, the law as man's response to God is itself God's gift of guidance, a sign of his infinite care for his people. Far from being a heteronomous imposition which attacks human freedom, the moral law is an aspect of autonomy. The self-regulating person is truly free. The laws which direct him are freely accepted as suited to the kind of being he is. Thus we also made reference to the example of Jesus, whose autonomy was to be found in his obedient relationship to his Father. One could even talk of the special covenant between Jesus and the Father as the paradigm covenantal model. A simplistic reading of the promisory covenant, then, which reduces the human response to a minimum, gives us a picture of a paternalistic God who spoils his children with gifts, while denying them the opportunity to grow up as mature, responsible adults.

The law covenant, on the other hand, takes up the best elements of both types of covenant, God's promise of faithful love is partly revealed in the gift of the Old Testament law, and perfectly fulfilled in the New Testament law of love. Sometimes the best gift is the giving of responsibility to another, and this is exactly what God does. In demanding a free response from us God shows a great respect for his creation, a respect which comes to a climax in the waiting of Jesus in Gethsemane for the response of the Jewish leaders to his ultimatum. An important aspect of our response to God concerns our claiming rights and fulfilling obligations. As members of a covenant relationship with God we have obligations to claim our own rights in many cases in order to highlight our own God-given dignity. The same principle applies to our obligation to claim for others and to enable others to claim for themselves.

This discussion of covenant has focused on the relationship between God and humanity, which is the primary religious and moral relationship emphasised in the Christian tradition. But this divine–human covenant is expressed fundamentally in the associated human covenants or interpersonal relationships. Thus the rights and duties arising from each covenant, while having a bearing on our relationship with God, actually benefit persons in their earthly life, rather than God. God has entrusted others to us and us to others – this is an essential characteristic of covenant – and rights with their correlative duties and obligations form an indispensable aspect of this mutual trust.

COVENANT LOVE AS THE BASIC MORAL STANDARD

According to Joseph Allen in the work we have been discussing, covenant has more to do with love than with justice. In fact, covenant love is said to be the basic moral standard for Christian ethics, on a par with the principle of utility or the categorical imperative in secular ethics. The second chapter of Allen's book is dedicated to an explication of this position.

God is the source of this basic standard and Christian ethics is a response to the God who cares for us with this covenant love. For Allen the best way of expressing this response is in terms of what he calls the 'divine exemplar theory' (p. 57). This means that Christian ethics is patterned after the being and action of God. For instance, the Sabbath is kept holy in imitation of the God who rested after creation. We are encouraged in scripture to 'be holy as God is holy' (Lev. 19.2; Mtt. 5.44–5) and to imitate the one who allows his rain to fall on good and bad alike. But what exactly is this divine love like so that we might emulate it?

In the Old Testament God's covenant love is described with the aid of two words. First, there is the term 'ahabah' which 'refers to love that is unconditioned by covenant, the "election-love" of God, who freely chose to make covenant with the people' (*ibid.*, p. 60). And secondly, there is the word 'hesed' which 'refers to love within the covenant and thus love that includes faithfulness to the covenant; the Revised Standard Version appropriately translates this term as 'steadfast love' (*ibid.*). The frequently used Greek term 'agape' includes both Hebrew meanings, according to Allen.

Taking these very basic expressions of God's love, Allen expands on them, drawing out more specific aspects. Thus, God binds us together as members of a covenant community, reminding us of our social nature (p. 61). He creates and affirms the worth of each covenant member (p. 62). The covenant love is extended inclusively to embrace the gentiles (p. 68). Covenant love seeks to meet the needs of its members (p. 69). And God's covenant love is both steadfast and reconciling (pp. 72–3). This standard must be the basis for our moral action. To be a Christian is to have good reasons for not being a 'loner'; for affirming the worth of others as well as one's own worth; being inclusive; meeting the needs of others; being faithful to commitments; and seeking reconciliation when relationships break down. And, in turn, we can apply each of these aspects to our analysis of rights. Rights too remind us of our social nature; speak to us of the individual worth of each person as an end in himself or herself; focus on basic needs; demand commitment and loyalty over time, and so on.

What of the two types of love that express the divine agape? Do these challenge us too? One wonders if the first kind mentioned by Allen has much application to human morality. It centred on God's decision to enter into covenant in first place by his work of creation. It is the love of election, which precedes the inclusive covenant. This can't apply strictly to human moral choice, since that is always made within the context of the inclusive covenant. As creatures the inclusive covenant is a 'given' in our life. But this type of love does apply to human decisions when we must decide on entering into or creating special covenants. To initiate or build a new moral community by marriage, procreating, forming a religious community, even founding a club, is a matter of free choice. Since it involves entrusting others, putting oneself in the hands of others, it is a risky business, so that there is often the temptation to draw back and to live a safer and more comfortable existence. However, from the Christian perspective the example of God must be followed. His choice of inclusive covenant, within which there is the special covenant with the chosen people, was quite a risk, especially in view of his gift of freedom. Yet God, according to Christian religious tradition took this risk in love, accepting the consequences of human abuse of free will. Greater love no God hath than to give his creatures freedom.

The Christian life follows this example, being ready to enter into new covenants as well as respecting the inclusive covenant which is the basis of all moral choice. Entering into new covenants involves the giving of special rights to others, extending their freedom and power, often at great personal expense to oneself. It can mean both a limitation of one's own freedom and power, and an extension of that same freedom and power. It is at this level in particular that the gift element of covenant, mentioned by May above, is most obvious. When we construct a set of relationships which bind us to others, allowing others to expect certain behaviour from us, so that they can claim against us when we default on the original promise or arrangement, the motive or reason may vary. On occasion selfish motives may predominate, but the Christian ideal stresses the unselfish gift of self to others in a spirit of service. The granting of human rights as a result of the inclusive covenant is God's gift and no one else's. Thus, our respect for human rights is not something for which others need be grateful (except to God who gave the rights in first place). But the granting of special rights to others, as in marriage, is typically accompanied by a sense of the gift involved, the gift of trust and the faith, hope and love which are elements of that trust.

The impression given so far could be that covenants are simply normative relationships made up of rights and duties with a religious twist or interpretation appended. The further impression may also have been given that rights and duties can only be elucidated morally from the covenant perspective. Are these impressions valid?

In reply to the first problem, it must be said that covenants are not simply reducible to rights and duties, and that this applies both to the inclusive covenant and special covenants. It is perhaps most obvious in the case of the more personal special covenants mentioned so frequently, marriage, family, friends, religious groups and so on. Certainly legalistic views of marriage which would describe it as a mere contract, consisting of the mutual exchange of rights and duties are no longer in vogue in the Western World, where a more romantic view of matrimony has caught on. We have already mentioned the view that rights are usually claimed only when a relationship is on the verge of breakdown. Then they act as a safety net, attempting to salvage something from the relationship. Of course, this is not to deny that personal relationships and special covenants in part depend for their survival and growth on the spontaneous respect for rights and obligations. People can exercise their rights without being aware of it, especially when those who respond are equally unaware that they are fulfilling correlative obligations. Becoming aware of one's rights and duties may in fact be a bad sign in a personal relationship, an indication that all is not well. So special covenants involving intimate relationships involve much more than respect for rights and duties. Specifically, special covenants require a willingness to go beyond one's duty, to transcend the language of claiming, and to be willing to 'go the extra mile'.

But this is also true to some extent of the inclusive covenant and human rights. Many human rights, we saw, are not respected because they appear to be of the type we have called 'manifesto rights'. An important good or benefit such as food is due to every human being, we feel, so that talk of a human right to food sounds reasonable, even mandatory. But we are frightened of translating this rhetoric into action by nominating those with a duty to respect this right. So we put the matter on the long finger by creating a neat philosophical category. We say that there is a right indeed, but that conditions beyond our control make it impossible to respect it absolutely at present; but it is only a matter of time...and we are working on it...Here again, the inclusive covenant may act as a criticism of an approach which depends overmuch on the concept of human rights, and argues instead for an approach which stresses the notion of imperfect obligation and supererogation.

COVENANT AND CONTRACT

Regarding the second problem, whether covenant is the only moral model for elucidating rights and duties or obligations, it is plain that it is not. In fact, the more obvious model might be that of a contract. William May has an interesting discussion of the relative advantages and disadvantages of using covenant and contract as terms to describe the doctor–patient relationship.[41] May sees contract as a relationship 'in which two parties calculate their own best interests and agree upon some joint project in which both derive roughly equivalent benefits for goods contributed by each' (*ibid.*, p. 33). This has a number of advantages over the more traditional medical approach to patients which tended towards authoritarianism, playing down informed consent and often undermining the dignity of the patient. One of the advantages listed is that a contractual approach 'allows for a specification of rights, duties, conditions, and qualifications limiting the agreement. The net effect is to establish some symmetry and mutuality in the relationship between doctor and patient' (*ibid.*). Further advantages include provision for legal enforcement of terms for both parties which gives some protection; and a movement away from what May calls 'the pose of philanthropy, the condescension of charity', (*ibid.*) as if doctors owed nothing to their patients, but acted as their benefactors.

While recognising that 'some of these aims of the contractualists are desirable', May argues that 'it would be unfortunate if professional ethics were reduced to a commercial contract without significant remainder' (*ibid.*, p. 33). Covenant has some distinct advantages over contract, according to May:

But, in spirit, contract and covenant are quite different. Contracts are external; covenants are internal to the parties involved. Contracts are signed to be expediently discharged. Covenants have a gratuitous, growing edge to them that nourishes rather than limits relationships. (p. 34)

And further along on the same page May declares that:

There is a donative element in the nourishing of covenant – whether it is the covenant of marriage, friendship, or professional relationship. Tit-for-tat characterizes a commercial transaction, but it does not exhaustively define the vitality of that relationship in which one must serve and draw upon the deepest reserves of another.

Surely the impression we get in reading many philosophical attempts at rights analysis is that the concept of contract is most suited to reflect the relationship between claimant and the bearer of obligations. For rights to be efficient tools in normative ethics, law and politics, they must be made precise, tidied up, pinned down. And the notion of contract appears well fitted to perform this task. In fact, it may be suggested that the contract model can act as a severe critic of much of our language of rights, even reducing the number of rights we can claim. Many so-called human rights would lose their status as rights because they lack the precision of a detailed contract between named parties. The proliferation of rights-claim would be curtailed and the limits of rights-language accepted. To some extent this suggestion is attractive, and certainly the contractual aspect of the right–duty relationship can be seen as primary in many relationships, especially commercial–business ones. But such an approach would, arguably, limit the language of rights to a small corner of moral reality. A great price would be paid for the advantage of tidiness. The heart would be cut out of the concept of rights once one sees them as external, tit-for-tat exchanges of services.

This is where the notion of model is so important. We recall that models are a form of metaphorical thinking; they are extended metaphors. As such they are not a literal description of a reality. We speak of the tension between 'is' and 'is not'. War has something in common with a chess game, but is obviously very different from it at the same time. The differences as well as the similarities bring out the meaning of the object qualified by the metaphor or model. This too is why we have stressed the need for different models of complex realities, each of which corrects the others and also complements them.

Thus, to speak of a contract model of rights is not to say that rights and their correlative duties are just contracts, but that the notion of a contract has something in common with the possession of rights. But even more important is the qualification that rights and duties differ from contractual relationships in certain ways. The use of another model, say a covenant model of rights, may help to bring out the differences between rights and contracts.[42] And in turn a contract model may bring out the differences between rights and covenants.

CONCLUSION

We opened this chapter with a realistic appreciation of the ambiguity of the concept of power. The theologians we encountered, Tillich and Rahner, are convinced that power can be used positively and fits into God's providence regarding humanity. Falconer makes the same point when speaking of creative or positive conflict. The psychological analysis of power takes these ideas up and applies them to various conflict situations. The negative use of power is expressed in exploitative and manipulative relationships, and sometimes in competitive modes of behaviour. In some situations nutrient power expresses a justified paternalism, while in other cases it can degenerate into manipulation. Ideally, power should be of the integrative form, i.e. a form of co-operation with others, respecting their freedom by eliciting their consent through the use of reason.[43] This type of power, we said, is very close to the analysis of 'authority' in political science. I need not go into the connections with rights in detail, except to say that the exercise of rights shares in the ambiguity of the exercise of power in these different situations. Sometimes our claims are evidence of manipulation and exploitation; sometimes they reflect nutrient power used justifiably, and, ideally, they involve working with others in normative relationships made up of respective rights and duties.

The challenging perspective on God's power or authority, and the ways in which his Messiah reflects this in his human life, inspires a fresh understanding of how we might exercise rights morally. I feel specially attracted to the image of waiting which expresses the need for patience as the possibility of exercising rights properly develops. Because waiting is so closely connected with love, waiting for rights to be respected appears to me to be an appropriately Christian activity, though sometimes our waiting may have to give way to a more robust approach, especially when vital claims of others are at stake.

Regarding the long section on the value of a covenant model for the imaginative elucidation of the concept of rights, let us return to the initial point made by Allen when he declared that models go to the deepest ontological roots, the ultimate ground and meaning of moral life. The covenant concept claims to go this deep. The notion of an inclusive covenant, which is framed at creation and constantly renewed throughout history, is the most basic doctrine of Christian ethics. It draws attention to God's loving initiative which is further expressed in special covenants with individuals and groups. These two types of covenant are quite useful in bringing out the close relationships between human and special (moral) rights. As the inclusive covenant is the ground of special covenants, so human rights are the ground and foundation for the possibility of special rights. Unless we are persons of equal worth and dignity, with basic freedom and power, there can be no basis for entering into special relationships which further express that dignity. As special covenants flesh out the implications of the inclusive covenant in particular sets of just and loving relationships, so special rights are a particular application of human rights. I have a human right to a fair trial if I am accused of some crime, so I can enter into a special covenant with legal advisers who will vindicate both my human right and my special rights against them and the particular legal system within which I live.

The covenant model of rights relativises the distinction between human rights and special rights by insisting that this viewpoint refuses to accept any fellow human as a mere stranger. This does not entail being on intimate terms with millions of people; it simply involves the development of a frame of mind, an attitude, which refuses to cut off or ignore those in need because they live in distant lands or are not part of one's immediate family, or cultural group. The inclusive covenant uses the image of a family of brothers and sisters not in any vague, sentimental way, but as a challenge to see the truth of our common relationship to God, with the implication that we should imitate his attitudes to creation.

The promisory and law covenants together underline God's transcendence as well as his respect for his creatures. He initiates and gives backing to human covenants by refusing the paternalistic option and respecting our dignity by demanding our participation in the right–duty relationship. God entrusts persons to one another in these normative relationships. By means of these covenants and rights he creates situations where human freedom and power are both constrained and extended. Through them he exercises his own 'power with' people to further his Kingdom. Above all God waits for humanity to recognise the challenge implicit in the concept of inclusive covenant. For this covenant is not fully actualised until all people accept it with loyal trust. And until this covenant is respected we can hardly expect the cause of human rights to flourish.

Finally, we insisted that the covenant concept is not simply reducible to the correlativity between rights and duties. If it were so reducible it would no longer be a model or metaphor.

There are contractual elements to be found in rights which do not fit very well with the notion of covenant, but which are still necessary if rights-language is to have practical effect, even as a safety net when covenant relationships break down. One of the characteristics of covenant love was that it was reconciling, but it is hard to see how the claiming of rights would achieve this end in every case. When persons are threatened, often the first step one takes to help is to protect them from harm. Here rights are useful. Reconciliation is a further step one takes when the claiming of rights has redressed the balance of injustice. Nor is it the case that rights language falls between the language of covenant and contract; instead it participates in the advantages and disadvantages of each model. Contractual and covenantal models are rich enough and complex enough to clarify the meaning and value of rights language without claiming to give an exhaustive analysis, but the covenant model is the richer of the two for believer and non-believer alike.

CHAPTER 8

Theological foundations of rights-language

In this chapter my main intention is to take the major models of rights I have been using: freedom, power and covenant, and to relate them in turn to a further model which may be thought of as the ultimate foundation of rights. This model has been mentioned in passing throughout this work. It is the notion that humanity's dignity comes from being created in the image of God. I want to argue here that having and exercising rights are a vital aspect of that dignity, and that being made in God's image gives a specifically religious justifying reason for acting morally. I hope to show that the models of power, freedom and covenant are all related intimately to this ultimate model and are particular expressions of it.

Before examining this image model I need to treat briefly of the general debate, especially within Roman Catholicism, on the distinctiveness of Christian ethics. Then I shall mention some of the difficulties regarding the use of the language of God's rights and our having rights against God. Rejecting this approach as a foundation for rights I stress the view that rights are granted by God to human persons as part of our special status as images of his, partners in covenant, free and self-assertive co-workers with the Creator.

THE DISTINCTIVENESS OF CHRISTIAN ETHICS

Before I can consider the question of providing a Christian foundation for rights, the prior question of the possibility of a distinctive Christian ethics has to be faced. This debate has raged of late particularly among Roman Catholic theologians.[1]

233

In the following pages I shall rely heavily on Vincent Mac-Namara's discussion of the issues in his *Faith and Ethics*.[2]

I begin with MacNamara's account of the different ways in which religious faith may influence moral beliefs and practices. There may be a causal relationship between religious beliefs and moral beliefs. This means that a person may learn about moral right and wrong, what ought to be done morally, from some religious tradition, for example the commandments of the Old Testament or the teaching of Jesus in the Sermon on the Mount. There can be a psychological relationship between religion and morality in so far as religious beliefs can motivate someone to act in a particular way morally. Thus, for instance, a person may decide to forgive another following the example of Christ. Without this example the person may realise the goodness and rightness of forgiving in the abstract, but not be able to 'bring himself' to actually do it in practice. There is also a possible ontological relationship between religion and morals. This involves the belief that the goods or values of this life derive from a divine source, that created value depends on uncreated value – the goodness of God. The last relationship mentioned by MacNamara is that of 'epistemological dependence', and entails that at least some moral positions held by Christians 'cannot be intelligibly arrived at or supported without the framework of faith' (*ibid.*, p. 96). This is the most radical form of relationship between faith and morality, because it underlines the possibility that the content of morality may differ according to whether one is a religious believer or not.[3]

On the question of epistemological dependence of morality upon religious belief, MacNamara discusses the debate between two schools of thought in Roman Catholic moral theology. On one hand, the so-called 'Autonomy' school allows the possibility of there being causal, psychological and ontological links between religious belief and morality, while refusing to accept epistemological dependence.[4] On the other hand, there is the so-called '*Glaubensethik*' (Faith–Ethic) school which holds that all four types of relationship are possible, and thus that Christian ethics is highly specific.[5] Put simply, and perhaps simplistically, the 'Faith–Ethic school tends to claim that the content of morality may be different for Christians; while the 'Autonomy' school of thought tends to deny this, allowing that Christian belief is important in giving specific motivation and context to the moral life. As will be seen, the differences between these groups hinge largely on how one understands concepts like 'content' of morality and 'motives' for acting morally.[6]

The areas where the content of Christian ethics is supposed to be different from humanistic morality are mentioned by MacNamara as follows:

There are values, it [the Faith–Ethic school] says, such as poverty, virginity, renunciation of power, humility, modesty. There are demands to receive the Eucharist, do penance, preach the Gospel. There is the New Testament's new vision of marriage, of the world, of hope. There are attitudes of joy, thankfulness, prayer, indifference to the world.[7]

This list looks at first sight to give strength to the Faith–Ethic approach. However, the 'Autonomy' approach has its answer. First, it is not impossible for humanists to value poverty, in the sense of living a simple life in solidarity with the poor of the world. Also it is doubtful whether virginity is a style of life open to Christians alone. But what of specifically religious realities such as receiving the Eucharist and preaching the Gospel? One strategy used by the Autonomists to get around this objection is to make a separation between strictly moral values and religious values. Preaching the Gospel or receiving sacraments, if they are commands, are not moral commands. The point here, according to MacNamara, is that many contemporary moral philosophers are sceptical of any attempt to see acts directed towards God as truly moral. This is because of:

the widely accepted view about the definition of morality which requires that normative judgments, if they are to qualify as moral, must meet a material social criterion pertaining to the distribution or promotion of non-moral good or evil among sentient beings.[8]

One can see why the 'Autonomy' approach has such attraction for many theologians. In the first place, it is in line with traditional 'natural law' theory, which insists upon a common grasp of moral truth by all humans independently of divine revelation, though not independent of God's gracious gift – natural law is said to be a reflection of the eternal law after all. Secondly, it avoids the problem of two kinds of morality in the world, one a minimalist kind for non-believers, and the other a more challenging one for Christians. Related to this is the possibility of arguing rationally with other humans, believers and non-believers alike, regarding the requirements of the moral imperative.

Still, the odd thing about this debate is that in some ways all involved in it seem to agree on the fact that Christian ethics does have something distinctive to recommend it.[9] The disagreement is on where exactly this distinctiveness lies. Does it lie in the realm of content or in the realm of motivation?

The answer to this question depends on how one understands the content of morality, especially its scope, and also on distinguishing carefully the place of motivation in making moral judgements. In other words, one has to take into account both 'act-evaluation' and 'agent-evaluation' in humanistic and Christian ethics.

THE 'CONTENT' OF CHRISTIAN ETHICS

Regarding the content of morality, I pointed out that there is sometimes a tendency to separate off 'purely religious realities' like receiving sacraments and preaching the Gospel from ethics or morality. But it is easy to protest against such a compartmentalisation of life. Even in terms of the required 'material social criterion pertaining to the distribution or promotion of non-moral good or evil among sentient beings', a strong argument can be made in favour of including 'religious rituals' in the moral category. Much has been written of late concerning the relationship between liturgy and justice that shows the moral challenge involved in the Christian's sacramental life.[10] Reception of the Eucharist, for instance, cannot be so spiritualised that it enables Christians to forget that the 'body of Christ' is found starving in the world as well as in the sacred species offered on the altar. The sacraments are not just spiritual

nourishment for people, 'in this world, but not of it'; they point
to the divine interest in this world through creation, incarnation
and redemption, an interest which humans must imitate in
daily life.

So, too, with prayer: the traditional Thomistic view of prayer
of petition is that the Christian is included in a special way in the
providence of God, such that humans can actually bring about
certain goods in this world that would not come about if they
did not pray. This is the view of Aquinas; Christians pray, not
to change God's will, but within that will, in order to accomplish
it.[11] And some things will just not happen if Christians do not
pray. I see no problem in accepting that prayer is a strictly
moral obligation for those who accept such a doctrine of
petitionary prayer (In fact, St Thomas treats of prayer of
petition under the virtue of religion, which is that section of
justice that seeks to give God his due.)

In this way, prayer is both directed to God and can have
material effects on life in this earth (These issues have been
discussed widely in philosophy of religion in recent decades.)[12]
Moreover, since belief in the power of sacraments and prayer
demands religious belief, it would appear that part of the
content of morality is religiously specific. This argument
suggests that the differences between the two 'schools' of
thought must be distinguished with proper care shown for the
nuances of each position, even within each school.

MOTIVES AND REASONS IN RELATION TO CONTENT

The other major problem mentioned at the start concerns the
(more subjective) level of motivation. It is sometimes claimed
that Christianity offers a special motivation to do what is
morally right, though the particular act-type may be recognised
as obligatory by the non-believer. MacNamara argues that the
'Autonomy' school tends to mix up motives and reasons at this
stage, causing some confusion.[13] What is this distinction between
'motives' and 'reasons'?

A great deal of purely philosophical analysis has been applied
to the related notions of 'reason', 'motive', and 'intention'.[14]

In ordinary language in use each day, most people do not distinguish carefully between reasons and motives, and this is understandable since motives are always reasons in one sense of that term. By this I mean that a motive is at least an explanatory concept, explaining why a person acted in a certain way. However, in ethical deliberation one concentrates more on the justification of action than on its explanation. After all, an action may be explained by bad motives just as easily as by good ones. And in relation to justification, it is MacNamara's view that the language of 'reasons' is more appropriate than the language of 'motives'.

When one places the stress on reasons for acting, one is thinking of the reasons that justify an action or practice morally. When one does x for a morally justifying reason y, the reason y both explains why one acted and justifies the act. But the language of motives has a much closer connection with explanations of actions than with their justification. This is because motive is more akin to psychological and causal aspects of action than to the aspect of moral judgement. A motive characteristically 'moves' a person to act, hence the 'causal' element. From the psychological point of view, motives tend to refer to desires which move a person to do something. This does not necessarily mean that having a motive forces one to act. Detectives attempting to solve a crime may concentrate on a particular suspect, asking whether he had a motive for committing the crime. But this does not imply that the person actually performed the act. It is simply a way of limiting the number of suspects to be considered. The police want to find out initially who *could* have committed the offence. The language of motivation used here is not the language of moral judgement. It is more pragmatic, being related more to discovery of a cause and its explanation than with its justification. To be honest I suppose we could use the word 'reason' here instead of motive. The investigators want to know if so-and-so had any reason for doing x, but this use of the term is secondary, the primary use involving the aspect of justification.

Like having a motive, having a (justifying) reason to do something need not necessarily move one to act, even if one is conscious of the legitimacy of the reason from the moral point of view. However, failure to act on the basis of a justifying reason is more likely to give rise to moral criticism than failure to act on the basis of a particular motive. The language of motivation tends towards moral neutrality.

The ideal to be achieved in the moral life is always to act on the basis of justifying reasons, and this means being motivated by those reasons. This is an important distinction, since a person may have a notional grasp that an action is good, for example helping a poor man with alms, but may be moved to aid the man by a disreputable motive – to be admired by others as a 'charitable' individual. In this way, an agent can recognise a good reason for doing something and not be motivated to do it; for example a student who recognises that he ought to go to lectures, but gives in to the temptation to stay in bed. Or an agent can have a good reason for acting, and moves to achieve an object, but for another reason that fails to justify the act.[15]

I believe, then, following NacNamara's analysis, that it is misleading to talk of motives when attempting to justify actions. Particular types of reasons justify actions and make certain motives respectable from the moral point of view. Often, indeed, the idea of 'having a good motive' is used as a type of excuse when the act posited is of questionable moral worth. For instance, in the discussion of active euthanasia there is some-times this tendency to excuse acts of 'mercy killing' because of the alleged 'good motives' of friends or relations of the patient. Or consider the case of someone who kills another from the motive of revenge. Our reaction to this may be one of sympathy and understanding, but usually we would refuse to identify such a motive with a reason for killing someone. This is the case, I think, because of the tendency to associate reasons for acting with justification. I have no objection to arguments in this area if they are based on 'good reasons' instead of 'good motives'; in fact, my point all along has been that truly 'good' motives must be based on justifying reasons.

Now the point that MacNamara wishes to make against the Autonomists is that Christian beliefs offer certain reasons for acting which are not available to those not sharing those beliefs.

And this involves much more than the claim that Christian beliefs just motivate the believer. What MacNamara is saying, I think, is that one must take a step back beyond motives to the justifying reasons which move people. And if one looks at these, one will find reasons based on religious beliefs, which distinguish the actions of Christians from those of non-Christians.

Justifying reasons for acting can vary. If my neighbour offends me in some way and I discern that I have an obligation to forgive him, I may have a number of good reasons for doing this. I may argue that I have an obligation to myself not to bear a grudge over time and that I 'couldn't live with myself if I failed to forgive'. Or I may approach forgiveness from the point of view of the other person's right to be forgiven. Perhaps the harm done was small, and the other meant no harm in the first place. I may reason that this person should not have to bear the brunt of my exaggerated bitterness. Then again, I may consider wider issues such as the bad example given to family and neighbours and the long-term effects of personal feuds on later generations and the peace and harmony of the neighbourhood. All of these reasons for forgiving my neighbour are basically humanistic: there is yet no mention of religious reasons. So let me mention a few.

I am under an obligation to obey the command of Jesus to forgive others out of love (Luke 7.41ff.; 17.3–4). Partly the reason for this is the fact that the Heavenly Father allows his rain to fall on just and unjust alike (Mtt. 5.44ff.);[16] in other words, God is patient with all humans until their dying moment when they make their final option for or against him (2 Pet. 3.8–9, 15). Part of the reason for forgiving others is that God has forgiven me in a most dramatic way and expects me to imitate him spontaneously (Mtt. 18.23ff.). I should also forgive if I wish to bring my gifts to the altar in worship and if I wish to pray the Lord's prayer honestly (Mtt. 5.24–5; 6.14–15).

These religious reasons for forgiving my neighbour are also moral reasons, not only in the basic effect of bringing about a reconciliation here and now between persons, but also in so far as there are obligations of gratitude to God as to any other person when another does one a good turn. Moreover, if one knows something of one's benefactor's wishes, one should consider the possibility of acting appropriately. It also seems to be a good thing morally to follow the example of a man (Jesus) widely recognised to be a good model from the moral point of view.

Note that I am not saying that the religious reasons mentioned contradict the non-religious reasons for acting. There is an overlap between the reasons such that Christians may act from all of these reasons at different times. Obviously people very often act morally without considering all the possible good reasons for acting. Often it suffices that a person has at least one justifying reason for acting morally. What I am arguing here is that Christians should try to consider the religious reasons for acting, as well as the reasons held in common with humanists. I believe that there can be a set of justifying reasons for acting morally, and that the religious reasons offer a deeper, an ultimate grasp of the significance of the actions intended.[17] This is simply because of the basic Christian insight that moral behaviour is a vital part of the most important relationship a human being has, the relationship with God.

I believe, then, that it is necessary to distinguish among the justifying reasons for acting the secular or humanistic reasons available to all men and women of good will, and the reasons stemming from revelation which are available only to those adhering to a specific religious tradition. The fact that the latter bring one closer to the ultimate truth about human life, its divine origin and its supernatural destiny, does not mean that the former are unimportant or can be ignored. The Christian has access to both kinds of reason; the non-believer, by definition, has access only to the former. Does this mean that the Christian has a superior morality to that of the non-believer?

The answer must be affirmative and negative. The affirmative answer depends on there being a situation where the Christian looks carefully at the elements making up the moral judgement, all the facts open to any human observer of rational discernment, and also consults the community's tradition for the relevant values. The resultant judgement takes together the best of human judgement with God's wisdom as revealed in scripture and tradition. The negative answer applies to situations where believers attempt to force moral problems into a framework where traditional principles do not apply so easily, and where general values in the tradition are misapplied in relation to new problems. Sometimes, then, religious justifying reasons offer little practical guidance in particular areas of moral controversy.[18]

I want to be clear about the general trend of my argument over the preceding pages. I am claiming that, because of the gap that may exist between reasons for acting morally and being motivated to act morally, it is tempting to say that religious beliefs typically act as an extra pressure to do what is right when the natural law or humanistic reasons fail to give the essential motivation. This, of course, may be part of the role of religious beliefs, but it is not in my opinion the only role or the most important role they play in moral deliberation and action. I am claiming that religious beliefs provide ultimate justifying reasons for acting morally without contradicting the fundamental natural law reasons. I use two different terms – 'ultimate' and 'fundamental' – to qualify the different kinds of reasons here, because I want to maintain their complementary roles in moral reasoning within Christian ethics. Moreover, it must be clear that the meaning of 'content' of morality for me must involve reference to the agent's reasons for acting. In other words, I refuse to distinguish strictly between act and agent evaluation, making the former of key importance and making the latter peripheral. Any attempt to separate the two makes the analysis of moral actions too abstract. In fact, without consideration of the mentality of the agent, one must talk of human 'behaviour', but not of human 'action'.

The religious justifying reasons are an aspect of the content of morality, for it is the content that moves us to act. But it is a mistake to reduce content to a narrow consequentialism, which is what happens when one places too much emphasis on 'the distribution or promotion of non-moral good or evil among sentient beings'. Certainly this is vital and necessary, but it is not sufficient, at least for the Christian, as a definition of content. Those who prefer to speak of the morality of virtue or character may well argue that the creation of people of character and a community of character is an essential aspect of the content of morality. What is necessary at this level is a whole vision of life, a philosophy of existence, a world-view within which our moral actions find meaning and justification.[19] For the Christian then, the moral focus will be on patterns of action which reflect the truth about human life in this world. And central to this truth is the existence of a God in whom one lives and moves and has one's being. In this light there can be no firm distinction between content, motivation and justifying reasons. All three are inseparable aspects of one's ultimate vision of life's significance. Religious beliefs, according to this view, are not peripheral aids to move us to act morally. They are the ultimate ground of our moral activity, without which our moral life takes on a different shape and colour.

CHRISTIAN REASONS FOR RESPECTING RIGHTS

If it is granted that Christian beliefs influence the ways in which members of the Church see the content of morality, how does this apply to the Christian's attitude towards rights? One possible way of thinking about this has been mentioned earlier, for instance in Donal Murray's discussion of the right to religious freedom. It can be argued that all rights pertaining to human beings are really derivative from God's rights. The concept of God 'having rights' may be said to be distinctively religious. As well as discussing God's rights against man one can also discuss the question of man's rights against God, and whether this makes sense or not.

'GOD'S RIGHTS'

In my discussion of the relationships between faith and ethics I have argued that religious morality is authentic morality in so far as its doctrines relate in part to human good in this world. At the same time the morality of Christians must be distinctively religious, because moral acts and practices must be seen in some basic sense as God-directed. Any person committed to being moral must not be satisfied with merely bringing about certain good effects deriving from a deliberately limited process of moral discernment. What is required is an attempt to discern the best justifying reasons for acting morally. For the Christian, these reasons ought to transcend the fundamental humanistic reasons available to all persons of good will. The reasons should have God as their object, not in the sense that God benefits from the actions, but in the sense that Christian ethics recognises an obligation of gratitude to God for creation and redemption;[20] that life has an eschatological perspective in which Christians wait in longing for Christ's second coming; and that moral activity can be part of the process of deification.[21] These are just some central feature of a Christian 'vision' of reality.

Regarding the language of rights in particular, I would now like to discuss an approach which stresses the God-directed nature of all rights, since the basis of all rights is said to be God's right against his creation. Among the theologians holding this position I shall mention three in particular: Emil Brunner, Jurgen Moltmann, and Franz Bockle.

Emil Brunner discusses rights in the context of justice in his classic work, *Christianity and Civilisation*.[22] In ancient civilisation, Brunner informs his readers, justice and religion were closely linked, the civic order was expected to copy the divine order, the *lex naturae* to mirror the *ius divinum*. Thus, 'Justice is something holy; it is backed by divine order, divine necessity.'[23] The *lex naturae* represents the orders of creation, which the church fathers connected with the *logos*, in whom the world is created and finds its order. 'That is to say, the Christian Church never had a *lex naturae* conception other than a Christological one' (*ibid.*). Of course he admits that the pagans could know the moral law based on the orders of creation. They know something of justice, 'although the depth of Christian justice remains hidden from them' (*ibid.*).

The proper understanding of justice and rights, then, is, for Brunner, a theological one. He blames Grotius for the demise of the theological understanding of justice by driving a wedge between natural law and divine law. From then on, morality becomes increasingly secularised and is separated from its religious and metaphysical base. Brunner wants to retain the concept of 'natural right', but understood in a religious context, since all persons are sharers in the same dignity given in creation. The sovereignty of God above all must be stressed: 'Man has no rights over against God being his creature and property; he lives entirely from God's grace and mercy. Rights he has only in so far as God gives them' (pp. 117–18). And in the second volume of this work, Brunner insists on this point:

The first pronouncement about 'belongings' or 'rights' is this: that all things belong to God. The *ius divinum* is not in the first place the right which God gives, but the right which God has, and this right alone is absolute.[24]

In this passage, Brunner appears to be anxious lest people should think that God's gift of rights to them involves some claim against God, thus undermining his sovereign freedom.

A similar stress on the primacy of God's rights is central to Moltmann's view: 'We see the theological contribution of the Christian Church in the grounding of the fundamental human rights upon God's right to man.'[25] Such a right is revealed, says Moltmann, in salvation-history especially in the scriptural concept of covenant. Here Moltmann tends to underline the rights and duties of those who enter into covenant, but he does not make clear whether rights under the covenant are against God as well as against one's neighbour. One might think that this reference to God's rights is universally held in Christian theology, whereas in fact it is not, and Moltmann is realistic enough to recognise that this view is not even *the* Protestant view, least of all *the* Christian view. For instance, the Lutheran approach to this question as expressed by W. Todt and H. E. Huber rejects the notion of a 'Christian foundation' of human rights.[26] Moltmann remains true to the Reformed tradition of Brunner in stressing a theological foundation in God's rights.

Franz Bockle makes plain the primacy of God's claim as central to the whole study of fundamental moral theology. Under the heading 'The Question of the Ultimate Basis of Moral Claim', Bockle has this to say:

Instead of asking about the ultimate basis of moral claim, we could well ask about the limits of man's moral autonomy. This is also the special concern of our own enquiry. It is a simple matter of course for theological ethics that the ultimate basis of man's moral obligation is found in God's radical claim imposed on man. But everything depends on the way we understand this divine claim.[27]

One wonders, having seen the admission of Moltmann about the controversy over the question of a Christian foundation for rights, whether Bockle can afford to be so certain of the ultimate basis of man's obligation in God's claim. In fact, he does not appear to recognise the major problems of talking about God's claims or rights. He is more concerned, in the section from which the quotation has been lifted, to harmonise human dependence on God with human autonomy. Bockle does not really follow up the question of God's claims as such. It is fairly clear that he transfers as soon as possible to the correlative language of obligation, a wise move indeed, but of little help in the analysis of what 'God's rights' could mean.

What then are the problems of using the language of rights in relation to God? John A. Henley[28] provides a valuable service to Christian ethics in his discussion of this question. First, he speaks of the way in which talk of God's rights must be analogical. Prescinding from consideration of the putative 'rights' of animals, rights are usually held to be predicable only of persons. Moving from the known to the unknown the question now arises, 'Is God sufficiently like human persons to allow the predication of the language of rights?' Henley points to the Christian doctrine of the Trinity where the term 'person' is used in a relational sense. The term 'Father' seems to permit some view of God as having rights on the analogy of any earthly father having rights against his children, rights to gratitude and loyalty, for instance (p. 372). It is, however, difficult to know exactly how God's personhood is similar to human personhood, even when it is claimed that God became human in Jesus of Nazareth, who is the perfect image of the Father (Heb. 1.3; Col. 1.15). The least a Christian would wish to hold, I presume, is that God may be more than what is called a 'person', but certainly not less.

If God is in some sense a person, how might his 'rights' be categorised? Recalling the distinction between human rights and special moral rights, where does God fit into that schema? Henley shows that God's 'rights' cannot be like human rights for the simple reason that human rights are defined as those 'one has simply because of who one is and in order to become who one is' (p. 372). But God, as understood in traditional theistic terms, cannot change in order to become more, or less, divine. This is the single most difficult problem relating to the concept of the rights of God. Rights are required by humans because they are weak, and because there is a sense in which human dignity can be undermined by the actions of others. People need the protection of rights against one another, but God needs no such protection. He cannot be harmed in any way.[29]

A further reason why the human rights concept cannot apply to God is the fact mentioned earlier, that the notion of equality is built into the doctrine of human rights. Each human person has a similar basic dignity, and owes every other person the same respect. However, God is not on equal terms with his creatures, and there are theologians like Brunner who reject out of hand the idea of humans having rights against God.

If God's 'rights' are not of the 'human rights' type, is there any way in which they can be said to be like 'special moral rights'? Henley is equally sceptical of this approach, for 'special rights obtain only between those who share a particular relation, not between all and sundry' (p. 372). So it is doubtful whether the special relationship existing between God and those who accept the gift of faith can provide a very strong basis for speaking of the rights of God. Henley holds that 'this right of God exists only in relation to those whom in biblical terms he has chosen and this is not yet everyone' (*ibid.*). There is some point to this argument, since special moral rights tend to apply only to people who voluntarily enter into a relationship with some other person, and this is simply not the case in a world which often voluntarily rejects the existence of God.

However, it is arguable that some special moral rights arise without bilateral agreement. The relationship between parents and their offspring is a case in point. Children do not 'consent' to be born and to enter into a normative relationship with their parents, but it is common to hold that children as they grow up must respect, to some degree, their parents' rights. Analogously, it may be argued that all human beings are *de facto* God's children or God's creatures, and that God has rights against them, even if they do not recognise the existence of such rights. It must be remembered that rights can exist without any immediate hope of their exercise. Perhaps in the present world with its large proportion of non-believers in God, his 'rights' against such people are 'manifesto rights' in Feinberg's sense? Nevertheless, if one is interested in a universal respect for human rights in practice, it seems that giving them a theological foundation must fail from the start, given the wide disagreement on even the basic question of God's existence. This does not mean, however, that a theological foundation is impossible. In any case, even if it is accepted that God's 'rights' are more like special moral rights than human rights, one is still left with the fundamental problem of coping with the consequences of failure to respect God's 'rights' – is God harmed by the failure of his creation to obey him and give him his due? My conclusion is that talk of God's 'rights' is so divorced from the usual meaning of rights-language as applied to human persons, that such a usage is of very little, or no, help in Christian ethics.

'RIGHTS' AGAINST GOD

Is there more sense in talking of the rights of men and women against God in spite of worries about maintaining God's sovereignty? At first glance there does appear to be some sense to this notion, since rights are important for human beings in basic relationships they have with any powerful figure who can exercise some control over their lives. And surely God's omnipotence together with his interest in human life suggests that humans need some assurance that God will respect their freedom?

Thus, there are theologians who want to speak of the rights persons hold against God. Albert Knudson, for instance, takes

Brunner to task for his criticisms of the doctrine of natural rights from a theological point of view, for saying that rights have no place in the Christian ethic of love, and that all the goods of life are gifts of God's grace, not rights. To this Knudson responds:

But if this be true in an absolute sense, there is no moral order. Duties vanish as well as rights. The only way in which the idea of a moral universe can be maintained is by ascribing moral responsibility to God and a limited independence to man. As Creator of the world, God is a responsible being, and we his creatures have rights over against him as well as duties to him. The failure to see this is due to a one-sided and exaggerated conception of divine grace, a conception that is excluded by the fact of human freedom.[30]

Likewise, Christopher Wright refers to human rights against God in the context of scriptural examples. He thinks that 'the Exodus was a "declaration of right" inasmuch as *Israel had a right to be redeemed*'.[31] And he goes on to say:

For God had, in his sovereign freedom, chosen to *make himself responsible for Israel*. In his covenant with Abraham, God not only undertook a responsibility towards Abraham in the form of a promise, he also bound himself to himself, as it were. (*ibid.*)

Clearly the mention of a binding promise here implies that God has created a situation in which a special moral right comes into being with the covenant. But God's sovereignty remains, given that he is the dominant partner.

The major disadvantage in speaking of rights against God, and one which I think is insuperable, is mentioned by Joseph Allen in an article in the *Journal of Religious Ethics*.[32] He asks what could rights against God mean in practice? Can people claim long life, or health, or comfort? All that can be claimed, according to Allen, is what God has promised – steadfast love. But is this really significant, asks Allen?

But of what use is that claim? Of no use against God, because it is his nature to love, and we cannot conceive (from the standpoint of Christian faith) of circumstances in which we might ever have to assert that right, that is, of any instance when the promise would not be kept.[33]

The notion of claiming against God makes no sense, because the language of rights only fits a world where persons live under the shadow of ignorance and selfishness. Human beings need rights against others because of the general moral weakness of the whole race, which makes human living so vulnerable. But God is never a threat to personal welfare and flourishing, as fellow human beings can be.

The discussion so far has been designed to underline the difficulties of speaking analogously about rights in relation to God. It is exceedingly difficult to know how the language of rights can be applied strictly in this area when the differences between God and humanity are noted. It appears that the very features of human life which make the language of rights essential are not features of God's life as he has been traditionally conceived. I shall leave to others the possibility of applying the language of rights to God from less traditional perspectives.

GROUNDING RIGHTS IN HUMAN DIGNITY

While accepting that respect for human rights in practice does not require a theological justification, but essentially secular–humanistic reasons which are open to all men and women who have reached the age of moral discernment, I am still interested in the question of theological foundations for the language of rights. I feel that there are particularly distinctive religious justifying reasons which derive from Christian tradition and which change the content of respect for rights for the believer. Having rejected the approach which tries to derive human rights from God's rights, I now wish to explore what I believe is a more favourable approach, namely, that God gives rights to human beings against one another because of his providential care for his children, whether they believe in him or not. This allows for the protection of human dignity, and also foils any attack on God's sovereignty.

The first point I can make is that God creates a world in which conflict is possible and in which that conflict is actualised by human freedom. And what interests me most in this context is the issue of moral conflict arising from human selfishness and pride. Though God does not will human sin, he is said to allow sin to occur with all its bad consequences, near and remote. But Christian revelation speaks of a God who, in a sense, 'responds' to human disobedience and alienation, through the grace of forgiveness and through moral and religious guidance in the 'old law' and the 'new law'.

Alan Falconer expresses the manner in which God uses conflict, with reference to the work of André Dumas on political theology:

In his analysis of the Old and New Testaments, André Dumas, in *Political Theology and the Life of the Church*, sees a recurrent pattern of conflict in the events recorded – a conflict which arises primarily because of the differences between individuals and groups. Such conflict possessed then, as it does now, both destructive and creative elements. It is particularly in the creative element of conflict that God is seen active. In such conflicts, God appears as the 'Disturber' or 'praesentia explosiva'.[34]

Thus, the concept of conflict is ambiguous from the Christian point of view. It appears that creative conflict is a valuable aspect of human becoming and human dignity. Falconer locates this creative conflict in the necessary self-assertion each individual needs to develop in order to flourish as a unique being (p. 199ff.). One's own self-assertiveness naturally comes up against the assertiveness of others in positive and negative ways, and the positive ways are an expression of this creative conflict. The language of rights, at its best, can be understood as part of this creative conflict, a response to oppressive and negative conflict as found in the selfish assertiveness which is injustice. The creative conflict, revealed in particular in the power to claim against others, is God's gift and task to those who often seem trapped in the web of destructive conflict. Thus, Falconer sums up the argument so far:

Human rights emerge as attempts to regulate the conflict between human beings or groups of human beings in such a way as to *protect* the individual or group and also in such a way as to *enable* human beings and groups to grow to maturity. Human rights reflect, then, and engage the two effects of conflict, viz. the destructive and the constructive or creative. (p. 201)

What is most interesting in Falconer's analysis above is the positive function given to rights in bringing about human maturity. Respect for rights in human life is not just a defensive need, though this is important as 'protection' against oppression (destructive conflict); it is also a positive, personal need with regard to 'enablement' (creative conflict) directed towards the attainment of maturity. Though Falconer does not stress the function of claiming as much as I would like, it seems to me that the 'enablement' mentioned above must include the capacity to claim for oneself basic goods necessary for personal flourishing. But such claiming itself entails struggle in so far as it is part of the process of maturation. Falconer does not say that the way in which rights regulate the conflict between human beings will be painless. I assume there will often be a difficulty in achieving a proper balance between creative and destructive conflict. It is only realistic to admit that claim-rights can themselves be morally jarring, contributing to the destructive conflict they are meant to overcome. However, such dangers must not be used to obscure the central point that without some conflict there can be no truly human life.

The position just enunciated is not Feinberg's position on claiming in another guise, though it bears a close enough relationship to his approach. The specifically theological colour involves the idea of God as 'Disturber' and as '*praesentia explosiva*'. How does this disturbing presence of God make itself felt through the language of rights? One answer must be that God disturbs the powerful of this world through the claims of the weaker members of the human race. This is one of the major insights of current theology of liberation, which refuses to accept a fatalistic approach to suffering arising from injustice. This form of theology seeks to enable the poor of the world to recognise their obligation to claim in God's name against oppressive forces. According to this vision, it is better to be crucified in the process of claiming basic rights, than to be crucified in cowardly silence.[35]

I believe that Falconer was influenced in his reference to God as 'Disturber' by the writing of David Jenkins, who tends to see rights as a weapon in 'God's warfare on behalf of men and women created in his image, and as part of his judgment on the inhumanities of societies and institutions, including those of the Church'.[36] If this position is valid, then it sheds a further light on the question of the moral content of rights. Here is an essential justifying reason, a further dimension of a vision, for the Christian who wishes to understand in a deeper way why respect for rights is important.

Allen, who has been mentioned already in relation to his critique of talk of rights against God, is quite prepared to accept that rights are God-given:

The right that corresponds to God's promise, along with the rights that correspond to the structure he has bestowed upon us in creation, reflects, from a Christian point of view, what is essential to true humanity. Therefore, whether because it is God's command, or because it is right to affirm one's true humanity, such fundamental rights need to be vindicated when they are brought under attack.[37]

The clear implication here is that rights, far from being an attempt to undermine God's sovereignty, are in fact a significant expression of respect for God's sovereignty over creation. This point is stressed as follows:

To speak of rights in these relationships, though, is not at all to compromise God's sovereignty, but to express it, because the rights that reflect what it is truly to be a person and therein a child of God are the expression of how God in his sovereign will has bound himself in steadfast love toward his creatures. The Christian understanding of God and man, far from being contradictory to the concept of moral rights belonging to persons, is inseparably connected with it. (p. 132)

DIGNITY AND THE IMAGE OF GOD

All that has been said so far in this section can be brought under the general heading of respect for human dignity. In Christian ethics it is extremely common to express this dignity in terms of humanity being created in God's image. A number of theologians mention this link between rights, dignity and the image of God in humankind.[38]

Now talk of human dignity and of humanity being a reflection of God's own life sounds highly impressive at a general level; it is when one tries to pin this kind of language down that difficulties begin to arise. James Childress summarises some of the controversies surrounding this concept in his article on the subject in the *New Dictionary of Christian Ethics*.[39] For instance, there is the basic question of how far the image of God in humankind has been damaged by original sin. Reformation theology tends to underline the essential damage done to the image itself, while Roman Catholic theology has tended to distinguish between a basic image which remains untouched and an added quality of grace which is lost in the Fall. (Sometimes this is based on a distinction found as early as Irenaeus between the 'image' and the 'likeness' of God and humanity.) However, it is again dangerous to speak of a unified 'Protestant' approach to this question, since Childress points out how Lutherans and Calvinists interpret the effects of original sin on man differently. Lutherans talk in terms of loss of the image; Calvinists in terms of corruption, not loss, of the image (p. 292).

The other major issue is that of locating the image of God in some distinctive feature of human nature. Childress has this to say:

Although the image of God is often construed as reason and free will, it has also been interpreted as spiritual capacities, such as self-transcendence or the capacity for and the call to relationship with God, and as excellences, such as righteousness. (p. 292)

Either approach mentioned in this quotation gives rise to embarrassing problems in grounding human dignity on this concept of image. If image is related to reason and free will, then there are the problems of grounding the dignity of humans lacking these capacities – embryos, young children, the severely retarded, the comatose, the demented. On the other hand, if the image of God in humanity is dependent on a person's actual response to others in spiritual and moral relationships, then as well as the same problems with the categories just mentioned, one may also have problems maintaining the dignity of solitary persons, those suffering from psychopathic and sociopathic disorders and persons who make a radically self-centred fundamental option. If the image of God in man and woman is dependent on one's moral record in terms of responsibility to others, then it seems likely that the image of God will come and go, grow stronger and weaker in the course of daily life.

I think it would be a pity to allow ourselves to be distracted at this point by the exceptions to the rule. My suggestion is that we should first of all explore the meaning of God's image as this applies in normal cases, and then deal with the problematic exceptions. In this work I shall only deal with the general application of the theme of image to morally mature adults. In the following I shall adopt a scriptural approach which, likewise, does not take exceptional cases into account.

THE IMAGE OF GOD IN SCRIPTURE

According to M. Flick and Z. Alszeghy, there are three main aspects to be underlined when studying the theme of image, especially in the opening chapters of Genesis.[40] First, there is the declaration that humankind is the high-point of God's creation. In particular humans are superior to the members of the animal kingdom (p. 62). This is seen in the change in the description in the Genesis account – from saying that the creation of all material reality before mankind is 'good' (for example Gen. 1.25), to saying that with the creation of man something 'very good' has come to light (Gen. 1.31). Man's feeling of loneliness in the midst of the animals, which is overcome only by the creation of woman from man, is another sign of human superiority, as is the bringing of the animals to man by God to be named (Gen. 2.20–1).

Second, the image of God is found in humanity's capacity to enter into dialogue with the Deity. Man is dignified with the possibility of entering into a personal relationship with his Lord. As Martin Buber declares: 'The great achievement of Israel is not to have taught the one true God ... it is to have shown that it was possible in reality to speak to Him, to say "Thou" to Him, to stand upright before his face.'[41] Adam and Eve walk with their God in the cool of evening in paradise.

And third, Flick and Alszeghy point to man's special role as God's co-worker and vice-regent in relation to the universe. All the rest of creation is ordered to him and placed under his command (Gen. 1.28).[42] Thus, man has duties to work in co-operation with God in a creative way, if he is to be in a right relation to the rest of creation.

In his treatment of this theme in scripture, Albert Gelin[43] makes much of the superiority of humanity in relation to the animals. He refers to the theory that man's upright posture differentiates him from the animals and represents his likeness to God, only to reject such an interpretation as too anthropomorphic for the priestly writer.[44] He prefers to follow the theory of Edmund Jacob, which interprets the image of God as 'a royal function, a delegation to be lord of the animal kingdom'.[45] This same idea is found highlighted in Psalm 8, where it is said that man has been made 'little less than a god' in the context of his dominion over material reality. From the wisdom literature Sirach also refers to Genesis and man's power over creatures:

> The Lord created man out of earth,
> and turned him back to it again...
> He endowed them with strength like his own,
> and made them in his own image.
> He placed the fear of them in all living beings,
> and granted them dominion over beasts and birds...
> (Sir. 17.1ff.)

But Gelin now adds an interesting twist to the interpretation. He suggests that the animals dominated by humanity may be symbols of evil. For in oriental literature evil is often portrayed in this way. Psalm 74 refers by name to monstrous beasts – dragons and serpents. Apocalyptic works favour this imagery too, as in the Books of Daniel and Revelation (the beast with seven heads). So Gelin concludes:

Man rules over the beasts, but he is also the conqueror of evil: he is, by his very nature, the imitator of God, ready to fight against evil. In the expression 'image of God,' there is consequently something like a call to arms, a dynamic invitation to action. (p. 33)

Here then the notion of image is given a moral meaning. Man is the imitator of God in fighting against evil. Gelin argues that strictly speaking this moral imperative comes from the covenant theme not from the theme of image, but what he has said already leads him to state that 'the moral imperative of imitation can be said to have been derived from the theme of the image if we take the term "imitation" in a very broad sense: imitate God in his battle against evil, in his labour, and be the humble reproduction of God's activity' (*ibid.*, p. 34). The command to rest on the sabbath (Exod. 20.11), for instance, seems to take the Genesis account of creation as a model for human as well as divine activity. Gelin wishes to keep separate the ideas of image and covenant, but I can see little reason to do so. I would prefer to say that creation is the first and primary covenant. Creation is promisory in offering the possibility of freely accepting a loving relationship with God. It is like a law covenant in that humanity is expected to work with God against all that would try to return creation to chaos. From the beginning in the Garden, conditions are laid down for the first parents, obedience to which would maintain their relationship with God. Disobedience involves the breaking of covenant and the obscuring of the image of God in man.

There is a degree of irony in saying that God made humanity in his image in order to share in his battle against evil, since the very possibility of evil comes from the creation of free creatures. One major response to this in Christian theodicy is the 'Free-Will Defence' theory which says that God permits evil as a real possibility if freedom is to be real.[46] Thus God does not will evil directly, but recognising its possibility and probability he creates persons with the capacity to fall and to pick themselves up again.

To be made in God's image is to participate in the struggle to use freedom properly. The abuse of freedom is, according to Gelin, the failure to recognise the limits of the power given by God in making humankind in his image. 'The first Adam was the image of God; he became arrogant and forgot that image does not imply equality with God but relationship with him, a delegation of power.'[47] The perfection of freedom lies by contrast in the example of Christ, the second Adam, who 'did not exalt himself, on the ground of his likeness to God, but, on the contrary abased himself'.[48]

The 'original sin', then, is a failure to respect the original covenant of creation, which makes persons in God's image.[49] This is a twofold failure, firstly in relation to God and secondly in relation to fellow humans. The concept of religious covenant, we saw, is characterised by a fundamental inequality between the partners, with the emphasis on the superior status of the one who initiates the covenant, God. According to the traditional myth of original sin, what I have called the 'covenant of creation' is broken by the attempt on the part of people from the beginning to establish a false sense of equality between themselves and their creator. But once this basic relationship is misunderstood and perverted there follows a perversion of the relationship between persons. Specifically, this involves a failure to recognise the equal dignity of others, exemplified in the murder of Abel by Cain – 'Whoever sheds the blood of man, by man shall his blood be shed; for God made man in his own image' (Gen. 9.6). This first murder is the first failure to respect a human right. Not only is it a matter of depriving a person of life, but it is also an insult to the person in the sense that it refuses to treat another as one's equal, as an end in himself rather than as a means to the fulfilment of one's own projects.

So we have brought together a number of models which seem to be intimately interconnected. Creation in God's image can be understood with the help of the covenant model, with the suggestion that man's creation is the first covenant he experiences. To reflect the nature of God in truth, men and women must recognise the limitations of their status as unequal to God, but as equal to all other persons. Unfortunately, however, these two aspects of the truth were, and still are, too often ignored.

The reference to human status must remind us of the freedom model we have also used above. Absence of constraint and opportunity to act are basic to freedom, but as a model of rights the freedom we are interested in is that which we can validly claim against others, not simply that which is allowed or given

by the kindness of others. This freedom which is an aspect of the
theme of image and of the creation-covenant implies that, as
made in God's image, we do not have rights against God or
against the lower orders of creation, but only against our fellow
humans. This is because the lower orders (plants and animals)
do not enjoy moral freedom; God's freedom is so perfect that
speaking of rights against him makes little sense, as Allen
argued; so that rights are only claimable against those whose
freedom has both positive and negative potential, namely other
persons.

Freedom's negative potential is expressed in the rejection of
our status as made in God's image, and is seen both in the
exploitation of our environment and the injustice shown
towards people. The violation of rights is then an offence
against the creation-covenant and a betrayal of our own natural
dignity. It involves the living out of a double lie, that we are
equal to God and superior to those fellow humans who are weak
and easily bullied. Respect for rights, on the other hand, is an
aspect of freedom's positive potential, because it stands for the
truth of the implications of being made in the image of God, and
thus remaining faithful to the primary covenant. The language
of rights is made possible by the reality of freedom. Abuse of
freedom is part of the causal definition of rights as we mentioned
earlier. Because we are tempted to forget the equal status of
those around us, the claiming of rights is necessary as a salutary
reminder of the dignified treatment due to all. Making just
claims for ourselves and for others (or enabling them to make
claims for themselves) is an antidote to the negative use of
freedom and an expression of the human dignity which, as
God's image, is concerned with reflecting God's struggle against
all that would distort his original creation. And this brings us
back to the set of arguments mentioned earlier in this chapter by
Alan Falconer and David Jenkins, namely, that rights are
weapons in God's warfare on behalf of men and women made in
his image, or the human attack on evil under God's inspiration.

The idea that men and women have a special status, inferior
to God, yet reflecting his divinity, and equal to one another in
basic worth, is a uniting factor in bringing together the models

of image, covenant and freedom. But what of the other major
model we have employed – power? Does it have relevance in
relation to these other models? Pretty clearly it does, since
power and freedom are closely related as we have noted. And,
above all, the concept of image has been interpreted as a
'delegation of power' by God. This power is of course partly
physical, the kind used to actually adapt creative forces to the
needs and wants of persons. However, in the context of Christian
ethics, our emphasis has been on the moral aspects of our being
made in the image of God, so what concerns us primarily is the
way in which this status delegates moral power to us in day to
day living.

First, in relation to the world of nature, (what I have called
the 'lower orders of creation'), the use of power by humanity
must have a positive moral quality. What was said earlier about
exploitative and manipulative forms of power in human
relationships also applies to some extent to our relationship with
our natural environment. As stewards of creation we do not
have absolute moral power over the plants and animals, such
that any destruction we visit on non-rational creatures would be
judged to be morally neutral. It must be remembered that other
creatures have their own ends to pursue, their own laws to
follow, not as important as human projects perhaps, but
relatively important all the same.[50] This is a conclusion we
might draw from a statement included in a document from the
Second Vatican Council which speaks about the value and the
limits of human autonomy *vis-à-vis* our environment: 'By the
very nature of creation, material being is endowed with its own
stability, truth and excellence, its own order and laws. These
man must respect as he recognises the methods proper to every
science and technique.'[51] The authors seem to have in mind the
supposed conflict between scientific knowledge of our world and
knowledge by revelation, wishing to dissociate themselves from
those who subordinate the former to the latter. In the same
passage, however, they criticise a false form of autonomy:

However, if by the term 'the autonomy of earthly affairs' is meant that
material being does not depend on God and that man can use it as if
it had no relation to its creator, then the falsity of such a claim will be

obvious to anyone who believes in God. Without a creator there can be no creature. In any case, believers, no matter what their religion, have always recognised the voice and the revelation of God in the language of creatures. Besides, once God is forgotten, the creature is lost sight of as well. (*ibid.*)

The Roman Catholic Church here teaches that humanity's treatment of nature must follow God's will not human whims. If nature is used by God to reveal his truth, then it too has a dignity which we ignore at our peril. Furthermore, one can turn around the final statement in the passage just quoted and declare that 'once the creature is forgotten, God is lost sight of as well'.

Second, we arrive at the central issue of how power is to be exercised between people in such a way that we remain faithful to our identity as images of God. In our discussion of human power and its various types, we tended to stress the moral superiority of those types which respected human freedom to the greatest degree. Though power often has to bypass consent and rely on force, the ideal form of power we claimed was what we called 'authority'. This does not rely on threatened sanctions or actual force to change the behaviour of others, but depends on reason to win over others to a certain way of thinking and acting. The presumption is that authority is the highest form of moral power, and this is why our translations of the New Testament speak often of the 'authority' of Jesus in his preaching.[52] Thus we argued that the authority model is useful for our understanding rights, since these normative relationships are best exercised in a voluntary context, where claimants and duty-bearers act for the best reasons and not out of compulsion.

It may be objected that the image theme refers mainly to the power which God has delegated to humankind over nature, which is inferior in status, and not to the relationship between humans who enjoy the same basic status. In other words, does the image theme offer any justification for the exercise of personal power over others?

To answer this objection we must recall the different types of power relationships mentioned by Rollo May. The ideal type of power relationship, he argued, was the one called 'power with'.

This type is experienced in situations where we are in relationship with mature adults who have a desire to act in a morally responsible way. Exercising rights can be an example of such power with others. I claim a right in a particular instance by calling on another to perform a particular duty or obligation for my benefit. To some extent this may involve a burden on the duty-bearer (and also on myself, especially if the right is of the 'mandatory' type), but the underlying quality of this normative relationship is expressed by saying that two people are co-operating morally in achieving a common value. The claimant exercises 'power with' the duty-bearer, so that in the same action both agents respect each other equally.

But not all relationships are in this category. 'Nutrient power' or 'power for' another is typical of the more paternalistic relationship. While recognising that the other has equal worth with myself, I am forced to accept an inequality at the level of maturity and moral responsibility. The other person may be incompetent to some degree and needs me to protect him. When I claim rights on behalf of another in this way, as a parent for a child, for instance, then the power exercised is nutrient power or 'power for' another. Furthermore, this type of power may fit those occasions when we claim rights against those who are competent, but for various reasons simply will not respect the rights of others. In enforcing rights, then, we are not really manipulating or exploiting others, we are not using 'power over' or 'against' these stubborn individuals. We are simply treating them like naughty children who do not know what is best for themselves or for other people. They are in need of education, the kind provided by our exercise of nutrient power. And in time they may even be grateful to us for pointing out their mistakes.

Now this type of power relationship sounds like the ideal for a person made in God's image. If God is a father who cares for his children, then to be made in his image surely includes a similar relationship not only to the world of animals and plants, but in particular to those humans who refuse to be guided by the Father's will and by the helpful rules he gives for our flourishing. Working for rights seems to involve a use of nutrient power when we are facing people who seem to have little or no respect for rights. God, in creating us according to his image and likeness, delegated his fatherly power to us, a power which is partially expressed in the language of rights. Struggling against evil in imitation of God is like a father struggling to make his children see sense.

I do not wish to deny the value of this model completely, but I think that its major disadvantages must be obvious. Paternalism concerning adults is always extremely dangerous as a moral position. It easily leads to a patronising stance, and to a pride which refuses to listen to the experience of others. When the paternalism is given a religious justification, and involves the imposition of moral positions said to have divine authority, then the dangers increase. What may begin with good intentions to respect rights actually achieves the opposite – the treatment of the morally mature in an infantile manner.

Therefore, my suggestion is that, if we accept the view that the delegation of power is an aspect of the image of God in us, we should emphasise that this is of the type we have called (following May) 'integrative power' or 'power with'. This, rather than nutrient power, is the form chosen by God when dealing with his people. We have called it power-in-weakness, and noted its presence in God's seemingly infinite capacity for waiting on his personal creation to respond to the constant offer of covenant. God has the power to overcome all evil in an instant, according to the traditional interpretation of omnipotence, but he prefers to involve human weakness in the ongoing struggle. In the example of Christ the stature of waiting is given special value in his painful waiting for the human response to his offer of love. Thus, he refuses to act in a paternalistic mode, but prefers to rely on the model of friendship to describe his expectations of his disciples.[53]

There is, of course, an important difference between the integrative power employed by God and his Christ, and the version of this power employed by us. We do not have the same moral strength or perfection as our models. Thus, we cannot afford to claim that we are always waiting for others to respect the truth of our moral position, that we alone have full respect for rights and that we are waiting in frustration for non-believers to catch up with Christian insights. This is not required doctrine for those who hold that Christian ethics is distinctive. Integrative power or power with others is an essential aspect of the 'inclusive' covenant which is made with all persons created by God. All participate in this covenant in so far as they are made in God's image. All are delegated the power to work with God and others to overcome evil, not merely religious believers. Although particular religious moral traditions may be helpful in fulfilling our role as images of God, there must be room for learning from those who do not belong to institutional Christianity, but still have important insights derived from their experience of the inclusive covenant. Power with others is open to learning from all who are made in God's image.

CONCLUSION

Various interconnected models of rights have been used to throw light on the nature of claims or entitlements. Some, like freedom and power, are basically humanistic metaphors or models, but derive additional insight from Judaeo-Christian themes, such as covenant and image. These in turn, of course, are important metaphors or models for religious ethics. The covenant model, while having special religious connotations, is also useful at the humanistic or secular level of discussion, as we saw in the case of the doctor–patient relationship. No doubt, parallel applications could be worked out for other associated roles and relationships without any necessary reference to God. The model of image, however, is fundamentally theological (even though older than either Judaism or Christianity), and will cause the greatest problems for the secular thinker. Even for the Christian believer or theologian this model has its difficulties, as we have pointed out. Still, as a model it has great synthetic value, i.e. it draws together in a comprehensive way the essential characteristics of the other models of freedom, power and covenant.

Each model appears to exist at a different level of generality. The most general is that of image, where the resemblance between God and his creatures is partly shrouded in mystery, and where the very fact of there being a resemblance is awe-inspiring. The temptation is to simply sit back in silent worship. But the theologian cannot afford this luxury, at least not for long. The image model must be cashed at the further levels of covenant, freedom and power. Covenant relationship is the most basic form in which humanity experiences the reality of being moulded in the image of God. But it is freedom and power which further specify the nature of covenant. God supposedly gives power and freedom to his human creation in relation to himself. He gives his name to the Israelites (Exod. 3.14–15) and the freedom to be either obedient or disobedient. In the language of rights we notice the same freedom and power bestowed on humans in their normative relationships. Therefore we are moving down a religious and ethical scale from the more abstract level to the more concrete, depending on the model being used. At the most concrete level, to treat others as slaves implies a refusal to apply the models of image and covenant to them, for the lack of basic freedom and power of the slave makes it impossible for him or her to represent God or to enter into (human) relationships characterised by an essential equality.

Each model is a mixture of image and concept which reveals something of the nature and value of rights-language. Yet none of them is a literal description or explanation of rights. In line with the nature of metaphorical thought, rights are not identical with moral freedom and power; they do not exhaust the covenant relationship or the theme of being made in God's image. However, these notions do help underline the specific nature of rights, and at the same time rights-talk goes some way towards elucidating the meaning of these major models.

Finally, the imaginative use of models has contributed to the effort of justifying the language of rights. This has been made possible by the recognition of fundamental value judgements concerning human life and relationships in each model studied. None of these models is morally neutral. All of them are based on some normative position regarding our existence. This is most obvious perhaps in the models of freedom and power, but it is not difficult to find profound moral value judgements in any discussion of covenant and image. The distinction between covenant and contract, the various types of covenants and their intimate connection with different types of rights – human and special – should alert us to such positive moral connotations. Similarly, with the model of image: the possibility of understanding this in ideal terms as a sharing of God's authority; of participating in integrative power or power with God and others; of struggling with God against chaos; and of alerting others, as well as ourselves, to the existence of a special dignity which is ultimately a gift – all of these features contribute to an overall vision of life and morality into which the language of rights fits rather appropriately.

Epilogue

In my study of the role of imagination, the debt I owe to scholars like McFague, Black and Barbour, among others, must be evident. In particular I have derived great benefit from reading Sallie McFague's writings on models and metaphorical theology. In conclusion I would like to comment briefly on some important issues McFague introduces concerning the proper criteria for judging the success of theological models.[1] I want to relate these issues to my metaethical models of rights.

Some of the criteria mentioned by McFague have been implicit in the initial discussion of metaphors and models in chapter five. For instance, a good model is fairly comprehensive, taking into account diverse dimensions of experience, being 'extensible', i.e. capable of expansion and application to novel areas or topics. In relation to rights-language we applied this criterion when trying to judge the value of simple metaphors or models like the 'safety net', 'the flashing light', and 'the chain'.

Another criterion used to judge models involves consistency. Here we can think of internal consistency, where the concern is with the ways in which various parts of the model fit together without contradiction; and we can also consider external consistency whereby one model does not contradict another related model. Thus, we have been interested in showing that the 'freedom' and 'power' models of rights are consistent in themselves and between themselves. Another criterion is implicit in the criterion of external consistency. It follows from the point that one model is hardly ever sufficient on its own to express the full meaning of the topic being explored. We tend to need a number of different models to help us to understand some complex area of human behaviour. The criterion I have in mind here is one of 'humility'. I realise that this would be better predicated of the user of a model than of the model itself, but the basic point must be clear. A successful model does not think too highly of itself, recognises its limitations, and the help it requires from other models if a full picture of the reality in question is to appear. It does not regard itself as the literal truth or the full truth on any complex matter.

From these simple examples of criteria, McFague presents two further examples which are of key importance (p. 139). First, she stresses the importance of the complementarity of our models. Consistency and complementarity are related, but not identical. To be consistent it is sufficient that one model does not contradict another. To be complementary one model must be able to add to the knowledge derived from other related models. Cumulative imaginative power is in question at this level.

The four main models of rights used in this work appear to be complementary as well as consistent. As McFague expresses the general point, 'The major models in a theology... must share characteristics which identify them as belonging to the same syndrome.' So, when we turn to the models of 'image', 'covenant', 'freedom' and 'power', we find fundamentally similar characteristics. Each model is personal and interpersonal or relational. Each has a key reference to moral or normative relationships, their protection and promotion. Each speaks of moral ambiguity, of respect for persons and their dignity, and of an ultimate relationship to God as the ground of all value. More important still, each model adds to our understanding of rights and normative relationships by providing a slightly different perspective from its companions. The model of image requires the covenant model to flesh it out. According to Judaeo-Christian tradition, persons were created for covenant-style relationships. The covenant model is rich enough to cover all types of relationships from the universal and inclusive to the particular and relatively exclusive. It offers a religious perspective on human rights and special rights. But the other models – 'freedom' and 'power' – provide an extra viewpoint on the actual exercise of rights. In many situations, though not all, claiming rights is a prime example of free choice, and protects this form of human autonomy. We noted that a particular type of power – authority or power-with others – contributes a helpful perspective on the healthy or ideal exercise of rights. This is not to say that these four models together provide the complete picture of the nature and value of rights-language, but, arguably, they do present us with a useful framework within which we can paint in further details, or add in more skilful brush strokes.

Another criterion of the good model which McFague regards as important is 'the ability of models to cope with anomalies, with "contra-factors"'.[2] She is thinking here of certain relevant events, situations, or experiences which a model fails to cover. This seems to be an aspect of the criterion of comprehensiveness, but it is worth a further emphasis. Of the examples used by McFague the most striking are the Jewish Holocaust, which places 'considerable strain on traditional models of evil'; and some forms of feminist critique which challenge what is thought of as a patriarchal model of God (p. 140). The more efficiently a model copes with such anomalies the more satisfying it will be.

Do the models of rights we have used cope with such 'contra-factors'? In one major way I feel they do help us. I have in mind a point made above regarding the complementarity of our models, namely, that they have in common a recognition of moral ambiguity. By this I mean that each model not only helps to organise our images and concepts of how rights might operate ideally, but they also provide an awareness of how the language and the exercise of rights can go morally astray. The image model is aware of the dignity implied in sharing in God's power over and with others which rights involve. But it is also painfully aware of the distortion of that image in the sin of idolatry. This occurs when our self-image is faulty, especially when we think of ourselves as equal to God and superior to other humans at a fundamental level.[3] The covenant model is aware of the challenge to pass beyond our special moral relationships and special rights, to wider, universal relationships and human rights, but the history of covenant shows a reluctance to accept the latter trend. Still, that universalism is inherent in the model.

And obviously similar points can be made regarding freedom and power models. Not every claim or demand will be an expression of human freedom and power. At times, even our claims on behalf of others will use positive sounding moral terms like 'justified paternalism' and 'authority', when in fact our activity will be manipulative or exploitative. So these models need to be distinguished carefully and applied with caution in individual situations.

Finally, there is the criterion of 'empirical fit'. McFague states that, 'Models must "fit" with "data," not scientific but human data' (p. 141.). A theological model, or a metaethical model for that matter, is valuable only in so far as it can exist outside the rarefied atmosphere of academic discussion and metaphysical systems. It must relate to experience. And this experience, according to McFague, 'is not life as conventionally lived or usually understood, but at its deepest level, or as it could be or ought to be, might have been' (*ibid.*). This is a useful remark in that it gives us some protection in using imaginative models against the off-hand rejection by those who live life superficially and who are not used to the imagination at work. It is also a support for those who profess Christian belief, but whose 'experience' may seem irrational and bizarre to the non-believer. Empirical fit does not refer to the lowest common denominator of everyday experience, or to some crude form of positivism, whereby only the evidence of our physical senses is believed. It refers to life 'at its deepest level', and, more tantalising still, it can refer to a form of life which beckons to us, but does not yet exist.

For the Christian the 'human data' mentioned by McFague, against which our models must be tested for their 'empirical fit', is not merely what actually is, but what has been in the human life of Jesus of Nazareth and remains as a challenge due to his resurrection from the dead. In his resurrection, Jesus as God's image becomes the model of humanity for the believer.[4] But this reality is, for the eyes of faith, more than simply a human datum. The traditional orthodox Christology, from Chalcedon on, stresses the inseparability of the humanity and divinity of Jesus, even if the two 'natures' can be distinguished. Hence, when we pointed to the example of the human life of Jesus in our discussion of models of rights, we were also pointing to a mode of divine action. It is the God–Man who is free through his obedience, and who waits for the human response of love. And when his present-day disciples use the language of rights, that vision of the ways in which the Lord related to people colours their experience of normative relationships; it can even transform the practice or exercise of rights.

At this stage, of course, the language of experience has been stretched to its limits. Some may say that such an extension of the concept is extreme. Even imagination will not lead us to this point. This is true. Imagination is not faith. The non-believer can use his or her imagination to attempt to stand in the shoes of the believer. The models of rights used may help in that process. They build on human experience common to believer and non-believer, but ultimately they bring us to the edge of a precipice where the secular imagination faces its limit. However, even to arrive at that point means that Christian ethics and secular ethics have much in common regarding the meaning and value of rights.

Notes

1 Joel Feinerg, 'The Nature and Value of Rights', in his *Rights, Justice and the Bounds of Liberty: Essays in Social Philosophy* (Princeton, New Jersey, Princeton University Press, 1980), pp. 143-57, quotation at p. 143.

2 *Ibid.*, p. 143.

3 P. H. Nowell-Smith, *Ethics* (Baltimore, Penguin, 1954).

4 Gilbert Harman, *The Nature of Morality: An Introduction to Ethics* (New York, Oxford University Press, 1977), Preface, p. viii. For general discussions of the distinction see: W. D. Hudson, *Modern Moral Philosophy*, Modern Introductions to Philosophy series (London/Basingstoke, Macmillan, 1970), ch. 1; H. J. McCloskey, *Meta-Ethics and Normative Ethics* (The Hague, Martinus Nijhoff, 1969); Alan Gewirth, 'Meta-Ethics and Normative Ethics', *Mind*, 69 (1960), pp. 187–205; Kai Nielsen, 'Ethics, Problems of', in Paul Edwards (ed.), *The Encyclopedia of Philosophy* (London, Collier/Macmillan, New York, Free Press/Macmillan), cxi, pp. 117–34; W. Frankena, *Ethics*, 2nd edition (Foundations of Philosophy series) (New Jersey, Prentice-Hall, 1973), ch. 6; R. M. Hare, *Moral Thinking: Its Levels, Method and Point* (Oxford, Clarendon Press, 1981), pp. 25–6; From a religious perspective see: N. H. G. Robinson, *The Groundwork of Christian Ethics* (London, Collins, 1971); Garth L. Hallett, *Christian Moral Reasoning* (Notre Dame, Indiana, Notre Dame University Press, 1983); Gerard J. Hughes, *Authority in Morals*, Heythrop Monographs (London, Sheed and Ward, 1978); Bruno Schuller, *Wholly Human: Essays in the Theory and Language of Morality*, trans. P. Heinegg (Dublin, Gill and Macmillan, Washington, Georgetown University Press, 1986); Ian C. M. Fairweather and James I. H. McDonald, *The Quest for Christian Ethics: An Inquiry into Ethics and Christian Ethics* (Edinburgh, Handsel Press, 1984).

5 Nielsen, 'Ethics, Problems of', p. 119.

6 John A. Henley, 'Theology and the Basis of Human Rights',

Scottish Journal of Theology, 39 (1986), pp. 361–78, quotation at p. 367.

7 Lisa Sowle Cahill, 'Toward a Christian Theory of Human Rights', *Journal of Religious Ethics*, 8/2 (1980), pp. 277–301, quotation at p. 277.

I METAETHICS: MEANING AND JUSTIFICATION

1 W. Frankena, *Ethics*, 2nd edition (Foundations of Philosophy series) (New Jersey, Prentice-Hall, 1973), p. 96.

2 *Ibid.*

3 Alan R. White, *Rights* (Oxford, Clarendon Press, 1984), p. 16.

4 On the subject of the relationship between morality and etiquette see P. Foot, 'Are Moral Considerations Overriding?' in her *Virtues and Vices and Other Essays in Moral Philosophy* (Oxford, Basil Blackwell, 1978), and W. D. Hudson, *A Century of Moral Philosophy* (Guildford and London, Lutterworth, 1980), ch. 7.

5 Cf. J. L. Austin, *How To Do Things With Words* (Oxford, University Press, 1965). See also J. Searle, *Speech Acts* (Cambridge, University Press, 1969).

6 For some of the philosophical problems related to promises see Annette Baier, 'Promises, Promises, Promises', in her *Postures of the Mind: Essays on Mind and Morals* (London, Methuen, 1985) and P. S. Atiyah, *Promises, Morals and the Law* (Oxford, Clarendon Press, 1981).

7 For the 'Right/Good' distinction see Frankena, *Ethics*, ch. 1, where he connects 'right' with 'judgements of moral obligation' or 'deontic' judgements, and 'good' with 'judgements of moral value' or, as he calls them, 'aretaic' judgements (p. 9). A classic reference to this distinction is W. D. Ross, *The Right and the Good* (Oxford, Clarendon Press, 1963), chs. 2 and 5, esp. p. 137. For some objections to the distinction, see Michael Stocker, 'Rightness and Goodness, Is There a Difference?', *American Philosophical Quarterly*, 10 (1973), pp. 87–98; Elizabeth Pybus, 'False Dichotomies: Right and Good', *Philosophy*, 58 (1983), pp. 19–27; Peter Geach, 'Good and Evil', in P. Foot (ed.), *Theories of Ethics*, Oxford Readings in Philosophy (Oxford, University Press, 1967), pp. 64–73, esp. p. 72.

8 For a bibliography on definition, see John Hospers, *An Introduction to Philosophical Analysis*, 2nd edition (London, Routledge and Kegan Paul, 1967) p. 100; especially Richard Robinson, *Definition*, (New York, Oxford University Press, 1950), and W. V. O. Quine, *Word and Object*, (New York, John Wiley and Sons, Inc., 1960);

R. M. Hare, *The Language of Morals* (London/Oxford/New York, Oxford University Press, 1967), pp. 86–93. Whether ethical terms such as 'good' can be defined was the subject of impassioned discussion among philosophers at the turn of this century. In his *Principia Ethica* (Cambridge, University Press, 1903), G. E. Moore claimed that 'good' is a simple, non-natural property, incapable of definition in either naturalistic or metaphysical terms. To define 'good' in terms of pleasure, for instance, was for Moore, a prime example of the 'Naturalistic Fallacy'. The 'good' is known through direct intuition, not by means of analysis or definition. Moore did hold, however, that other ethical terms, 'right' for instance, could be defined, and there is nothing in his work which would suggest that the language of rights is intractable from the point of view of definition.

9 See Quine, who calls into question the possibility of translating terms by means of synonyms in his famous article 'Two Dogmas of Empiricism', in *From A Logical Point of View: 9 Logico-Philosophical Essays*, 2nd revised edition (New York and Evanston, Harper and Row, 1961), pp. 20–46.

10 Hospers, *Philosophical Analysis*, p. 24.

11 *Ibid.*, pp. 56–62.

12 M. B. Cohen and E. Nagel, *An Introduction to Logic* (New York, Harcourt, Brace and World, 1962). They distinguish between 'subjective', 'essential' and 'objective' intension, while stressing 'essential intension' – the necessary and sufficient conditions for the application of a word, pp. 31–2). The traditional notion of connotation is discussed by John Stuart Mill in *A System of Logic* (London, Longman's Green and Co., 1884), Bk. 1, ch. 2, s. 5.

13 See Hospers, *Philosophical Analysis*, pp. 32–3.

14 Wesley Hohfeld, *Fundamental Legal Conceptions*, W. W. Cook (ed.) (New Haven, Connecticut, Yale University Press, 1919).

15 Carl Wellman, 'A New Conception of Human Rights,' in E. Kamenka and A. E. S. Tay (eds.), *Human Rights* (London, Edward Arnold, 1978).

16 This distinction is found in Joel Feinberg, 'A Postscript to The Nature and Value of Rights', in *Rights Justice and the Bounds of Liberty: Essays in Social Philosophy* (Princeton, New Jersey, University Press, 1980), pp. 156–7. The author is sceptical concerning 'mandatory rights' because they do not give a person full liberty to act or forbear. 'But so-called "mandatory rights" to do x confer only the half-liberty to do x without the other half-liberty not to do x. Why then are they called "rights" at all?' (p. 157). This point is echoed by L. W. Sumner in *The Moral Foundation of Rights*

(Oxford, Clarendon Press, 1987), where he claims that mandatory rights may be 'deviant or oxymoronic', p. 34.

17 Hospers, *Philosophical Analysis*, p. 30.

18 Jeremy Bentham, *The Limits of Jurisprudence Defined*, C. W. Everett (ed.) (New York, 1945), pp. 57–9, cited in White, *Rights*, p. 2.

19 Hohfeld, *Fundamental Legal Conceptions*, p. 30.

20 White, *Rights*, p. 2.

21 H. L. A. Hart, 'Definition and Theory in Jurisprudence', in *Essays in Jurisprudence and Philosophy* (Oxford, Clarendon Press, 1983), pp. 21–48.

22 The American realists include jurists such as Oliver Wendell Holmes (1841–1935), Jerome Frank (1889–1957) and Karl Llewellyn (1893–1962).

23 The Scandinavian realists include Axel Hagerstrom (1868–1939), Alf Ross (1899–1979), and Karl Olivecrona (1897–1980).

24 Hart, 'Definition', p. 31.

25 Ludwig Wittgenstein, *Philosophical Investigations*, trans. G. E. M. Anscombe (Oxford, Blackwell, 1953). W. D. Hudson provides a brief summary of the development of Wittgenstein's theory of meaning in *Modern Moral Philosophy* (London, Macmillan, 1970), pp. 44ff., 'Wittgenstein believed that he had been wrong in the *Tractatus* because he had tried to impose on language a preconceived idea of what its meaning ought to be. He came to think that what he should have done instead is to "*look at* its use and learn from that".' (*Philosophical Investigations*, 340); Hudson, p. 45. We must be careful when dealing with philosophical slogans like 'Don't ask for the meaning; ask for the use.' About this slogan J. N. Findlay comments: '... the use for which it bids us ask, is of all things the most obscure, the most veiled in philosophical mists, the most remote from detailed determination or application, in the wide range of philosophical concepts'. 'Use, Usage and Meaning', in G. H. R. Parkinson (ed.), *The Theory of Meaning*, Oxford Readings in Philosophy (Oxford, University Press, 1968), pp. 117–18. Findlay argues that the 'use' of language is a wider concept than the 'meaning' of language, but presupposes it and builds upon it.

26 I assume here that ostensive definition plays little or no part in uncovering the meaning of rights because of the relative abstraction of the concept. Verbal definitions are more appropriate in dealing with the subtle distinctions between various normative relationships.

27 Hart, 'Jhering's Heaven of Concepts and Modern Analytical Jurisprudence,' in *Essays in Jurisprudence*, p. 274; F. Waismann,

'Verifiability,' in Parkinson (ed.), *The Theory of Meaning*, pp. 35–60, esp. p. 37. The term 'open-texture' was suggested as a translation of *Porositat der Begriffe* by the logician W. C. Kneale.

28 Hart, 'Jhering's Heaven', pp. 274–5.

29 Waismann, 'Verifiability', p. 38.

30 Hart, 'Jhering's Heaven', p. 275.

31 Hospers, *Philosophical Analysis*, p. 26.

32 The literature on the rights of animals is immense but see especially T. Regan and P. Singer (eds.), *Animal Rights and Human Obligations* (Englewood Cliffs, New Jersey, Prentice-Hall Inc., 1976).

33 See C. D. Stone, *Should Trees Have Standing? Towards Legal Rights for Natural Objects* (New York, Avon Books, 1975).

34 See J. Feinberg, 'The Rights of Animals and Unborn Generations,' in *Rights, Justice and the Bounds of Liberty*, esp. pp. 180–2; R. I. Sikora and B. Barry (eds.), *Obligations to Future Generations*, Philosophical Monographs, 2nd annual series (Philadelphia, Temple University Press, 1978).

35 See M. A. Warren, 'Do Potential People Have Moral Rights?', in Sikora and Barry, *Obligations*, pp. 14–30.

36 Feinberg discusses this issue in 'The Rights of Animals', pp. 173–6.

37 See the discussion in Onora O'Neill, *Faces of Hunger: An Essay on Poverty, Justice and Development* (London, Allen and Unwin, 1986), esp. ch. 6; also P. Alston and K. Tomasevski (eds.), *The Right to Food* (Dordrecht, Nijhoff, 1984).

38 Feinberg, 'The Nature and Value of Rights,' p. 153.

39 Hospers, *Philosophical Analysis*, p. 27.

40 G. J. Warnock, *The Object of Morality* (London, Methuen, 1971), ch. 2; though T. M. Scanlon argues that 'One common view of the place of rights, and moral rules generally, within utilitarianism holds that they are useful as means to the co-ordination of action. The need for such aids does not depend on imperfect motivation; it might exist even in a society of perfect altruists.' 'Rights, Goals and Fairness,' in J. Waldron (ed.), *Theories of Rights* (Oxford, University Press, 1984), pp. 137–52, esp. p. 144.

41 Sometimes the treatment offered as a cure for some malady itself becomes a problem, as when tranquillizers prescribed for depression or anxiety become addictive. In a world fast becoming more and more litigious, claiming rights may become literally addictive and thus a symptom of 'moral disease'.

42 Typical of this approach is G. J. Hughes, *Authority in Morals: An Essay in Christian Ethics*, Heythrop Monograph (London, Sheed and Ward, 1978), where he states:
'I am assuming a cognitivist position in ethics. That is to say, I believe that moral utterances can be true or false, and that it is

perfectly legitimate to speak of moral views as being mistaken, well-founded, or ill-supported, and of moral arguments as being valid, invalid, or inadequate, just as it is in other areas of rational discourse' p. xiii. For a radically different view see Don Cupitt, *The New Christian Ethics* (London, SCM, 1988), ch. 1, 'Christian Ethics as the Creation of Human Value'.

43 The term 'murder' is an example of language which is both descriptive and evaluative. To say that 'Murder is wrong' is a tautology because the term 'murder' already has the notion of wrongness applied to it; 'murder' means 'unjust killing', so that a negative moral judgement is implied. On the other hand, the proposition 'Killing is wrong' is synthetic because the connection between killing and wrongness is looser than the connection between murder and wrongness. Not all killings are morally wrong. A positive example of a term with justification 'built in' is 'flourishing'. We would find it difficult to deny that 'human flourishing' is a morally good state of affairs to promote. Similarly, nearly any name of a virtue has the same positive moral meaning. The difficulties we experience in using these evaluative terms is in coming to agreement as to what counts as an instance of 'murder' or 'human flourishing' or 'justice'.

44 Jeremy Waldron, '*Nonsense Upon Stilts' Bentham, Burke and Marx on the Rights of Man* (London and New York, Methuen, 1987), p. 163.

45 On the subject of 'natural rights' see two articles, H. L. A. Hart, 'Are There Any Natural Rights?' and Margaret MacDonald, 'Natural Rights', both in Waldron (ed.), *Theories of Rights*; John Finnis, *Natural Law and Natural Rights* (Oxford, Clarendon Press, 1980); and J. Maritain, *The Rights of Man and Natural Law*, Doris C. Anson, trans. (San Francisco, Ignatius Press, 1986).

46 Waldron, *Nonsense Upon Stilts*, p. 163.

47 Hosper's stipulative definition of 'connotation' echoes what Cohen and Nagel have called 'subjective intension' – 'sum total of attributes present to the mind of the person using the term, which may vary widely'. In, *Introduction to Logic*, p. 31.

48 Hospers, *Philosophical Analysis*, p. 48.

49 *Ibid.*, p. 49.

50 On the theory of emotivism in ethics see the classic work of J. O. Urmson, *The Emotive Theory of Ethics* (London, Hutchinson Library, 1968). There is a useful critical discussion in W. D. Hudson, *Modern Moral Philosophy*, ch. 4.

51 The language of 'pro-attitudes' is associated with P. H. Nowell-Smith, *Ethics* (Baltimore, Penguin, 1954).

52 Hospers, *Philosophical Analysis*, pp. 49–53.

53 Sallie McFague, *Metaphorical Theology: Models of God in Religious Language* (London, SCM, 1983).

54 McFague's reference to images 'feeding' concepts finds an echo in a remark by the liberation theologian Juan Luis Segundo. Discussing the 'Images of Liberty in Literature', he has this to say: 'It is not enough to attempt to work out a terminology. We must let the image bring something of its richness to the abstract concept. The image of liberty which finds expression in man's imaginative works contains hues and overtones that are useful to us here', in *A Theology for Artisans of a New Humanity*, 5 vols., (Maryknoll, New York, Orbis Books, 1973), II, *Grace and the Human Condition*, p. 39.

55 In David Tracy's analysis of 'The Classic' we find this remark: 'The artist knows that we dare not allow timidity in entering the "game" of expressing a truth of existence. Here we must enter, play and be played until we have experienced and recognized where and how we belong, where and how we participate in the fundamental questions and responses to life itself.' *The Analogical Imagination: Christian Theology and the Culture of Pluralism* (London, SCM, 1981), p. 129.

56 Philip S. Keane, *Christian Ethics and Imagination: A Theological Inquiry* (New York/Ramsey, Paulist Press, 1984).

57 *Ibid.*, p. 103.

58 Stanley Hauerwas, *The Peaceable Kingdom: A Primer in Christian Ethics* (London, SCM, 1984), p. 120.

59 John Howard Yoder, 'What Would You Do If?', *Journal of Religious Ethics*, 2/1 (1974), pp. 82–3 cited in Hauerwas, *The Peaceable Kingdom*, p. 125.

60 J. J. Thomson, 'Self Defense and Rights', in *Rights, Restitution and Risk: Essays in Moral Theory*, William Parent (ed.) (Cambridge, Massachusetts and London, Harvard University Press, 1986), pp. 33–48.

2 INITIAL ELUCIDATION OF RIGHTS-LANGUAGE

1 This approach is borrowed from R. Martin and J. W. Nickell, 'Recent Work on the Concept of Rights', *American Philosophical Quarterly*, 17 (1980), pp. 165–80.

2 See Joel Feinberg, 'The Nature and Value of Rights', in *Rights, Justice and the Bounds of Liberty: Essays in Social Philosophy* (Princeton, New Jersey, University Press, 1980), p. 149; Alan Gewirth, 'The Epistemology of Human Rights', in Ellen Frankel Paul, Fred D. Miller, Jun. and Jeffrey Paul (eds.), *Human Rights* (Oxford, Blackwell, 1984), p. 1; Bernard Mayo, 'Human Rights', *Proceedings of the Aristotelian Society* (*Suppl.*), 39 (1965), pp. 219–

36; Richard Wasserstrom, 'Rights, Human Rights, and Racial Discrimination', in James Rachels (ed.), *Moral Problems: A Collection of Philosophical Essays*, 3rd edition (New York, Harper and Row, 1979), p. 10.

3 Feinberg, 'The Nature and Value of Rights', p. 149.

4 Cf. Alan R. White, *Rights* (Oxford, Clarendon Press, 1984), p. 117, where he labels this use a 'subjunctive claim'. 'A subjunctive claim is a call for acceptability of the proposal that something (*should*) *be* the case…'.

5 White calls this the 'indicative use', *ibid.*, p. 116.

6 Here White refers to the 'possessive use' of the language of claiming, p. 121; cf. David Jenkins, 'Theological Inquiry Concerning Human Rights – Some Questions, Hypotheses and Theses', *The Ecumenical Review*, 28/2 (1975), pp. 97–103; 'I doubt if human rights should be thought of at all as either hypostatized or absolutized. Human rights are not the sort of "things" that exist on their own. They refer rather to relationships and possibilities enabling human development.' p. 100.

7 H. J. McCloskey, 'Rights', *Philosophical Quarterly*, 15 (1965), pp. 115–27; and 'Rights – Some Conceptual Issues', *Australian Journal of Philosophy*, 54 (1976), pp. 92–115.

8 McCloskey, 'Rights', p. 116.

9 *Ibid.*, p. 118; and see G. Marshall, 'Rights, Options and Entitlements', in A. W. B. Simpson (ed.), *Oxford Essays in Jurisprudence*, 2nd series (Oxford, Clarendon Press, 1973), pp. 228–41, quotation at p. 228.

10 Wasserstrom, 'Rights, Human Rights and Racial Discrimination', p. 10.

11 Feinberg, 'The Nature and Value of Rights', p. 150.

12 White, *Rights*, p. 121.

13 See, for instance, Tom L. Beauchamp and James F. Childress, *Principles of Biomedical Ethics*, 2nd edition (New York/Oxford, Oxford University Press, 1983): 'Most recent writers in ethics recognize that "rights" should be defined in terms of claims. In our framework, rights are best understood as justified claims that individuals and groups can make upon others or upon society' p. 50. Cf. Raanon Gillon, *Philosophical Medical Ethics* (Chichester, John Wiley and Sons, 1985), p. 54.

14 Feinberg, 'The Nature and Value of Rights', pp. 154–5.

15 S. I. Benn and R. S. Peters, *Social Principles and the Democratic State* (London, George Allen and Unwin, 1959), pp. 90–3.

16 McCloskey, 'Rights', p. 116.

17 Michael Bertram Crowe, *Human Rights* (Dublin, Veritas Publications, 1978), pp. 4–5.

18 White, *Rights*, p. 133 refers to Hobbes, *Leviathan*, ch. 14, and Spinoza, *Tractatus Theologico-Politicus*, ch. 16.

19 T. D. Perry, 'A Paradigm of Philosophy: Hohfeld on Legal Rights', *American Philosophical Quarterly*, 14 (1977), pp. 41–50, quotation at p. 41. For a critique of Perry see, S. D. Hudson and D. N. Husak, 'Legal Rights: How Useful is Hohfeldian Analysis?', *Philosophical Studies*, 37 (1980), pp. 45–53.

20 Samuel Stoljar, *An Analysis of Rights* (London, Macmillan, 1984), p. 51.

21 John Finnis, *Natural Law and Natural Rights* (Oxford, Clarendon Press, 1980), p. 199.

22 Stoljar, *An Analysis of Rights*, pp. 51–2.

23 H. L. A. Hart speaks of 'special rights' in his essay 'Are There Any Natural Rights?' in J. Waldron (ed.), *Theories of Rights* (Oxford, University Press, 1984), p. 84.

24 Called 'general rights' by Hart, *ibid.*, p. 87.

25 For a discussion of 'inalienable' rights, see William Frankena, 'Natural and Inalienable Rights', *Philosophical Review*, 64 (1955), 212–32; B. A. Richards, 'Inalienable Rights, Recent Criticism and Old Doctrine', *Philosophy and Phenomenological Research*, 29 (1969), pp. 391–404. There is a logical distinction between 'inalienable' rights and 'absolute' rights. Inalienable rights cannot be waived or relinquished by those who hold them, but may in theory be forfeited or taken away as punishment. Absolute rights can be neither waived nor taken away.

26 Hart, 'Are There Any Natural Rights?', p. 81.

27 *Quinn v Leathem* (1901), A. C., 495, 534; Hohfeld, *Fundamental Legal Conceptions* (New Haven, Connecticut, Yale University Press, 1919), pp. 42–3.

28 It seems that Lord Lindley ruled in favour of the employer on the grounds that the interference he suffered was unlawful, in so far as the union acted maliciously, with the intent to punish Leathem for taking on non-union labour in the first place.

29 Stoljar, *An Analysis of Rights*, pp. 52–3.

30 Hohfeld, *Fundamental*, pp. 50–64.

31 J. W. Harris, *Legal Philosophies* (London, Butterworths, 1980), p. 77.

32 C. Wellman, 'A New Conception of Human Rights', in E. Kamenka and A. E. S. Tay (eds.), *Human Rights* (London, Edward Arnold, 1978), pp. 49–58, quotation at p. 55.

33 *Ibid.*, p. 51; The terminology used to describe the components of a right can vary. Thus, for instance, A. Fagothey uses the following terms: 'subject' – the one who possesses the right; 'term' – those

bound to respect or fulfil the right; 'matter' – that to which one has a right; and 'title' – the reason why a subject has the right to x. Austin Fagothey, *Right and Reason: Ethics in Theory and Practice* (4th edition) (St Louis, C. V. Mosby Company, 1967), pp. 199ff. L. W. Sumner also speaks of the subjects of rights. To ask about the 'scope' is to ask who are the subjects. He uses 'content' for 'matter' and 'object' for Fagothey's 'term' in *The Moral Foundation of Rights* (Oxford, Clarendon Press, 1987), pp. 11–12. In these pages I tend to avoid the use of these technical terms in favour of simpler language, for instance that of 'right-holder' and 'duty-bearer'.

34 R. S. Downie and E. Telfer, *Caring and Curing: A Philosophy of Medicine and Social Work* (London, Methuen, 1980), p. 41.

35 S. I. Benn and R. S. Peters, *Social Principles and the Democratic State*, pp. 88ff.; D. D. Raphael, 'Human Rights', *Proceedings of the Aristotelian Society Suppl.*, 39 (1965), pp. 205–18; G. Grisez, *The Way of the Lord Jesus: Volume 1 – Christian Moral Principles* (Chicago, Franciscan Herald Press, 1983), pp. 264–5; Simone Weil, *The Need for Roots: Prelude to a Declaration of Duties Towards Mankind* (London/New York, Ark Paperback, 1987), p. 3.

36 C. H. Whitely, 'On Duties', *Proceedings of the Aristotelian Society*, 53 (1953), pp. 95–104.

37 Cf. White, *Rights*, pp. 51–3.

38 Joel Feinberg, 'Duties, Rights and Claims', *American Philosophical Quarterly*, 3/2 (1966) pp., 137–44.

39 Hart, 'Are There Any Natural Rights', p. 80, n. 7.

40 John Stuart Mill, *Utilitarianism*, Mary Warnock (ed.) (London, Collins/Fount, 1962), pp. 304–5.

41 See the treatment of this question in O'Neill, *Faces of Hunger* (London, Allen and Unwin, 1986), pp. 110–13. And cf. George Sher, 'Ancient Wrongs', *Philosophy and Public Affairs*, (1981), pp. 3–17.

42 Tom Regan, 'The Case for Animal Rights', in P. Singer, (ed.), *In Defence of Animals* (Oxford, Blackwell, 1985), pp. 13–26; Joel Feinberg, 'The Rights of Animals and Unborn Generations', in *Rights, Justice and the Bounds of Liberty*, pp. 159–84; G. R. Grice, *The Grounds of Moral Judgement* (Cambridge, University Press, 1967), pp. 147–8; Finnis, *Natural Law*, pp. 194–5. McCloskey, 'Rights', pp. 123–4.

43 McCloskey, 'Rights', p. 122, note; cf. J. Raz, 'Right-Based Moralities', in Waldron, *Theories of Rights*, pp. 182–200. He says that owning a valuable painting involves a right to destroy it if one wishes. There is no correlative duty to someone to maintain the

work in existence. 'Nevertheless, while I owe no one a duty to preserve the painting I am under such a duty. The reason is that to destroy it and deny the duty is to do violence to art and to show oneself blind to one of the values which give life a meaning', p. 197.

44 White, *Rights*, pp. 60–1; Though odd to speak of a right to be punished, this idea is not unheard of. See Weil, *The Need for Roots*: 'Punishment is a vital need of the human soul... Punishment must be an honour. It must not only wipe out the stigma of the crime, but must be regarded as a supplementary form of education', p. 20 – and education is surely a basic right?

45 David Lyons, 'The Correlativity of Rights and Duties', *Nous*, 4 (1970), pp. 45–55.

46 *Ibid.*, p. 47.

47 Note an opposing view from Paul Ramsey, 'Individuals have a right to speak freely because society has a right to hear freely from all its members.' And he goes on to say that 'Any right is also a duty', *Basic Christian Ethics* (New York, Scribners, 1950), pp. 360–1. Thus, Ramsey claims that there is a strict correlativity between the right of free speech and the duty to listen.

48 David Braybrooke, 'The Firm but Untidy Correlation of Rights and Obligations', *Canadian Journal of Philosophy*, March (1972), pp. 351–63. Quotation at p. 352.

49 *Ibid.*, pp. 358–60; cf. R. Frey, *Rights, Killing and Suffering* (Oxford, Blackwell, 1983), p. 78.

50 Feinberg, 'The Nature and Value of Rights', p. 153.

51 Glanville Williams, 'The Concept of a Legal Liberty', *Columbia Law Review*, 56/8 (1956), pp. 1129–50.

52 *Ibid.*, p. 1140.

53 H. L. A. Hart, 'Bentham on Legal Rights', in A. W. B. Simpson (ed.), *Oxford Essays in Jurisprudence*, pp. 171–201, esp. pp. 179–81.

54 Williams, 'The Concept of a Legal Liberty', p. 1150.

55 Harris, *Legal Philosophies*, p. 85.

56 Hart, 'Bentham on Legal Rights', p. 192.

57 The Choice Theory is also advocated by Wellman, in 'A New Conception of Human Rights', and more recently in Sumner, *The Moral Foundation of Rights*.

58 Hart, 'Introduction', *Essays in Jurisprudence and Philosophy* (Oxford, Clarendon Press, 1983), p. 17; see Jeremy Waldron, 'Critical Notice' (review of Hart's *Essays*), *Mind*, 94 (1985), p. 292.

59 See Marshall, 'Rights, Options and Entitlements', p. 234.

60 Carl Wellman, 'Consent to Medical Research on Children', *Archives für Rechts-und-Socialphilosophie*, 12 (1979), pp. 85–103; cf. Grice, *The Grounds of Moral Judgement*, pp. 147–8.

61 D. N. MacCormick, 'Childrens' Rights: A Test Case for Theories of Rights', *Archives für Rechts-und-Socialphilosophie*, 62 (1976), pp. 305–17; Raz, 'Right Based Moralities' in Waldron, *Theories of Rights*; Lyons, 'Rights, Claims and Beneficiaries'; On Bentham, see Hart, 'Bentham on Legal Rights'.

62 MacCormick, 'Childrens' Rights', p. 311.

63 Waldron, 'Introduction', *Theories of Rights*, pp. 9–10.

64 J. Feinberg, 'Voluntary Euthanasia and the Inalienable Right to Life', in *Rights, Justice*, pp. 221–51, esp. pp. 232–8; Martin P. Golding, 'Towards a Theory of Human Rights', *The Monist*, 52 (1968), pp. 521–49, esp. p. 546.

65 John Finnis, *Natural Rights*, p. 200, insists that powers and immunities should not be overlooked when discussing human rights, but he does not give a clear indication why the language of claims and liberties needs to be complemented by such concepts. His general example of a Hohfeldian power – 'wherever A can grant B permission to do something that otherwise he (B) would have the (moral) duty not to do' – could be equally well described in terms of waiving a claim or exercising a liberty. So, for instance, in cases of informed consent, Mrs Smith has a claim-right not to be operated on without her consent, while having the liberty-right, under certain circumstances, to give permission to Dr Jones to perform that operation. Samuel Stoljar, *An Analysis of Rights*, p. 66, reinterprets the notion of power: 'The true logical secret of a power...is that it is a combination of rights and duties: a combination designed to give the power-holder the right to perform an office, but a right qualified by fiduciary duties controlling the performance of his tasks.' In this way powers are supposed to be distinct from claims and liberties. In my opinion, the work done by Stoljar's powers can be done just as well by the concept of a 'mandatory right' which brings together claims and duties. Why multiply entities?

3 CONCEPTUAL SCEPTICISM AND RIGHTS

1 Alan Gewirth, 'Why Rights Are Indispensable?', *Mind*, 95 (1986), pp. 329–44, quotation at p. 329; cf. two further works of Gewirth, *Human Rights* (Chicago, University Press, 1982); *Reason and Morality* (Chicago, University Press, 1978).

2 Opposition to the language of rights on the part of theologians tends to be normative rather than conceptual. Moral and theological scepticism will be discussed in the next chapter.

3 Gewirth, 'Why Rights', p. 330; Christopher Arnold, 'Analyses of

Rights', in E. Kamenka and A. E. S. Tay (eds.), *Human Rights* (London, Edward Arnold, 1978) pp. 74–86, esp. pp. 82ff; J. Finnis, *Natural Law and Natural Rights* (Oxford, Clarendon Press, 1980) speaking of the shift in meaning and use from duty to right he declares that: 'there is no cause to take sides as between the older and the newer usages, as ways of expressing the implications of justice in a given context. Still less is it appropriate to argue that "as a matter of juristic logic" duty is logically prior to right (or vice versa)' p. 210.

4 Gewirth, 'Why Rights', p. 333.

5 'Burden' is used here in a logical, not psychological, sense. Some duties are psychologically pleasant; some rights psychologically burdensome. The logical sense refers to the main direction of the benefit – towards another. Needless to say, the duty-bearer may also benefit, though in a secondary or indirect way.

6 D. N. MacCormick, 'Childrens' Rights: A Test-Case for Theories of Rights', *Archives für Rechts und Socialphilosophie*, 62/3 (1976), pp. 305–17, esp. p. 312.

7 Gewirth, 'Why Rights', p. 333.

8 Ronald Dworkin, *Taking Rights Seriously*, second impression with appendix (London, Duckworth, 1978), pp. 150–83, quotation at p. 171.

9 Utilitarians differ in their attitudes towards rights. Jeremy Bentham was hostile to any rights other than legal rights; see his 'Anarchical Fallacies', in J. Waldron (ed.), *Nonsense Upon Stilts: Bentham, Burke and Marx on the Rights of Man* (London/New York, Methuen, 1987), pp. 46–76; a contemporary utilitarian sceptical about rights is Raymond Frey, *Rights, Killing and Suffering* (Oxford, Blackwell, 1983). More favourable to rights-language from a utilitarian point of view is R. M. Hare, *Moral Thinking: Its Levels, Method and Point* (Oxford, University Press, 1981), ch. 9; John Gray, 'Indirect Utility and Fundamental Rights', in Ellen Frankel Paul, Fred D. Miller, Jun. and Jeffrey Paul (eds.), *Human Rights* (Oxford, Blackwell, 1984), pp. 73–91; and L. W. Sumner, *The Moral Foundation of Rights* (Oxford, Clarendon Press, 1987), 'Any viable form of consequentialism, when combined with a realistic picture of the nature of moral agents and of the world in which they operate, must make room for rights', p. vii.

10 Ronald Dworkin, 'Rights as Trumps', in J. Waldron (ed.), *Theories of Rights* (Oxford, University Press, 1984), pp. 153–67, quotation at p. 153.

11 Dworkin, *Taking Rights Seriously*, p. 172; For all Dworkin's emphasis on individual rights as trumps over collective interests he

still refuses to treat all of the former as absolute. 'I must not overstate the point. Someone who claims that citizens have a right against the Government need not go so far as to say that the State is *never* justified in overriding that right.' *Taking Rights Seriously*, p. 191. What he is opposed to is the overriding of rights, such as free speech, 'on the minimal grounds that would be sufficient if no such right existed', pp. 191–2.

12 Braybrooke, 'The Firm But Untidy Correlativity of Rights and Obligations', *Canadian Journal of Philosophy* (March 1972), pp. 351–63, quotation at p. 357.

13 Frey, *Rights, Killing and Suffering*, p. 49.

14 Gewirth, 'Why Rights', p. 334.

15 A. I. Melden expresses the issue quite well as follows: 'For the possessor of the right orders and conducts some portion of his life in such a way that a failure on the part of the person obliged to him is not merely to disappoint him or visit some misfortune on him, but to wrong him, i.e. to commit an offence against him as a moral agent', *Rights and Persons* (Oxford, Blackwell, 1977), p. 53.

16 Charles Fried, *Right and Wrong* (Cambridge, Massachusetts, Harvard University Press, 1978), p. 85; cf. the discussion of interests in White, whether they are the necessary and/or sufficient condition for possessing rights, *Rights* (Oxford, Clarendon Press, 1985), pp. 79ff.

17 Feinberg, 'The Nature and Value of Rights', in *Rights, Justice and the Bounds of Liberty* (Princeton, University Press, 1980), p. 154.

18 Robert Young, 'Dispensing with Moral Rights', *Political Theory*, 6 (1978), pp. 63–74.

19 Frey, *Rights, Killing and Suffering*, p. 51.

20 See Sean MacBride, 'The Universal Declaration – Thirty Years After', in A. Falconer (ed.), *Understanding Human Rights: An Interdisciplinary and Interfaith Study* (Dublin, Irish School of Ecumenics, 1980), pp. 7–20, quotation at p. 11; and in the same collection see Michael O'Boyle, 'Strasbourg – A System of Supervision for the Protection of Human Rights in Europe', pp. 130–47; Maurice Cranston, *Human Rights To-day* (London, Ampersand Ltd., 1962), chs. 3 and 4.

21 See Maurice Cranston, 'Human Rights, Real and Supposed', in D. D. Raphael (ed.), *Political Theory and the Rights of Man* (London, Macmillan, 1967), pp. 43–53, for the argument that social and economic rights are in a different logical category to political and civil rights. The former are a category mistake. They are not real human rights at all. Cf. also in Raphael, the essay by P. Schneider, 'Social Rights and the Concept of Human Rights', pp. 81–94.

22 See Richard E. Flathman, 'Moderating Rights', in E. Frankel Paul, F. D. Miller, Jun. and J. Paul (eds.), *Human Rights* (Oxford, Blackwell, 1984), pp. 149–71.

23 Marcus Singer, 'Moral Rules and Principles', in A. I. Melden (ed.), *Essays in Moral Philosophy* (Seattle, University of Washington Press, 1958), pp. 160–97, quotation at p. 160.

24 *Ibid.*, p. 164.

25 Maguire, *The Moral Choice* (Minneapolis, Winston Press, 1978), p. 258, n. 45.

26 Jeremy Waldron, 'A Right to Do Wrong', *Ethics*, 92 (1981), pp. 21–39; William A. Galston, 'On the Alleged Right to Do Wrong: A Response to Waldron', *Ethics*, 93 (1983), pp. 320–4.

27 Eric D'Arcy, in the course of a discussion on the dictum 'error has no rights', points out that rights are derived, not immediately from what is objectively of moral obligation, but from what is subjectively so. *Conscience and the Right to Freedom* (London, Sheed and Ward, 1979), pp. 253ff.

28 Williams, 'The Concept of a Legal Liberty', *Columbia Law Review*, 56 (1956), pp. 1129–50, quotation at p. 1145.

29 Stephen Toulmin, 'The Tyranny of Principles: Regaining the Ethics of Discretion', *Hastings Center Report*, December, 1981, pp. 31–9, quotation at p. 31.

30 See the discussion of 'epicheia' in John Mahoney, *The Making of Moral Theology: A Study of the Roman Catholic Tradition* (Oxford, Clarendon Press, 1987), pp. 231–45. Especially interesting is the contrast between the view of equity held by Plato – necessary because of human inability to keep law perfectly – and Aristotle's view – the virtue which copes with laws that are typically imperfect, pp. 235–6. In the face of law, rules or principles which fail to apply perfectly to every possible situation, the language of rights may well be a key aspect of *epicheia*/equity. Reinhold Niebuhr is surely speaking about equity when he declares that 'Imaginative justice leads beyond equality to a consideration of the special needs of the life of the other', *An Interpretation of Christian Ethics* (New York, Seabury Press, 1979), p. 66.

31 To be fair, it must be said that the language of obligation is not totally inflexible. See our discussion earlier of the distinction between 'perfect' and 'imperfect' obligation, especially O. O'Neill's essay, 'Childrens' Rights and Childrens' Lives', *Ethics*, 98 (1988), pp. 445–63.

32 See A. Fagothey, who makes the following claim: 'If I have a right, everyone else has the duty to respect my right', *Right and Reason: Ethics in Theory and Practice* (St Louis, Mosby, 1967), p. 209.

This does not apply in the case of special rights, and is controversial in the case of at least some human rights, for example 'civil' rights.

33 R. Wasserstrom, 'Rights, Human Rights and Racial Discrimination', in James Rachels (ed.), *Moral Problems* (New York, Harper and Row, 1979), p. 12.

34 Kai Nielsen, 'Scepticism and Human Rights', *The Monist*, 52 (1968), pp. 573–94.

35 See Gregory Vlastos, 'Human Worth, Merit and Equality', in Joel Feinberg (ed.), *Moral Concepts*, Oxford Readings in Philosophy (Oxford, University Press, 1969), pp. 141–52; and in the same volume, Bernard Williams, 'The Idea of Equality', pp. 153–71.

36 The term is coined by Richard Ryder, 'Speciesism in the Laboratory', in P. Singer (ed.), *In Defence of Animals*, pp. 77–88; cf. James Rachels, *The End of Life: Euthanasia and Morality*, Studies in Bioethics, general ed., P. Singer (Oxford, University Press, 1986), where he refers to 'The unimportance of being human', p. 72. 'It is individual characteristics, and not species membership, that makes beings morally special', p. 73; Mary Warnock answers: 'I would argue, on the other hand, that the concept of 'speciesism' as a form of prejudice is absurd. Far from being arbitrary it is a supremely important moral principle. If someone did *not* prefer to save a human being rather than a dog or a fly we would think him in need of justification', cited by John Harris, *The Value of Life* (London, Routledge and Kegan Paul, 1985), p. 23.

37 Wellman, 'A New Conception of Human Rights', in Kamenka and Tay, *Human Rights*, pp. 55–6.

38 *Ibid.*, p. 56.

39 Raphael, 'Human Rights', *Proceedings of the Aristotelian Society Suppl.*, 39 (1965), pp. 205–18, esp. p. 216.

40 Margaret MacDonald, 'Natural Rights', in Waldron, *Theories of Rights*, pp. 21–40, quotation at p. 34.

41 Jacques Maritain, *Christianity and Democracy and The Rights of Man and Natural Law*, trans. Doris C. Anson (San Francisco, Ignatius Press, 1986), pp. 140–1.

42 MacDonald, 'Natural Rights', p. 30.

43 To say that humans possess a 'fixed human nature' does not lead logically to the conclusion that we necessarily know this nature in detail. Simon Tugwell insists on the Thomistic doctrine that we can never know, directly, the essence of our own soul. The context of this remark is the problem of knowing for certain whether anyone is in the state of grace or not, but surely the doctrine can apply as well to the knowledge of whether we are living in accordance with our God-given nature. Where our personal

288 *Notes to pages 77–83*

ontology is mysterious, our epistemology of the self is likely to be far from clear-cut. *Reflections on the Beatitudes: Soundings in Christian Tradition* (London, Darton, Longman and Todd, 1980), 'If man is made in God's image and likeness, man must be prepared to find himself as elusive and as unfathomable as God himself is', p. 50.

44 See Mahoney, *The Making of Moral Theology*, pp. 113ff., for an account of this transition from nature to person. Note his reference to the distinction in Aquinas between nature in general and nature in particular individuals, *Summa Theologiae.*, 1a q99; a.2 ad 1. Mahoney states that 'it appears that it is in this sense that he can refer to nature being changeable in individuals on account of particular circumstances', p. 111, n. 143.

45 Bernard Williams, *Ethics and the Limits of Philosophy* (London, Fontana, 1985), p. 17.

4 MORAL AND THEOLOGICAL SCEPTICISM

1 Gewirth, 'Why Rights Are Indispensable?', *Mind*, 95 (1986), pp. 329–44, quotation at p. 332.

2 On the history of the concept see: R. Tuck, *Natural Right Theories: Their Origins and Development* (Cambridge, University Press, 1979); Otto Gierke, *Natural Law and the Theory of Society*, 2 vols. (Cambridge, University Press, 1934); Ian Shapiro, *The Evolution of Rights in Liberal Theory* (Cambridge, University Press, 1986); A. P. d'Entrèves, *Natural Law: An Introduction to Legal Philosophy* (London, Hutchinson, 1951), esp. chs. 1 and 3; J. Finnis, *Natural Law and Natural Rights* (Oxford, Clarendon Press, 1980), ch. 8; Leonard Swidler, 'Human Rights: A Historical Overview', in Hans Kung and Jurgen Moltmann (eds.), *The Ethics of World Religions and Human Rights*, Concilium, 1990/2 (London, SCM; Philadelphia, Trinity Press International), pp. 12–22; Wolfgang Huber, 'Human Rights – A Concept and Its History', in A. Muller and N. Greinacher (eds.), The Church and the Rights *of Man*, Concilium, 1979 (New York, Seabury Press), pp. 1–9.

3 Eugene Kamenka, 'The Anatomy of an Idea', in E. Kamenka and A. E. S. Tay, *Human Rights* (London, Edward Arnold, 1977), pp. 1–12, quotation at p. 6.

4 Thomas Hobbes, *Leviathan*, John Plamenatz, ed. (Glasgow, Collins, 1962), pp. 145–6.

5 Quoted in C. B. Macpherson, 'Natural Rights in Hobbes and Locke', in D. D. Raphael (ed.), *Political Theory and the Rights of Man* (London, Macmillan, 1967), p. 3.

6 Raphael, 'Human Rights', *Proceedings of the Aristotelian Society Suppl.*, 39 (1965), pp. 205–18, esp. pp. 207ff.

7 Macpherson, 'Natural Rights', p. 6.
8 *Ibid.*; also see his *The Political Theory of Possessive Individualism: Hobbes to Locke* (Oxford/New York, Oxford University Press, 1964), pp. 197ff.
9 Macpherson, 'Natural Rights', p. 9.
10 Kamenka, 'The Anatomy of an Idea', p. 5.
11 But see Raphael's remark on the view of Paine who saw old-age pensions as a right and not as charity, due to the fact of the payment of taxes throughout life. Thus, Paine comes close to the notion of the Welfare State, 'The Rights of Man and the Rights of the Citizen' in Raphael, *Political Theory*, pp. 113ff.
12 J. Waldron, *Nonsense Upon Stilts: Bentham, Burke and Marx on the Rights of Man* (London/New York, Methuen, 1987), p. 40.
13 See Waldron, *ibid.*, for the text of Burke's, *Reflections on the Revolution in France*, pp. 96–118, and a useful introduction, pp. 77ff.
14 Karl Marx, 'On the Jewish Question', in Waldron, *Nonsense Upon Stilts*, pp. 137–50. For socialist/Marxian critique of the language of rights see: I. Meszaros, 'Marxism and Human Rights', in A. Falconer, *Understanding Human Rights: An Interdisciplinary and Interfaith Study* (Dublin, Irish School of Ecumenics, 1980), pp. 47–61; and Tom Campbell, *The Left and Rights* (London, Routledge and Kegan Paul, 1983).
15 David Hollenbach, *Claims in Conflict; Retrieving and Renewing the Catholic Human Rights Tradition* (New York, Paulist Press, 1979), p. 15. For a trenchant criticism of rights-talk from a liberation theology perspective, see A. Pieris, 'Human Rights and Liberation Theology', in Marc H. Ellis and Otto Maduro (eds.), *The Future of Liberation Theology: Essays in Honour of Gustavo Gutierrez* (Maryknoll, New York, Orbis Books, 1989), pp. 299–310. He tends to view the language of rights as a form of theological imperialism imposed by Western social ethics. Third World theologians prefer the language of liberation – 'God's specific language', p. 299.
16 Jose Miguez Bonino, 'Religious Commitment and Human Rights', in Falconer, *Understanding Human Rights*, pp. 21–33. Quotation at p. 25.
17 Huber, 'Human Rights – A Concept and Its History', in Muller and Greinacher, *The Church and the Rights of Man*, p. 5.
18 A classic statement of class/group selfishness is found in Reinhold Niebuhr's, *Moral Man and Immoral Society: A Study in Ethics and Politics* (New York, Scribners, 1960):

> While it is possible for intelligence to increase the range of benevolent impulse, and thus prompt a human being to consider the needs and rights of other than those to whom he is bound by organic and physical relationship, there are definite limits in the capacity of ordinary

mortals which makes it impossible for them to grant to others what they claim for themselves. (p. 3).

Niebuhr's point of view appears to recognise the relative ease with which we accept special rights, involving those to whom we are 'bound by organic and physical relationship', in contrast to the reluctance we sometimes feel regarding the demands made by general/human rights, where comparative strangers make claims upon us. I shall argue later, however, that some special rights may involve us in relatively impersonal normative relationships.

19 Gewirth, 'Why Rights', pp. 338ff.
20 Dorothy Emmet, *Rules, Roles and Relations* (London, Macmillan, 1966), p. 59; cf. R. M. Hare, *Moral Thinking : Its Levels, Method and Point* (Oxford, Clarendon Press, 1981): 'Moral judgements are, I claim, universalizable in only one sense, namely that they entail identical judgements about all cases identical in their universal properties', p. 108.
21 The 'ethics of strangers' does not necessarily have a pejorative meaning. Richard Titmus, for instance, sees the Welfare System in our society as one which gives help precisely to strangers. He laments the fact that in the area of blood donation the market in blood has deprived poor and rich alike of the right to give, not to a named individual, but to a stranger who remains anonymous. Giving blood is, he says, an example of 'creative altruism'. Thus, feelings of altruism and benevolence can be directed towards others, who, in one sense, remain strangers, i.e., anonymous, but in another sense are not 'mere' strangers because of the bond created by our giving. *The Gift Relationship : From Human Blood to Social Policy* (Harmondsworth, Penguin, 1973), esp. ch. 14, 'The Right to Give'.
22 Huber, 'Human Rights – A Concept and Its History', p. 6.
23 For a useful discussion of individualism from the perspective of Christian ethics see Michael K. Duffey, *Be Blessed in What You Do : The Unity of Christian Ethics and Spirituality* (New York, Paulist Press, 1988), pp. 82–5.
24 Steven Lukes, *Individualism* (Oxford, Blackwell, 1973), p. 99.
25 Alan Falconer, 'Theological Reflection on Human Rights', in Falconer, *Understanding Human Rights*, pp. 196–223, quotation at p. 204.
26 Daniel Callahan, *Honesty in the Church* (London, Constable, 1965), p. 163. Cf. John Drury, 'Christian Individualism', *Theology*, September/October (1991), pp. 332–7.
27 Thomas Ogletree, *Hospitality to the Stranger : Dimensions of Moral Understanding* (Philadelphia, Fortress Press, 1985), p. 51.

28 *Ibid.*, p. 53.

29 Jurgen Moltmann, 'Christian Faith and Human Rights', in Falconer, *Understanding Human Rights*, pp. 182–95, esp. p. 188; cf. Pierre Teilhard de Chardin who presents the maxim '"First, develop yourself", Christianity says to the Christian' and comments on this, 'It is a truly Christian duty to grow, even in the eyes of men, and to make one's talents bear fruit, even though they be natural.' *Le Milieu Divin: An Essay on the Interior Life* (London, Collins/Fontana, 1964), p. 96.

30 Robert A. Burt underlines the fear, commonly felt, that we are losing our individuality in the context of a discussion of the rights of the mentally handicapped. He suggests that the conditions suffered by many institutionalised patients – isolation, lack of privacy, lack of flexibility and conformity to the institution's schedule – are in fact the daily lot of many 'ordinary' Americans. When Judge Broderick condemned the conditions in one such institution, Pennhurst, Pennsylvania, he declared that these conditions were not reflective of society and thus not conducive to the 'normalization' of its inmates. But Burt refutes this, arguing that in fact places like Pennhurst are a microcosm of society as a whole. People are frightened of such places because they mirror the lack of individuality in society. And, unfortunately, this fear is projected unto the handicapped themselves, leading to the violation of their basic rights. 'Constitutional Rights of Handicapped People and the Teaching of the Parables', in Stephen E. Lammer and Allen Verhey (eds.), *On Moral Medicine: Theological Perspectives in Medical Ethics* (Grand Rapids, Eerdmans, 1987), pp. 582–90.

31 Finnis, *Natural Law*, p. 140.

32 *Ibid.*, p. 144.

33 Jeremy Waldron makes a distinction between individualism and egoism. To say that rights are individualistic is to say something of their fundamental logical form, and as a statement of logic is morally neutral. 'By its very nature, a theory of rights is an individualistic theory. Rights purport to secure goods *for individuals*: that is an elementary consequence of their logical form.' *Nonsense Upon Stilts*, p. 185. To say that rights involve egoism, on the other hand, is to make a normative moral statement.

34 See Waldron, *Nonsense Upon Stilts*, p. 196:

> If we look at the way in which moral claims are put forward in the real world (as opposed to what philosophers say about them), in cases where rights really matter, what is striking is that, on the whole, claims are put forward by people *on other individuals' behalf*. The demand for human rights in the USSR, Eastern Europe, South Africa, Chile and

elsewhere is often a demand by western governments or by pressure groups (like Amnesty International) based in the west, put forward not on behalf of their own constituents, but on the basis of a concern for the well-being and freedom of people they have never met and from whom they are not expecting to receive any benefit in return.

35 Gewirth, 'Why Rights', p. 332.

36 Stanley Hauerwas, *Suffering Presence: Theological Reflections on Medicine, the Mentally Handicapped and the Church* (Edinburgh, T. and T. Clark, 1986), p. 128.

37 *Ibid.*, p. 125; Hauerwas may be correct in saying that it is somehow morally repugnant to treat children as '*merely* another interest group', but I can't see why children cannot be taken in any way as an interest group. What is wrong with this view as long as it is *just one aspect* of how we treat children? In a discussion of the respective rights of parents and children, Simon Lee cites Lord Denning: the legal right of parents ends when the child becomes eighteen, but before then 'it is a dwindling right which the courts will hesitate to enforce against the wishes of the child, and more so the older he is. It starts with a right of control and ends with little more than advice.' *Law and Morals: Warnock, Gillick and Beyond* (Oxford, University Press, 1986), p. 52. And what is said here of legal rights applies, other things being equal, to moral rights. As children grow older, their interests may conflict with parental interests, and it is difficult to state a priori that the latter automatically take precedence.

38 Toulmin, 'The Tyranny of Principles', *Hastings Center Report*, December 1981, p. 35.

39 *Ibid.*

40 Robin Downie, 'The Right to Criticise', *Philosophy*, 44 (1969), pp. 116–26, especially pp. 122–3; cf. C. Fried, *Right and Wrong* (Cambridge, Massachusetts, Harvard University Press, 1978), ch. 7, 'Rights and Roles'.

41 Feinberg, 'The Nature and Value of Rights', in *Rights, Justice, and the Bounds of Liberty* (Princeton, University Press, 1980), p. 153.

42 See O'Neill, *Faces of Hunger* (London, Allen and Unwin, 1986), 'Holders of rights can press their claims only when the obligations to meet these claims have been allocated to specified bearers of obligations', p. 100.

43 Feinberg, 'The Nature and Value of Rights', p. 151.

44 Peter Winch, 'Can A Good Man Be Harmed?', in his *Ethics and Action* (London, Routledge and Kegan Paul, 1972), pp. 193–209.

45 Ludwig Wittgenstein, 'A Lecture on Ethics', *Philosophical Review*, 74 (1965), pp. 3–12; see Antony Duff, 'Must a Good Man Be Invulnerable', *Ethics* (1975), pp. 294–311.

46 See Gerard Watson, 'Pagan Philosophy and Christian Ethics', in James Mackey (ed.), *Morals, Law and Authority: Sources and Attitudes in the Church* (Dublin, Gill and Macmillan, 1969), pp. 39–57; cf. Lisa Sowle Cahill, 'Toward a Christian Theory of Human Rights', *Journal of Religious Ethics*, 8/2 (1980), pp. 277–301, esp. p. 290, 'Material claims, in contrast to claims on moral goods, do not constitute absolute rights.' Personal integrity is *the* absolute right.

47 See Jack Sanders, *Ethics in the New Testament* (London, SCM, 1986); Rudolf Schnackenburg, *The Moral Teaching of the New Testament*, trans. J. Holland Smith (London, Burns and Oates, 1965), Part II, ch. 1; Thomas Ogletree, *The Use of the Bible in Christian Ethics* (Oxford, Blackwell, 1984), chs. 4 and 6; J. L. Houlden, *Ethics and the New Testament* (London/Oxford, Mowbrays, 1973), pp. 9–13.

48 John Ferguson, *The Politics of Love: The New Testament and Violent Revolution* (Cambridge, James Clarke, 1973), p. 73.

49 See I Cor. 6.2; Houlden, *Ethics and the New Testament*, p. 11.

50 Schnackenburg, *The Moral Teaching of the New Testament*, p. 370.

51 Barnabas Ahern, 'The Fellowship of His Sufferings', in Carroll Stuhlmueller (ed.), *New Horizons: Studies in Biblical Theology* (Indiana, Fides Dome, 1965), pp. 95–131, quotation at p. 95.

52 *Ibid.*, p. 107.

53 See Hauerwas, *Suffering Presence*, pp. 165ff. for a good description of human ambivalence in the face of suffering.

54 See John Hick's contention that the virtues of compassion, courage, unselfishness and determination 'all presuppose for their emergence and for their development something like the world in which we live. They are values of personal existence that would have no point, and therefore no place, in a ready-made utopia.' 'A World Without Suffering', in Michael J. Taylor (ed.), *The Mystery of Suffering and Death* (New York, Doubleday, 1974), p. 45.

55 On the poverty issue, see Cajetan Esser, *Origins of the Franciscan Order*, trans. A. Daly and I. Lynch (Chicago, Franciscan Herald Press, 1970), pp. 228–40; John Moorman, *A History of the Franciscan Order: From Its Origins to the Year 1517* (Oxford, Clarendon Press, 1968), chs. 16 and 25.

56 Simon Tugwell 'Francis of Assisi' in *Ways of Imperfection: An Exploration of Christian Spirituality* (London, Darton, Longman and Todd, 1985), pp. 125–37, quotation at p. 129.

57 Hauerwas, *The Peaceable Kingdom* (London, SCM, 1984), p. 104.

58 H. R. Niebuhr, 'The Grace of Doing Nothing', *Christian Century*, 49 (March 23) 1932, pp. 378–80; Reinhold Niebuhr, 'Must We Do Nothing?', *Christian Century*, 49 (30 March) 1932, pp. 415–17. Cited in Hauerwas, *The Peaceable Kingdom*, ch. 8.

59 Yoder, *The Politics of Jesus* (Grand Rapids, Michigan, Eerdmans, 1972), p. 133–4.

60 *Ibid.*, p. 132.

61 See Tugwell, *Reflections on the Beatitudes* (London, Darton, Longman and Todd, 1980), p. 61, reflecting on the beatitude of those who mourn the author states: 'The naive hedonism by which some of our contemporaries seem to want to live has not been obviously successful in producing any results except frustration, and our libertarian age with its frantic quest for pleasure and excitement, is oddly characterized by an increase in the number of people complaining to their doctors that they can no longer feel anything at all.'

62 P. Foot, 'Moral Beliefs', in her *Virtues and Vices and Other Essays in Moral Philosophy* (Oxford, Blackwell, 1981), pp. 101–31.

63 In the meantime Mrs Foot has considerably reworked her ideas; see her preface to *Virtues and Vices*, pp. xi–xiv, where she regrets her insistence on self-interest as the fundamental moral reason. 'Where I came to grief was, predictably, over justice', p. xiii. In spite of her emphasis on prudential reasons for acting well, Foot's naturalism seems to reflect basic common sense. Certain states of affairs pertaining to human life provide essential evidence if we are to make sensible evaluative judgements. Our moral judgements must have a strict relationship to human needs and widely accepted social practices, otherwise, as Foot argues, we will have to accept as moral commands such as 'not to look at hedgehogs in the light of the moon'. Even religious morality cannot divorce itself entirely from socially perceived needs and preferences. Just because Christian ethics has an ultimate supernatural reference does not mean that it contradicts the sphere of the natural. But some forms of anti-naturalism tend in this direction.

64 D. Z. Phillips and M. O. Mounce, *Moral Practices* (London, Routledge and Kegan Paul, 1970).

65 See a number of essays in C. Curran and R. McCormick (eds.), *Readings in Moral Theology No. 1 : Moral Norms and Catholic Tradition* (New York, Paulist Press, 1979), esp. Louis Janssens, 'Ontic Evil and Moral Evil', pp. 40–93; Joseph Fuchs, 'The Absoluteness of Moral Terms', pp. 94–137; Bruno Schuller, 'Direct Killing/ Indirect Killing, pp. 138–57. For the purposes of our discussion I regard 'pre-moral', 'non-moral' and 'ontic' as synonymous qualifications of value (and 'dis-value'). They are like building materials out of which the edifice of morality is constructed.

66 See Simon Tugwell, *The Way of the Preacher* (London, Darton, Longman and Todd, 1979), pp. 134–9.

67 Cahill, 'Towards a Christian Theory of Rights', p. 277.
68 David Little, 'Human Rights: An Exuberant Disarray', *Hastings Center Report*, 18/2 (1988), pp. 40–2, quotation at p. 40.

5 IMAGINATION, METAETHICS AND RIGHTS

1 Hospers, *An Introduction to Philosophical Analysis*, 2nd edition (London, Routledge and Kegan Paul, 1967), pp. 48ff.
2 See Susanne K. Langer, *Philosophy in a New Key: A Study in the Symbolism of Reason, Rite, and Art* (New York, Mentor/New American Library, 1942): 'The end of a philosophical epoch comes with the exhaustion of its motive concepts', p. 6. For Langer, a philosophical movement depends on the strength and vigour of its 'generative ideas', and there comes a time when they have outlived their usefulness. Christianity suffers this process too, Langer points out: 'The wonderful flights of imagination and feeling inspired by the rise and triumph of Christianity, the questions to which its profound revolutionary attitude gave rise, provided for nearly a thousand years of philosophical growth...But, at last, its generative ideas – sin and salvation, nature and grace, unity, infinity, and kingdom – had done their work', p. 7.
3 James Mackey, *Modern Theology: A Sense of Direction* (Oxford, University Press, 1987), p. 25. On Theology and the value of imagination see also: John McIntyre, *Faith, Theology, and Imagination* (Edinburgh, The Handsel Press, 1987); Julian Hartt, *Theological Method and the Imagination* (New York, Seabury Press, 1977); Ray Hart, *Unfinished Man and the Imagination: Toward an Ontology and a Rhetoric of Imagination* (New York, Herder and Herder, 1968); D. Tracy, *The Analogical Imagination: Christian Theology and the Culture of Pluralism* (London, SCM, 1981).
4 Mary Warnock, *Imagination* (Oxford and London, Faber, 1976). And see, Gilbert Ryle, 'Thought and Imagination' in K. Kolenda (ed.), *On Thinking*, (Oxford, Blackwell, 1979).
5 Philip Keane, *Christian Ethics and Imagination: A Theological Inquiry* (New York/Ramsey, Paulist Press, 1984), pp. 23–6.
6 Hans Georg Gadamer, *Truth and Method* (New York, Crossroads, 1982).
7 '...distance is necessary for *interpretation* to fulfil its proper task.' Sallie McFague, *Metaphorical Theology: Models of God in Religious Language* (London, SCM, 1983), pp. 120–1.
8 Paul Ricoeur, 'Creativity in Language: Word, Polysemy, Metaphor', in C. E. Reagan and D. Stewart (eds.), *The Philosophy of*

Paul Ricoeur: An Anthology of His Work (Boston, Beacon Press, 1978); *Hermeneutics and the Human Sciences*, ed. and trans. J. B. Thompson (Cambridge, University Press, 1981).

9 Mary B. Hesse, *Science and the Human Imagination: Aspects of the History and Logic of Physical Science* (London, SCM, 1954).

10 Daniel Maguire, *The Moral Choice* (New York, Doubleday, 1979), esp. pp. 190–5.

11 Jacob Bronowski, *Science and Human Values* (New York, Harper Torchbook, 1965), p. 15.

12 Arthur Koestler, *The Act of Creation* (New York, Dell Publishing Co., (Laurel Edition), 1967), p. 96.

13 *Ibid.*, p. 96, cited in Maguire, *The Moral Choice*, p. 192.

14 Max Black, *Models and Metaphors* (Ithaca, New York, Cornell University Press, 1962), ch. 13.

15 *Ibid.*, p. 236.

16 *Ibid.*, p. 237.

17 Ian Barbour, *Myths, Models, and Paradigms: A Comparative Study in Science and Religion* (New York, Harper and Row; London, SCM, 1974), p. 6.

18 *Ibid.*, p. 12.

19 Black, *Models and Metaphors*, pp. 238–9.

20 Stephen Toulmin, *The Philosophy of Science* (London, Hutchinson, 1953), pp. 38–9; cited by Black, *Models and Metaphors*, p. 239.

21 Barbour, *Myths, Models and Paradigms*, p. 15.

22 See the notion of 'root metaphor' in Stephen Pepper, *World Hypotheses* (Berkeley and Los Angeles, University of California Press, 1942).

23 As in Langer, *Philosophy in a New Key*, p. 113, 'In a genuine metaphor an image of the literal meaning is our symbol for the figurative meaning, the thing that has no name of its own.'

24 John Macquarrie, *God-Talk: An Examination of the Language and Logic of Theology* (London, SCM, 1967), p. 194.

25 *Ibid.*, p. 196.

26 McFague, *Metaphorical Theology*, pp. 177ff.

27 *Ibid.*, p. 198.

28 Tracy, *The Analogical Imagination*, p. 410.

29 McFague accepts Ricoeur's distinction between metaphor and symbol. 'Symbols are rooted in reality at a cosmic, prelinguistic level, while metaphors are the linguistic innovation of symbols, interpreting and reinterpreting them.' McFague, *Metaphorical Theology*, p. 202; see Ricoeur's *Interpretation Theory: Discourse and the Surplus of Meaning* (Fort Worth, Texas, Christian University Press, 1976), pp. 45–69. Cf. Bernard Lonergan, *Method in Theology*

(London, Darton, Longman and Todd Ltd., 1971): 'The symbol, then, has the power of recognizing and expressing what logical discourse abhors: the existence of internal tensions, incompatibilities, conflicts, struggles, destructions. A dialectical or methodical viewpoint can embrace, of course, what is concrete, contradictory and dynamic. But the symbol did this before either logic or dialectic were conceived.' p. 66; Avery Dulles discusses the value of symbol from the point of view of the theology of revelation in *Models of Revelation* (New York, Doubleday, 1983), ch. 9.

30 See Baruch A. Brody, 'Morality and Religion Reconsidered', in Paul Helm (ed.), *Divine Commands and Morality* (Oxford Readings in Philosophy) (Oxford, University Press, 1981), pp. 141–53; and in the same volume, R. E. Swinburne, 'Duty and the Will of God', pp. 120–34; D. Z. Phillips, 'God and Ought', pp. 175–80.

31 Max Black, 'More About Metaphor', in A. Ortony (ed.), *Metaphor and Thought* (New York and Cambridge, Cambridge University Press, 1979), p. 31, cited by McFague, *Metaphorical Theology*, p. 38. Cf. Peter Geach, who applies the chess metaphor to the relationship between God and humanity. God is the 'supreme Grand Master' who can anticipate every move his creatures make, thus winning the game, *Providence and Evil* (Cambridge, University Press, 1977), p. 58.

32 See Monroe Beardsley, 'Metaphor', in Paul Edwards (ed.), *The Encyclopedia of Philosophy* (*Vol. V*) (London, Collier/Macmillan; New York, Macmillan/Free Press), pp. 284–8.

33 McFague, *Metaphorical Theology*, pp. 67–73.

34 See John D. Crossan, *The Dark Interval: Towards A Theology of Story* (Niles, Illinois, Argus Communications, 1975), p. 56, where he says that, 'Parable is always a somewhat unnerving experience. You can usually recognize a parable because your immediate reaction will be self-contradictory: "I don't know what you mean by that story but I'm certain I don't like it."'

35 Black, *Models and Metaphors*, pp. 222–3.

36 Barbour, *Myths, Models and Paradigms*, p. 6.

37 Beardsley comments on how precise and concise Gilbert Ryle's metaphor of 'the ghost in the machine' is in criticising Cartesian dualism. 'Metaphor', p. 286. The concepts of 'mind' and 'body' are represented in a captivating image. See Ryle's, *The Concept of Mind* (Harmondsworth, Penguin, 1973).

38 T. F. Torrance is critical of theological models which are over-dependent on the paradigm of vision and wishes to stress an alternative, auditory model, based on the notion of hearing God's Word: 'The outstanding characteristic of theology is that it

operates with a direct act of cognition in *hearing* God and engages in the act of conception through audition.' *Theological Science* (London, Oxford University Press, 1969), p. 23.

39 Black, *Models and Metaphors*, p. 233.

40 McFague, *Metaphorical Theology*, p. 94.

41 Barbour, *Myths, Models and Paradigms*, pp. 49–50.

42 Cf. Gibson Winter, *Liberating Creation: Foundations of Religious Social Ethics* (New York, Crossroads, 1981). Winter sees a fundamental clash between two models used to interpret the world. One is the mechanistic model, on which our modern technological world is based. The other is the more traditional organic/biological model. He claims that women identify with the latter model, men with the former, and that the clash between the two models is evident especially in the controversy over sexism in industry. In his book he argues in favour of a new model which transcends the two just mentioned – it is the metaphor of artistic process. pp. 10ff.

43 McFague, *Metaphorical Theology*, p. 74.

44 Douglas Berggren, 'The Use and Abuse of Metaphor', *Review of Metaphysics*, 16 (1963), pp. 450–72, quotation at p. 456, cited in McFague, *ibid.*, p. 203.

45 Mary B. Hesse, *Models and Analogies in Science* (Notre Dame, Indiana, University of Notre Dame Press, 1966), p. 170, cited in McFague, *Metaphorical Theology*, p. 93.

46 Alastair V. Campbell, *Rediscovering Pastoral Care* (London, Darton, Longman and Todd, 1981, ch. 2, esp. p. 23.

47 Hesse, *Models and Analogies*, p. 169, cited in McFague, p. 93.

48 See Beardsley, 'Metaphor', p. 285.

49 Black, *Models and Metaphors*, p. 233.

50 *Ibid.*

51 C. S. Lewis, 'Bluspels and Flalansferes', in Max Black (ed.), *The Importance of Language* (Englewood Cliffs, New Jersey, Prentice-Hall, 1962), pp. 38–9, cited in McFague, pp. 87–8.

52 A. I. Melden, *Rights and Persons* (Oxford, Blackwell, 1977). Cf. Hart, 'Are There Any Natural Rights', in Waldron, *Theories of Rights*, p. 82, '…the precise figure is not that of two persons bound by a chain but of one person bound, the other end of the chain lying in the hands of another to use if he chooses'.

53 John Hardwig, 'Should Women Think in Terms of Rights?', *Ethics*, 94 (1984), pp. 441–55. Quotation at pp. 442–3. Cf. A. Ingram, 'The Perils of Love: Why Women Need Rights', *Philosophical Studies*, 32 (1988–90), pp. 245–62, esp. p. 261, where she replies to Hardwig.

54 As can be seen in our earlier discussion of the distinctions between 'claims' and 'liberties', 'discretionary' and 'mandatory' rights.

55 Joel Feinberg, 'The Idea of a Free Man', in *Rights, Justice and the Bounds of Liberty: Essays in Social Philosophy* (Princeton, New Jersey, University Press, 1980), pp. 3–29.

56 See Isaiah Berlin, *Four Essays on Liberty*, (Oxford/New York, Oxford University Press, 1969), pp. 118ff.; G. C. MacCallum, Jun., 'Negative and Positive Freedom', *Philosophical Review*, 76 (1967), pp. 312–34.

57 Feinberg, 'The Idea', pp. 6–7.

58 *Ibid.*, p. 9.

59 Michael Meyer, 'Dignity, Rights, and Self-Control', *Ethics*, 99 (1989), pp. 520–34. Cf. John Rawls, *A Theory of Justice* (Oxford, University Press, 1973), who claims that 'perhaps the most important primary good is that of self-respect', p. 440. He relates this good to the experiences of shame and guilt. The latter is felt especially when, 'By wrongly advancing his interests he has transgressed the rights of others', p. 445. The former is felt 'because his conduct shows that he has failed to achieve the good of self-command', *ibid.* In other words, guilt tends to be other directed, while shame focuses on the self and the fear of what others may think.

60 *Ibid.*, p. 531.

61 Feinberg, 'The Idea', p. 11.

62 *Ibid.*, p. 12.

63 Berlin warns against any move to romanticise the 'freedom' of the destitute:

> First things come first: there are situations, as a nineteenth century Russian radical writer declared, in which boots are superior to the works of Shakespeare; individual freedom is not everyone's primary need … The Egyptian peasant needs clothes or medicine before, and more than, personal liberty, but the minimum freedom that he needs today, and the greater degree of freedom that he may need tomorrow, is not some species of freedom peculiar to him, but identical with that of professors, artists and millionaires. *Four Essays on Liberty*, pp. 124–5.

64 Henri Bergson, *The Two Sources of Morality and Religion*, trans. R. Ashley Audra and Cloudesly Brereton (New York, Doubleday, 1935), p. 76, cited in Maguire, *The Moral Choice*, p. 193; see also Hannah Arendt, *The Human Condition* (Garden City, New York, Doubleday/Anchor Books, 1959), p. 289, cited in Maguire, *ibid.*, p. 194.

65 Peter Bachrach and Morton S. Baratz, *Power and Poverty: Theory and Practice* (New York, Oxford University Press, 1970). One of the central theses in this book is the criticism of the view that power is seen centrally in decision-making. This is only 'one face' of power.

The other 'face' is the sphere of 'nondecisions', (p. 16) for instance, the limiting of discussion and decision to 'safe' issues. Issues seen as threatening to individuals and/or groups are buried.

66 According to Bachrach and Baratz, influence tends to involve persons who do not share the same values and where one party is (in one example) 'converted' to 'higher' values. They state that under their definition, 'it would be incorrect to say that Marx "influenced" Lenin, or that Haydn "influenced" Mozart, or that Jesus Christ "influenced" the Conquistadores. In each of these cases the second *shared* the values of the first, that is, the relationship involved neither power nor influence, but *authority*.' p. 31 n. 27. I find this distinction a bit forced and the least satisfactory in the schema. From the moral point of view, influence and authority may be indistinguishable.

67 On authority seen as 'formal power' see H. D. Lasswell and A. Kaplan, *Power and Society* (New Haven, Yale University Press, 1950), p. 133; as 'institutionalised power' see Robert Bierstadt, 'An Analysis of Social Power', *American Sociological Review*, 15 (1950), pp. 730–8.

68 This may be an example of what C. Wright Mills called 'latent power' in *The Power Elite* (New York, Oxford University Press, 1954), p. 8. This involves the situation in which people who have wealth and social position do not appear to actually exercise power. However their potential to use their position can and does have unintended effects in so far as the rest of society may defer to what they think the latently powerful want. See Bachrach and Baratz, *Power and Poverty*, p. 26. A right that is not claimed may still exist as a latent power and may be respected out of fear of possible sanctions.

6 THEOLOGICAL IMAGINATION AND RIGHTS

1 John McIntyre, *Faith, Theology and Imagination* (Edinburgh, The Handsel Press, 1987).

2 John Baillie, *Our Knowledge of God* (Oxford, University Press, 1939), p. 77, cited in McIntyre, *Faith*, p. 1.

3 McIntyre, *Faith*, p. 5.

4 John Calvin, *Institutio*, 1.xi.i, 'God rejects without exception all shapes and pictures, and other symbols by which the superstitious imagine they can bring God near to them. These images defile and insult the majesty of God', quoted in McIntyre, *Faith*, p. 6.

5 In *The Cloud* the author holds that contemplation must transcend the use of imagination, which is valid for beginners, for instance,

meditating on Christ's passion. Simon Tugwell is puzzled by this view: 'So, although our author insists that these things ['subtle and quaint imaginations and meditations'] are necessary before we come to the higher part of the contemplative life, it is not at all clear why, since it is not at all clear how they can possibly lead to anything except error', *Ways of Imperfection: An Exploration of Christian Spirituality* (London, Darton, Longman and Todd, 1984), p. 171.

6 McIntyre, *Faith*, p. 48.

7 George MacDonald, *A Dish of Orts* (Sampson Low, 1907), p. 3, cited by McIntyre, *Faith*, p. 14.

8 D. Maguire, *The Moral Choice* (Minneapolis, Winston Press, 1979) p. 189.

9 Leonardo Boff entitles a section of his work on Christology, 'Jesus, a Person of Extraordinary Creative Imagination, in *Jesus Christ Liberator: A Critical Christology of Our Time*, trans. P. Hughes (London, SPCK, 1980), p. 90:

> Is it not possible that for us this category "imagination" may not reveal the originality and mystery of Christ? Many understand little about imagination and think it is synonymous with dreams, a day dreamer's flight from reality, a passing illusion. In truth, however, imagination signifies something more profound. Imagination is a form of liberty... Perhaps in the whole of human history there has not been a single person who had a richer imagination than Jesus. pp. 90–1.

10 McFague, *Metaphorical Theology: Models of God in Religious Language* (London, SCM, 1983) p. 45. Reference to Ricoeur is an article, 'Biblical Hermeneutics', *Semeia*, 4 (1975), pp. 94–112.

11 Maguire, *The Moral Choice*, p. 190. It is not only religious parables which upset their hearers – secular parables can upset the believer. Consider, for instance, the reaction in theistic circles to John Wisdom's famous parable of the Gardener in his essay 'Gods', in A. Flew (ed.), *Logic and Language*, 1st series (Oxford, Blackwell, 1951), ch. 10.

12 Rubem Alves, *Tomorrow's Child* (New York, Harper and Row, 1972), pp. 67–8, cited by Maguire, *The Moral Choice*, p. 190. Note however the recognition of the ambiguity of imagination even in modern times. Maguire devotes a section of his chapter on ethics and creativity to 'Imagination Astray' where he says that 'We can be monstrously as well as morally imaginative', p. 213. Particularly in his mind is the (imaginative) development of weapons of destruction. See also Irish Murdoch, 'Ethics and Imagination', *Irish Theological Quarterly*, 52 (1986), pp. 81–95, esp. p. 81 for the statement: 'The word "imagination" cannot be taken to represent

a single faculty. Analysis reveals, even to start with, good and bad imagining, creative and mechanical imagining, conscious and unconscious imagining.'; cf. Richard Kearney, *The Wake of Imagination: Ideas of Creativity in Western Culture* (London/ Melbourne, Hutchinson, 1988), p. 3, where he states that 'One of the greatest paradoxes of contemporary culture is that at a time when the image reigns supreme the very notion of a creative human imagination seems under mounting threat.'

13 H. Richard Niebuhr, *The Responsible Self: An Essay in Christian Moral Philosophy* (San Francisco, Harper and Row, 1978), esp. pp. 149–60.

14 Niebuhr, *ibid.*, p. 159; consider traditional references to the 'Church militant' on earth; cf. W. W. How's hymn, 'Thou wast their rock, their fortress and their might; Thou, Lord, their captain in the well-fought fight', and consider the imagery of John Donne's fifth Holy Sonnet, 'Batter my heart, three-personed God... Reason your viceroy in me, should defend, But is captived and proves weak or untrue.'

15 On the pilgrimage theme see G. Hughes, 'The Poor Man's Mysticism', *The Tablet*, 9 March 1991, pp. 298–9.

16 Niebuhr, *The Responsible Self*, p. 154, 157. Note how 'symbol' and 'metaphor' are used interchangeably by this author, *pace* McFague and Ricoeur.

17 McFague, *Metaphorical Theology*, p. 44; cf. J. D. Crossan, *The Dark Interval: Towards a Theology of Story* (Niles, Argues, 1975), p. 124: 'Jesus announced the Kingdom of God in parables, but the primitive church announced Jesus as the Christ, the parable of God.'

18 See C. K. Barrett, *Freedom and Obligation: A Study of the Epistle to the Galatians* (London, SPCK, 1985); Dietmar Mieth and Jacques Pohier (eds.), *The Ethics of Liberation – The Liberation of Ethics*, Concilium 172 2/1984 (Edinburgh, T. and T. Clark); Oliver O'Donovan, *Resurrection and Moral Order: An Outline for Evangelical Ethics* (Leicester, Intervarsity Press/Grand Rapids, Eerdmans, 1986), chs. 5 and 8; Franz Bockle, *Fundamental Moral Theology*, trans. N. D. Smith (Dublin, Gill and Macmillan, 1980), pp. 114–23.

19 See Denis Carroll, *Toward A Story of the Earth: Essays in the Theology of Creation* (Dublin, Dominican Publications, 1987), pp. 158ff. – 'a theology of human rights can present the imperative for austerity, for simplicity, even for asceticism,', p. 158.

20 F. Gerald Downing, *Jesus and the Threat of Freedom* (London, SCM, 1987), pp. 3–4.

21 For further material on the Cynics see, F. Gerald Downing, *Christ and the Cynics* (Sheffield, Sheffield Academic Press, 1988); A. J. Malherbe, *The Cynic Epistles* (Missoula, Scholar's Press, 1977).

22 Dio (Chrysostom) of Prusa, *Discourse*, 12.61, Loeb edition (Harvard, 1932), trans. J. W. Cohoon and H. L. Crosby; cited by Downing, *Jesus*, pp. 96–7.

23 Epictetus, *Arrian's Discourses of Epictetus*, 1, 6.40–1, Loeb edition (Harvard, 1925), trans. W. A. Oldfather; cited by Downing, *ibid.*, p. 97.

24 Downing, *Jesus*, p. 58; cf. this statement from Austin Smith, *Journeying with God: Paradigms of Power and Powerlessness* (London, Sheed and Ward, 1990), p. 138:

> The power elites of this world, for the most part, don't mind your daydreaming, and they don't get too anxious about your visions. But if you start saying you are going to redefine the whole meaning of their power, and you seem to have some credibility and following among the oppressed and those seeking solidarity with the oppressed, then you are in trouble. That's when the crosses go up. Cited in Peader Kirby, 'The Cross, the Kingdom and the Looney Left', *Doctrine and Life*, 41/4 (1991), pp. 203–8, quotation at p. 203.

25 Downing, *Jesus*, p. 59.

26 Berlin, *Four Essays on Liberty*, (Oxford/New York, Oxford University Press, 1969), pp. 135–6; cf. Reinhold Niebuhr's remark, 'Classical idealism and mysticism in short understand the transcendent freedom of the human spirit; but they do not understand it in its organic relation to the temporal process. The natural and temporal process is merely something from which man must be emancipated.' *The Nature and Destiny of Man*, 2 vols. (London, Nisbet and Co., 1943), II, *Human Destiny*, p. 12.

27 Luise Schottroff, 'Experiences of Liberation. Liberty and Liberation according to Biblical Testimony', in D. Mieth and J. Pohier (eds.), *The Liberation of Ethics*, pp. 67–73, quotation at p. 68.

28 Donal Murray, 'The Theological Basis for Human Rights', *Irish Theological Quarterly*, 56/2 (1990), pp. 81–101.

29 Cf. Paul Ramsey, *Basic Christian Ethics* (New York, Scribners, 1951), p. 354: 'A Christian doctrine of rights likewise follows primarily from man's service of God, and not from man's nature as man.'

30 Paul Ricoeur, *La Philosophie de la Volunte* (*3 vols.*), I, *Le Voluntaire et la Involuntaire* (Paris, Aubier, Editions Montaigne, 1967), p. 45; cited by Murray, 'The Theological Basis', p. 83.

31 From the scriptural/exegetical point of view see especially Claus Westerman, *Genesis 1–11: A Commentary*, trans. J. J. Scullion (Minneapolis, Augsberg Publishing House, 1984), pp. 36–9; and detailed bibliography pp. 147–8; From the point of view of theology see Edmund Hill, *Being Human: A Biblical Perspective*, Introducing Catholic Theology series (London, Chapman, 1984), ch. 19; Reinhold Niebuhr, *The Nature and Destiny of Man*, 2 vols. (London, Nisbet, 1941), I, *Human Nature*, ch. 6; Edward Schillebeeckx, *God and Man*, trans. E. Fitzgerald and P. Tomlinson (London and Sydney, Sheed and Ward, 1969), esp. ch. 5, 'The Mystery of God as the centre of man's essence'.

32 McIntyre, *Faith*, p. 73.

33 Jose Miguez Bonino derives the universality of human rights from the concept of creation. Beginning with the affirmation of God's oneness he argues that:

> The consequence cannot be avoided: there is only one mankind. Within the New Testament this consequence is first drawn in relation to the new Christian community: all are one body, in which all members have equal dignity and value: social, ethnic, cultural, even sexual distinctions cannot justify any discrimination. But this universality overflows the limits of any community. Every human being bears the image of God; it is therefore absurd and sacriligious 'to bless the Lord and Father...and to curse men, who are made in the likeness of God'. (James 3.11)

'Religious Commitment and Human Rights', in Alan D. Falconer (ed.), *Understanding Human Rights: An Interdisciplinary and Interfaith Study* (Dublin, Irish School of Ecumenics, 1980), pp. 21–33, quotation at pp. 29–30.

34 See Jurgen Moltmann, 'Christian Faith and Human Rights', in Falconer, *Understanding Human Rights*, p. 186.

35 Unfortunately, Murray does not analyse the concept of equality in sufficient depth, so one is not sure exactly what he is criticising. There is no contradiction in stressing equality and at the same time holding that respect for freedom involves respecting the dialogue with the infinite. In fact Bishop Murray borders on inconsistency, for on p. 82 he claims that if any of the three elements – freedom, equality and participation – was studied in depth, it would sustain the whole structure on its own.

36 See Joseph Fletcher, 'Indicators of Humanhood: A Tentative Profile of Man', *Hastings Center Report*, 2/5 (1972), pp. 1–4.

37 Paul Ramsey, *The Patient as Person: Explorations in Medical Ethics* (New Haven/London, Yale University Press, 1970), p. 253.

38 See Judith Jarvis Thomson, 'Preferential Hiring', in W. Parent

(ed.), *Rights, Restitution and Risk: Essays in Moral Theory* (Cambridge, Massachusetts/London, Harvard University Press, 1986), pp. 135–53; George Sher, 'Justifying Reverse Discrimination in Employment', in J. Rachels (ed.), *Moral Problems: A Collection of Philosophical Essays*, 3rd edition (New York, Harper and Row, 1979), pp. 48–59.

39 Murray, 'The Theological Basis', p. 81. It's important to note that at a very general level certain rights are 'mandatory', while at a more personal level they can be 'discretionary'. Thus, the Christian has a mandatory right to choose a way of life or calling which will be the basis of his or her daily response to God. But each person has a discretionary right whether to marry or remain single. Thus, some way of life must be chosen, but individual discretion is permitted in making the particular choice.

40 Colin Gunton, *Enlightenment and Alienation: An Essay Towards a Trinitarian Theology* (Basingstoke, Marshall, Morgan and Scott, 1985), p. 90.

41 *Ibid.* p. 94. According to Leonardo Boff, Jesus never used the word 'Obedience'. Yet he was obedient to his Father's will, not merely in the scriptures, but by consulting the signs of the times: 'Obedience is a question of having our eyes open to the situation; it consists in deciding for and risking ourselves in the adventure of responding to God who speaks here and now.' *Jesus Christ Liberator*, pp. 92–3.

42 Jurgen Moltmann, *The Crucified God* (New York, Harper and Row, 1974).

43 Gunton, *Enlightenment*, p. 99.

44 Alan White, *Rights* (Oxford, Clarendon Press, 1984), p. 34ff.

45 'Jury service', according to Joel Feinberg, 'can be quite intelligibly described both as a duty *and* as a right, though it is more likely to be described as the former by a harrassed and annoyed citizen grudgingly performing the service, and as the latter by the victim of discrimination who is excluded from the process'. 'Voluntary Euthanasia and the Inalienable Right to Life', in *Rights, Justice and the Bounds of Liberty: Essays in Social Philosophy* (Princeton, New Jersey, University Press, 1980), p. 237.

46 Feinberg, 'The Idea of a Free Man', in *Rights, Justice*, p. 12.

7 RIGHTS, POWER AND COVENANT

1 Paul Tillich, *Love, Power and Justice* (Oxford, University Press, 1960), p. 8.

2 *Ibid.*, p. 12.

3 Karl Rahner, 'The Theology of Power', *Theological Investigations IV*, trans. Kevin Smyth (Baltimore, Helicon/London, Darton, Longman and Todd, 1966), pp. 391–409, quotation at p. 391.

4 *Ibid.*, p. 392.

5 Alan Falconer, 'Theological Reflection on Human Rights', in *Understanding Human Rights* (Dublin, Irish School of Ecumenics, 1980), pp. 199ff.

6 Rollo May, *Power and Innocence* (Glasgow, Collins/Fontana, 1976).

7 Edgar Z. Friedenburg, *Coming of Age in America* (New York, Random House, 1965), pp. 47–8, cited in May, *Power*, p. 24.

8 The challenge of pacifism is to use wisely the integrative power of non-violence. Far from being a position of weakness pacifism is founded on this morally superior type of 'power'.

9 See the profound remark of Simone Weil:

> Those who keep masses of men in subjection by exercising force and cruelty deprive them of two vital foods, liberty and obedience; for it is no longer within the power of such masses to accord their inner consent to the authority to which they are subjected.

The Need for Roots: Prelude to a Declaration of Duties Towards Mankind (London and New York, Ark Paperback, 1987), p. 14.

10 Murray, 'The Theological Basis for Human Rights', *Irish Theological Quarterly*, 56/2 (1990), pp. 81–101, quotation at p. 87.

11 See Anthony Kenny, *The God of the Philosophers* (Oxford, Clarendon Press, 1979), Part III; Nelson Pike, *God and Timelessness* (New York, Schocken Books, 1970); Brian Davies, *An Introduction to the Philosophy of Religion* (Oxford, University Press, 1982), ch. 8.

12 Janet Martin Soskice, 'God of Power and Might', *The Month*, November 1988, pp. 934–8, quotation at p. 935.

13 Maurice Wiles, *God's Action in the World* (London, SCM, 1986).

14 David Jenkins, *God, Miracles, and the Church of England* (London, SCM, 1987).

15 Gordon D. Kaufman, *God the Problem* (Cambridge, Massachusetts; London, Harvard University Press, 1972).

16 Jurgen Moltmann, *The Trinity and the Kingdom of God* (London, SCM, 1981), pp. 3–4, cited by Soskice, 'God of Power', p. 934.

17 Walter Kasper, *The God of Jesus Christ* (London, SCM, 1983), p. 148, cited by Soskice, p. 937.

18 W. H. Vanstone, *The Stature of Waiting* (London, Darton, Longman and Todd, 1982).

19 Soskice, 'God of Power', p. 938.

20 See Michael Prior, 'Paul on "Power and Weakness"', *The Month*, November 1988, pp. 939–44; The Christological basis of Paul's theology is made clear: 'It should not come as a surprise that

"weakness" should not be distant from "strength" in the thought-patterns of one whose Lord, in whom the fulness of the deity existed, suffered the despicable death of crucifixion', p. 942.

21 See Martin Hengel, *Christ and Power*, trans. E. R. Kalin (Belfast, Christian Journals, 1977), p. 15; see James Reese, 'The Event of Jesus – Power in Flesh', in Franz Bockle and Jacques Marie Pohier (eds.), *Power, Domination, Service*, Concilium, 10/9, 1973 (London, Burns and Oates), pp. 40–50.

22 See Werner Foerster, 'Exousia', in G. Kittel (ed.), *Theological Dictionary of the New Testament*, trans. and ed. G. W. Bromley (Grand Rapids, Eerdmans, 1964), pp. 562–75. For instance in Mark 2.10 Jesus is asked by the scribes to justify his 'power' ('*dunamis*', which connotes strength or a mighty act/miracle), and he replies using the term '*exousia*', a word which comprises both right and power.

23 Downing, *Jesus and the Threat of Freedom* (London, SCM, 1987), p. 70.

24 Epictetus (Arrian's Discourses of Epictetus), IV.1.127, cited in Downing, *ibid.*

25 Hengel, *Christ and Power*, p. 15.

26 Vanstone, *The Stature of Waiting*, p. 49.

27 See John L. MacKenzie, 'Covenant', in his *Dictionary of the Bible* (London/Dublin, G. Chapman, 1972), pp. 153–7; Denis J. McCarthy, *Old Testament Covenant; A Survey of Current Opinions*, Growing Points in Theology series (Oxford, Blackwell, 1972); Walther Eichrodt, *Theology of the Old Testament*, trans. J. A. Baker, 2 vols. (London, SCM, 1961), I, ch. 2; Robert P. Carroll, *From Chaos to Covenant: Uses of Prophecy in the Book of Jeremiah* (London, SCM, 1981); John Bright, *Covenant and Promise: The Future in the Preaching of the Pre-exilic Prophets* (London, SCM, 1977), esp. ch. 2.

28 Joseph Allen, *Love and Conflict: A Covenantal Model of Christian Ethics* (Nashville, Abingdon Press, 1984).

29 On the covenant model in Christian ethics see: Ian C. M. Fairweather and James I. H. McDonald, *The Quest for Christian Ethics: An Inquiry into Ethics and Christian Ethics*, (Edinburgh, Handsel Press, 1984), pp. 116–21; Thomas W. Ogletree, *The Use of the Bible in Christian Ethics* (Oxford, Blackwell, 1984), ch. 3; Philip S. Keane, *Christian Ethics and Imagination*, pp. 114–15, 121–3, 125–6; Philip Rossi, *Together Toward Hope: A Journey to Moral Theology* (Notre Dame, University of Notre Dame Press, 1983), pp. 149, 191; P. Ramsey, *The Patient as Person* (New Haven/London, Yale University Press, 1970), Preface, pp. xiiff.

30 As Wilfred Harrington puts it: 'The Hebrew word *torah* has a wider signification, one less juridical, than the *nomos* of the LXX or

the English "law"; it is a "teaching" given by God to men in order to regulate their conduct. That is why the whole Pentateuch, and not only the legislation, is called the Torah.' 'The Law, the Prophets, and the Gospel', in Enda McDonagh (ed.), *Moral Theology Renewed* (Dublin, Gill and Son, 1965), pp. 31–54, quotation at p. 32.

31 William May, *The Physician's Covenant: Images of the Healer in Medical Ethics* (Philadelphia, Westminster Press, 1983), p. 110.

32 See Loren Lomasky, 'Personal Projects as the Foundation for Basic Rights', in E. F. Paul, F. D. Miller and J. Paul (eds.), *Human Rights* (Oxford, Blackwell, 1984), pp. 35–55.

33 T. W. Manson, *Ethics and the Gospel* (London, SCM, 1960), p. 17.

34 *Ibid.*, p. 17.

35 Birger Gerhardsson, *The Ethos of the Bible*, trans. S. Westerholm (London, Darton, Longman and Todd, 1982), p. 21. See also the controversy regarding the love commandment in the Johannine literature of the New Testament. Does 'loving one another' (Jn. 13.34 and 15.12,17) mean one's neighbour in a very wide sense, or is its scope limited to fellow disciples? For discussion of this see, Jack T. Sanders, *Ethics in the New Testament: Change and Development* (London, SCM, 1986), ch. 5 and cf. Raymond F. Collins, '"A New Commandment I Give to You, That You Love One Another..." (Jn. 13:34)', *Christian Morality: Biblical Foundations* (Notre Dame, Indiana, University Press, 1986), ch. 5.

36 Gerhardsson, *The Ethos*, p. 21.

37 See Eugene B. Borowitz, 'The Torah, Written and Oral, and Human Rights: Foundations and Deficiencies', in Kung and Moltmann, *The Ethics of World Religions*, Concilium, 1990/2 (London, SCM/Philadelphia, Trinity Press International), pp. 25–33. This author refers to the Talmudic tradition which sees in the covenant God made with Noah and his children the basis of Jewish theology of the gentile. But the gentiles violated the covenant by their idolatry.

> The critical point is that they were not condemned merely because they were gentiles, religiously alien, but because of their behaviour. Thus, rabbinic tradition came to the authoritative position that pious individuals among the gentiles, like Jews, had 'a share in the life of the world to come'. Clearly, the beliefs which ground this point of view could in a later age, one of much greater human interaction and equality, make possible a Jewish ground for a universal declaration of human rights. (p. 29)

38 See Michael Sandel's comment on Rawls' theory of justice: 'The difficulty with Rawls' theory of the good is epistemological as well

as moral.' 'Justice and the Good', in M. Sandel (ed.), *Liberalism and Its Critics*, Readings in Social and Political Theory (New York, New York University Press, 1984), p. 159. And he continues:

> Only the person himself can 'know' what he really wants or 'decide' what he most prefers. 'Even when we take up another's point of view and attempt to estimate what would be to his advantage, we do so as an adviser, so to speak' (1971, p. 448), and given the limited cognitive access Rawls' conception allows, a rather unprivileged adviser at that. (p. 165, internal quotation from Rawls' *Theory of Justice* (Oxford, University Press, 1971)

39 An interesting question from the religious sphere, and especially in Roman Catholicism, is the putative right of believers to the Eucharist and to ministers who will celebrate it in a world experiencing a shortage of male and celibate clergy. Can we call this claim to have married priests and/or women priests a 'manifesto right'? Here the correlative obligation would appear to lie at the door of the church's hierarchy.

40 Cf. James Tunstead Burtchaell's mention of the tension between the two models of covenant, each with its own model of God:

> There seem to be two Gods here. On the one hand, there is a Lord who chooses Israel irrespective of Israel's merits. Yet there is also the Lord who will continue to cherish Israel only on the ground of her merits. The Old Testament oscillates between the two ideologies, trying to sidestep the hazards of each. If you have a God who is totally gratuitous, then what possible serious motive have you for being righteous? But if being at peace with God depends upon your being righteous, how can you call his blessing a gift?
> *Living with Grace* (London, Sheed and Ward, 1973), p. 26.

41 William May, 'Code, Covenant, Contract or Philanthropy: A Basis for Professional Ethics', *Hastings Center Report*, December 1975, pp. 29–38, esp. pp. 33–5.

42 Far from being a vague religious concept, covenant has a firm foundation in international law at a very practical level. Maurice Cranston reminds us that the United Nations Commission on Human Rights felt that the Declaration of Rights would need to be followed up with a covenant or covenants which would be legally binding on member states, *Human Rights To-day* (London, Ampersand, 1962), ch. 4. The General Assembly of the UN unanimously adopted 'The International Covenants for the Protection of Human Rights' in December 1966. Sadly it took ten more years before these covenants were ratified.

43 It is difficult to express in a short statement what is meant by 'reason' in this context. We should at least keep in mind the

remarks of W. Frankena, in his *Ethics*, 2nd edn. (New Jersey, Prentice-Hall, 1973), p. 13:

> I think that moral philosophers cannot insist too much on the importance of factual knowledge and conceptual clarity for the solution of moral and social problems. The two besetting sins in our prevailing habits of ethical thinking are our ready acquiescence in unclarity and our complacence in ignorance – the very sins that Socrates died combatting over two thousand years ago.

Reason, in this sense, is not simply the pre-condition for making sense in moral argument or in presenting an authoritative communication of a moral position, it is also a way of being a moral agent. Sticking to facts and trying to be clear in one's use of concepts and images form part of the process of overcoming bias, as well as reminding us how easily we become the prisoners of ideology.

8 THEOLOGICAL FOUNDATIONS OF RIGHTS-LANGUAGE

1 From the Protestant side see James M. Gustafson, *Can Ethics Be Christian?* (Chicago, University Press, 1975).
2 Vincent MacNamara, *Faith and Ethics: Recent Roman Catholicism* (Dublin, Gill and Macmillan, 1985).
3 For further discussion of the possible links between religion and morality see: Brian Davies, *An Introduction to the Philosophy of Religion* (Oxford, University Press, 1982), ch. 10; Peter Baelz, *Ethics and Belief* (London, Sheldon Press, 1977); Kai Nielsen, *Ethics Without God* (London, Pemberton Books, 1973); Paul Helm, 'Introduction' in Helm (ed.), *Divine Commands and Morality* (Oxford, University Press, 1981); Ian C. M. Fairweather and James I. H. McDonald, *The Quest for Christian Ethics: An Inquiry into Ethics and Christian Ethics* (Edinburgh, The Handsel Press, 1984), ch. 6.
4 See Joseph Fuchs, 'Is There a Specifically Christian Morality?', in C. Curran and R. McCormick (eds.), *Readings in Moral Theology No. 2: The Distinctiveness of Christian Ethics* (New York, Paulist Press, 1980), pp. 3–19; also in the same collection, Bruno Schuller, 'The Debate on the Specific Character of Christian Ethics: Some Remarks', pp. 207–33; and Charles Curran, 'Is There a Catholic and/or Christian Ethic?', pp. 60–89.
5 See these essays in Curran and McCormick, *Readings in Moral Theology No. 2:* Joseph Ratzinger, 'Magisterium in the Church, Faith and Morality', pp. 174–89; Ph. Delhaye, 'Questioning the Specificity of Christian Morality', pp. 234–69; and Norbert Rigali, 'Christ and Morality', pp. 11–20.

6 It should be noted that reference to a 'school of thought' does not assume an identity of opinion between those classed together, but a common trend or motif which sets them apart from other thinkers in the particular sphere of discussion.

7 MacNamara, *Faith and Ethics*, p. 96.

8 *Ibid.*, p. 102; among the philosophers he mentions are: William Frankena, 'The Concept of Morality' in G. Wallace and A. D. M. Walker (eds.), *The Definition of Morality* (London, Methuen, 1970), pp. 146–73; P. Foot, 'Moral Arguments' in her *Virtues and Vices and Other Essays in Moral Philosophy* (Oxford, Blackwell, 1978), pp. 96–109; and Bernard Williams, *Morality* (Harmondsworth, Penguin, 1973).

9 Oliver O'Donovan is rather dismissive of this debate in Roman Catholicism, accusing the faith–ethic school of being 'implicitly voluntarist in its foundation', while attacking the autonomists for allowing 'no critical distance on the moral commonplaces of our culture because it refuses to admit an authoritative perspective in revelation', *Resurrection and Moral Order: An Outline for Evangelical Ethics* (Leicester, Intervarsity Press/Grand Rapids, Eerdmans, 1986), p. 20.

10 See the essays in Mark Searle (ed.), *Liturgy and Social Justice* (Collegeville, Liturgical Press, 1980), esp. Edward J. Kilmartin, 'The Sacrifice of Thanksgiving and Social Justice', pp. 53–71, and Regis Duffy, 'Symbols of Abundance, Symbols of Need', pp. 72–90.

11 On the Thomistic doctrine of prayer see Simon Tugwell, 'Thomas Aquinas and Prayer' in P. Lemass (ed.), *Learning to Pray: Lessons from the Masters* (Dublin, Veritas, 1977), pp. 84–95.

12 See the discussion of 'Prayer and the moral life' in Vincent Brummer, *What Are We Doing When We Pray? A Philosophical Inquiry* (London, SCM, 1984), pp. 111–13. Another view of the relationship between prayer and morality is Kant's in *Religion within the Limits of Reason Alone*, trans. T. M. Green and H. H. Hudson (New York, Harper and Bros., 1960), p. 181, where prayer borders on auto-suggestion with a view to strengthening the will to do one's duty. See also: D. Z. Phillips, *The Concept of Prayer* (Oxford, Blackwell, 1981); Hugo Meynell, *God and the World: The Coherence of Christian Theism* (London, SPCK, 1971), ch. 5.

13 MacNamara, *Faith and Ethics*, p. 103ff.

14 See G. E. M. Anscombe, *Intention* (Oxford, Blackwell, 1957); Anthony Kenny, *Action, Emotion and Will* (London, Routledge and Kegan Paul, 1963); A. Flew, *God and Philosophy* (London, Hutchinson, 1966), ch. 9; C. H. Whitely, *Mind in Action: An Essay*

in Philosophical Psychology (London/Oxford/New York, Oxford
University Press, 1973), ch. 5; G. Ryle, *The Concept of Mind*
(Harmondsworth, Penguin, 1973); Alan White (ed.), *The Philosophy of Action* Oxford Readings in Philosophy (Oxford, University Press, 1968). From the point of view of Christian ethics see
the discussion of motive in Fairweather and McDonald, *The Quest
for Christian Ethics*, ch. 3.

15 For a helpful analysis of the function of reasons in ethics, see
Gilbert Harman, *The Nature of Morality: An Introduction to Ethics*
(New York, Oxford University Press, 1977), chs. 10 and 11; also
Kurt Baier, *The Moral Point of View* (Ithaca, New York, Cornell
University Press, 1958), ch. 3. P. Foot, in a postscript to her essay,
'Reasons for Action and Desires', *Virtues and Vices*, pp. 148–56,
states: 'I am sure that I do not understand the idea of a reason for
acting, and I wonder whether anyone else does either', p. 156. She
concludes that having a reason for doing something may be based
either on what is in the agent's interest, or on the agent's desire,
and these are independent sources. One does not always desire
what is in one's interest.

16 For an uncompromising statement of the importance of religious
justifying reasons see Reinhold Niebuhr's treatment of 'The Ethic
of Jesus', in particular his discussion of the command to forgive
and love one's enemies, 'The justification for these demands is put
in purely religious and not in socio-moral terms. We are to forgive
because God forgives [Mtt. 18:23]; we are to love our enemies
because God is impartial in his love. The points of reference are
vertical and not horizontal. Neither natural impulses nor social
consequences are taken into consideration.' *An Interpretation of
Christian Ethics* (New York, Seabury Press, 1979), p. 28.

17 According to P. J. McGrath, natural law moralists offer very
different reasons for judging certain courses of action to be wrong.
This is acceptable, he says, when treating of individual actions
(act-tokens), since an individual action may belong to several
moral species at once. However, this is unacceptable, in his
opinion, when treating of universal moral principles or species of
actions (act-types): 'a morally wrong species as such cannot be
morally wrong for a number of reasons for this would mean that it
was simultaneously both one species and several species'. 'Natural
Law and Moral Argument' in J. P. Mackey (ed.), *Morals, Law and
Authority: Sources and Attitudes in the Church* (Dublin, Gill and
Macmillan, 1969), p. 61. Does this imply that we must choose
between a 'religious reason' for respecting rights, rejecting the
humanistic or secular reasons for doing so? Not, I think, if we take

the doctrine of the image of God in humanity seriously – for in respecting individuals in themselves we respect the divine in them. In other words, we find only one species of reason for acting, consisting of two inseparable aspects, divine and human.

18 See the document of the Second Vatican Council, *Guadium et Spes*, 33, in Austin Flannery (ed.), *Vatican Council 11: The Conciliar and Post Conciliar Documents* (Dublin, Dominican Publications, 1975), 'The Church is guardian of the heritage of the divine word and draws religious and moral principles from it, but she does not always have a ready answer to every question', p. 933.

19 See Stanley Hauerwas, *A Community of Character: Toward a Constructive Christian Social Ethic* (Notre Dame/London, University of Notre Dame Press, 1981); also Fairweather and McDonald, *The Quest for Christian Ethics*, ch. 3, 'Is Motive the Measure', especially pp. 90–1.

20 See Ceslaus Spicq, *St Paul and Christian Living*, trans. Sr. Marie Aquinas (Dublin, Gill and Son, 1963), 'But our essential reaction in the face of divine goodness, the one which will be the inspiring force of our moral life, is clearly that of gratitude', p. 35. In part this gratitude is a response to the gifts of being made in God's image and being offered a covenant relationship.

21 See A. M. Allchin, *Participation in God: A Forgotten Strand in Anglican Tradition* (London, Darton, Longman and Todd, 1988); and V. Lossky, *In the Image and Likeness of God* (Oxford, Mowbrays, 1975).

22 Emil Brunner, *Christianity and Civilisation*, 2 vols. (London, Nisbet, 1947–8).

23 *Ibid.*, I, p. 108.

24 *Ibid.*, II, p. 112.

25 Jurgen Moltmann, 'Christian Faith and Human Rights', in Falconer, *Understanding Human Rights* (Dublin, Irish School of Ecumenics, 1980), p. 193. Cf. J. Maritain, *The Rights of Man and Natural Law* (San Francisco, Ignatius Press, 1986), 'The notion of a right is even more profound than that of moral obligation, for God has sovereign rights over creatures and he has no moral obligation toward them (although he owes it to Himself to give them that which is required by their nature)', p. 145.

26 See Moltmann, 'Christian Faith', p. 190; W. Huber and H. E. Todt (eds.), *Menschenrechte, Perspektiven Einer Menslichen Welt*, (Stuttgart, Kreuz Verlag, 1977); David Jenkins, 'Theological Inquiry Concerning Human Rights: Some Questions, Hypotheses and Theses', *The Ecumenical Review*, 27/2 (1975), pp. 97–103, where he states that 'the struggle for human rights requires no theological justification', p. 99.

27 Frank Bockle, *Fundamental Moral Theology*, trans. N. D. Smith (Dublin, Gill and Macmillan, 1980), p. 5.

28 John A. Henley, 'Theology and the Basis of Human Rights', *Scottish Journal of Theology*, 39 (1986), pp. 361–78.

29 Brian Davies argues from traditional theistic premises that God cannot be a moral agent, since this would imply that God is a being among other beings; because moral agents are usually said to have duties as well as rights; and due to the fact that moral agency is generally linked with the notions of success and failure in the moral enterprise. None of these criteria apply to God as understood traditionally. Thus, if God has rights, they are not of the type possessed by normal moral agents. *An Introduction to Philosophy of Religion*, pp. 22–4. In *The Need for Roots: Prelude to a Declaration of Duties towards Mankind* (London/New York, Ark Paperback, 1987) Simone Weil states categorically, 'Neither the notion of obligation nor that of right is compatible with God, but infinitely less so that of right. For the notion of right is infinitely farther removed from pure good.' p. 265.

30 Albert C. Knudson, *The Principles of Christian Ethics* (New York/Nashville, Abingdon-Cokesbury Press, no date), p. 29.

31 Christopher Wright, *Human Rights: A Study in Biblical Themes* (Bramcote, Nottinghamshire, Grove Books, 1979), p. 18.

32 Joseph Allen, 'A Theological Approach to Moral Rights', *Journal of Religious Ethics*, 2/1 (1974), pp. 119–41.

33 *Ibid.*, p. 131.

34 André Dumas, *Political Theology and the Life of the Church*, trans. John Bowden (London, SCM, 1978), chs. 2 and 4; cited by Falconer, 'Theological Reflection on Human Rights', in *Understanding Human Rights*, p. 212.

35 See Leonardo Boff and Clodovis Boff, *Salvation and Liberation: In Search of a Balance Between Faith and Politics*, trans. R. Barr (Maryknoll, Orbis Books, 1984), pp. 2–3; Jose Miguez Bonino, 'Religious Commitment and Human Rights', in Falconer, *Understanding Human Rights*, pp. 21–33.

36 Jenkins, 'Theological Inquiry Concerning Human Rights', p. 99.

37 Allen, 'A Theological Approach', pp. 131–2.

38 Jean-Marie Aubert, 'Human Rights: Challenge to the churches', *Theology Digest*, 33/1 (1986), pp. 139–44, esp. pp. 142–3; Bonino, 'Religious Commitment and Human Rights', p. 26; Joseph Blank, 'The Justice of God as the Humanisation of Man – The Problem of Human Rights in the New Testament', in A. Muller and N. Greinacher (eds.), *The Church and the Rights of Man*, Concilium, 1979 (New York, Seabury Press), p. 27; D. Carroll, *Towards A*

Story of the Earth: Essays in the Theology of Creation (Dublin, Dominican Publications, 1987), p. 148ff.; Moltmann, 'Christian Faith and Human Rights', p. 149; Walter Kasper, 'The Theological Foundations of Human Rights', *The Jurist*, 50 (1990), pp. 148–66, esp. p. 151ff.

39 James Childress, 'Image of God (Imago Dei)', in J. F. Childress and J. Macquarrie (eds.), *A New Dictionary of Christian Ethics* (London, SCM, 1986), pp. 292–3. See the brief discussion in ch. 6 and n. 31, p. 304.

40 M. Flick and Z. Alszeghy, *Fondamenti di una Antropologia Teologica*, Nuova Collana di Teologia Cattolica, 10 (Florence, Libreria Editrice Fiorentina, 1969), pp. 62–4; See references to the major commentaries in ch. 6.; Claus Westerman sounds a warning in saying: 'What is striking is that one verse about the person, almost unique in the Old Testament, has become the centre of attention in modern exegesis, whereas it has no such significance in the rest of the Old Testament and, apart from psalm 8, does not occur again. This interest does not derive from the Bible itself but from certain presuppositions in the spiritual order which we cannot overlook. *Genesis 1–11: A Commentary*, trans. J. J. Scullion (Minneapolis, Augsberg Publishing House, 1984), p. 148. From our point of view in relation to rights it is not essential that the biblical writers made an explicit connection between image, dignity and rights. We are treating of a set of models or metaphors which have some basis in scripture, but there is no intention of driving the point home in any dogmatic or fundamentalist manner.

41 Buber, cited in Carroll, *Towards a Story of the Earth*, p. 84. Cf. the view of Bruce Vawter, 'Man is not only a creature but a conscious creature, and in the consciousness of his creaturehood he mirrors in some fashion that supreme consciousness with whom he can dialogue.' *On Genesis: A New Reading* (London, G. Chapman, 1977), p. 57. In this Vawter underlines the ability of man to ask the question how he relates to God and to the rest of creation.

42 Flick and Alszeghy, *Fondamenti*, p. 63; cf. Gerhard Von Rad, *Genesis: A Commentary*, trans. J. H. Marks, 2nd edition (London, SCM, 1963), for a functional approach to the image concept. The text dwells more on the purpose of man as image rather than on the nature of the image. In question is man's dominance in the world, especially over animals. He says that this is not so much part of the definition of God's image as a consequence of it, i.e., 'that for which man is capable because of it', p. 57.

43 Albert Gelin, *The Concept of Man in the Bible*, trans. D. M. Murphy (London/Dublin/Melbourne, G. Chapman, 1968), ch. 2.

44 *Ibid.*, p. 43; cf. Walther Eichrodt, *Theology of the Old Testament*, trans. J. A. Baker, 2 vols. (London, SCM, 1961), II, pp. 122–31. Eichrodt comments on the Priestly writer's rejection of anthropomorphism, speaking of his 'advance from the idea of a tangible image to that of parabolic similarity', p. 124. We might perhaps replace the last two words with references to metaphor and model without any essential loss of meaning.

45 Edmund Jacob, *Theology of the Old Testament*, trans. A. W. Heathcote and P. J. Allcock (London, Hodder and Stoughton, 1958), pp. 166–71; cited by Gelin, *The Concept*, p. 31.

46 For a useful discussion see J. L. Mackie, *The Miracle of Theism: Arguments for and against the Existence of God* (Oxford, Clarendon Press, 1982), pp. 162–76.

47 Vawter stresses that human domination is seen here as royal rule and therefore absolute, 'But it is not to be domination of exploitation, not an arbitrary rule however absolutely it may be phrased ... It was to be, rather, a domination modelled on God's own, of which it was a part', p. 58. The character of God's rule is found in texts like Isa. 11.3–5, according to this author. *On Genesis*, p. 58.

48 The theme of image is no more prevalent in the New Testament than in the Old Testament. In 1 Cor. 11.7 Paul refers to man (as opposed to woman) as the 'image and glory of God' with Gen. 1.26–8 in mind. Col. 3.10 implies that God's original plan in creating humanity is now being progressively realised. In general the New Testament tends to concentrate on Jesus as the image of God (2. Cor. 4.4; Col. 1.15; cf. Heb. 1.3). The concept takes on an eschatological note in 1 Cor 15.49 where believers are promised that they will bear the likeness of the heavenly man. See J. Y. Campbell, 'Image', in Alan Richardson (ed.), *A Theological Word Book of the Bible* (London, SCM, 1977), pp. 110–11. The Christian life can be seen as a process of being conformed to the image of Christ. It is also instructive to keep in mind the social dimension of the image theme. See Flick and Alszeghy, *Fondamenti*, ch. 7, and J. Mahoney, *The Making of Moral Theology: A Study of the Roman Catholic Tradition* (Oxford, Clarendon Press, 1987), pp. 335–7, where we are told that the divine image is found not just in the individual person, but is 'impressed upon humanity as such, or in its totality, so that it is the completeness of human *koinoinia*, or of human persons in community, which will most fully image forth the interpersonal riches of the Creator' (p. 346). I think it is safe to say that this *koinonia* must be built on respect for the rights of persons.

49 Commenting on 'the New Exegesis' of the biblical doctrine/texts on original sin, James Mackey reminds us 'that the texts attempt to explain present and apparently permanent realities rather than the historical, or prehistorical, origin of things', 'New Thinking on Original Sin', in M. J. Taylor (ed.), *The Mystery of Sin and Forgiveness* (New York, Alba House, 1971), p. 225; See James Gustafson, *Theology and Ethics* (Oxford, Blackwell, 1981), p. 293ff.; Carroll, *Towards A Story*, ch. 5.

50 See the point of view of Austin Farrer:

> In some such fashion we may say that God respects the action or organization of nature's elements; he does not violate it by the higher levels of organization and higher modes of action he superimposes. Now in the political sphere a hundred per cent success for public order or for economic planning is unthinkable, so long as individual freedom is given its rights. So in the natural world a hundred per cent success for animal bodies is unthinkable, if the cellular, chemical and atomic systems of which they are composed are to retain their rights, and go on being themselves in their own way at every level. *Saving Belief: A Discussion of Essentials* (London, Hodder and Stoughton, 1964), p. 51.

I presume Farrer is using the language of rights in a loose analogical sense. Surely he does not mean to imply that individual cells or chemicals have strict claims or entitlements? He is saying, however, that, as humans, we cannot expect God to constantly place our comfort ahead of the rest of creation.

51 'Gaudium et Spes', 36, in A. Flannery, *Vatican Council II*, p. 935.

52 See Ian M. Ellis, 'Christian Authority', *The Furrow*, 42/10 (1991), pp. 557–65; Oliver O'Donovan, *Resurrection and Moral Order: An Outline for Evangelical Ethics* (Leicester, Inter-Varsity Press, 1986), ch. 7 ('The Authority of Christ'); Helmut Thielicke, *Theological Ethics*, W. H. Lazareth (ed.), 2 vols. (London, A. and C. Black, 1969), II, *Politics*, chs. 11 and 12, esp. pp. 178–202; John F. O'Grady, 'Authority and Power: Issues for the Contemporary Church', *Louvain Studies*, 10/2 (1984), pp. 122–40.

53 See Sallie McFague's discussion of the model of God as friend in her *Metaphorical Theology: Models of God in Religious Language* (London, SCM, 1983), pp. 177–92. She provides standard New Testament references, especially to the life and words of Jesus – Jn. 15.13; 17.21 and Mtt. 11.19. Of particular interest, in the light of our discussion of authority, McFague discusses the difficulty of reconciling the two concepts of authority and friendship when speaking of God and his relationship to humanity. Even in the case of Jesus, she admits, the friendship he shares with his disciples is not an equal one: Jesus gives more than he takes. The focus, she

argues, is not on equality, 'rather, identification with the needs and sufferings of others, regardless of difference of class, race, gender, nationality seems far more critical', p. 182. It is also interesting that McFague mentions as one aspect of the authority vested in friendship the right and duty to criticise one's friends in certain circumstances (*ibid.*). This, we recall, was an aspect of the 'integrative power' which Rollo May underlined.

EPILOGUE

1 McFague, *Metaphorical Theology* (London, SCM, 1983), pp. 137–44.

2 *Ibid.*, p. 140; the language of 'contra-factors' is coined by Jerry Gill, *Ian Ramsey: To Speak Responsibly of God* (London, George Allen and Unwin, 1976), pp. 113ff.

3 Concerning the feminist critique of patriarchal theological models it seems that the models of rights used in this work fare relatively well. In biblical terms the image-model in Genesis stresses the fundamental equality of men and women, for the image of God in humankind is bisexual. The new covenant in Christ is supposed to break down barriers between slave and free, Jew and Greek, male and female (Gal. 3.28; cf. Rom. 10.12; 1. Cor. 12.13), even though in practice, historically, the Christian Church has been slow to apply these models rigorously. This fundamental sexual equality should filter down to the models of freedom and power due to the essential unity of all four models of rights.

4 See Oliver O'Donovan, *Resurrection and Moral Order: An Outline for Evangelical Ethics* (Leicester, Inter-varsity Press/Grand Rapids, Michigan, Eerdmans, 1986), 'In proclaiming the resurrection of Christ, the apostles proclaimed also the resurrection of mankind in Christ; and in proclaiming the resurrection of mankind, they proclaimed the renewal of all creation in him', p. 31. O'Donovan suggests that before the resurrection of Jesus it might have been possible to see the creation as a lost cause, but not after (p. 14).

Index

Open-texture (of concepts), 8; 10–11;
16; 45; 118; 143; 276, n. 27
Ostensive definition, 5; 275, n. 26

Pacifism, Christian
see R. Niebuhr and H. R. Niebuhr
and J. H. Yoder
Parables, 123; 155; 157; 297, n. 34;
301, n. 11
Paternalism, 38; 192; 231; 262–3
Paul, St, 90–100; 101–3; 105; 108; 210;
207, n. 20
Perry, T. D., 34
Peter, Letter of, 100; 109
Phillips, D. Z., (and H. O. Mounce),
110–11
Pictorial/Poetic meaning, 18–19; see
Hospers
Poverty, St Francis' practice of, 104–6;
112–13
Power
and claiming, 146; 149
and dignity, 189; 193; 230
and freedom, 133–4; 186–7; 189; 191;
207; 257
and God, 193–6; 198
political analysis of, 143–50
psychological analysis of, 188–93
and rights, 143–50
theological analysis of, 183–7; 260–4
Powers
moral powers, 31
rights as, 30–2; 33
Pragmatics, 17–19
Prayer and morality, see Liturgy and
justice
Pre-moral goods, 98; 111–12; 113
Prior, M., 307, n. 20
Promising, 3

Quine, W. V., xvi; 274, n. 9
Quinn v. Leathem, 37

Rahner, K., 184–6; 193
Ramsey, P., 282, n. 47; 305, n. 37
Rawls, J., 281, n. 59; 309, n. 38
Raz, J., 458, n. 43
Raphael, D. D., 76; 83–5; 289, n. 11
Reasons
for acting, 68–9; 237–43
Christian reasons for respecting rights,
163–82; 243–8; 312, n. 16

fundamental/ultimate distinction,
241–2
justifying type of, 238–42
and natural law, 235–6; 250
from revelation, 82; 236–7; 239–40;
243–8
Ricoeur, P., 116–17; 155; 164; 297, n.
29
Rights
of aged parents, 219
of animals, 11; 43; 73–4; 281, n. 42
of children, see MacCormick
discretionary/option, 24; 53; 78; 95;
173; 305, n. 39
against God, 248–50; 253
human, 7; 14–15; 23; 24; 32; 36; 55;
56; 64; 72–6; 90; 131; 140; 142;
167; 168; 173; 178–9; 191–2;
213–15; 218; 226; 231; 247; 262;
279, n. 6
inalienable, 36; 51; 52; 280, n. 25
and interests, 61–3; 78
mandatory, 8; 24; 53; 68; 80; 95;
131; 173; 262; 274, n. 16; 305, n.
39;
manifesto, 11; 24; 46; 96; 136; 140;
205; 219; 226; 248; 309, n. 39
and moral principles, 12; 66–72; 78–9
natural, 14; 23; 76–7; 83–7
and reasons for acting, 68–9
of recipience and action, 83–4
and the right thing to do, 48; 59;
67–8; 78–9
and sin, 12–13; 91; 98–9
special, 3; 14; 35; 56; 63–4; 132;
140; 142; 168; 191–2; 213–15; 218;
225; 231; 247; 280, n. 23; 290, n.
18
theological foundations of, Ch. 8, see
Murray
as trumps, 59; 63
and Utilitarianism, 59; 61; 284, n. 9
see Claims, Entitlements, God,
Powers, Liberties, Freedom,
Authority
Root Metaphors, 121; 155; 296, n. 22

Sandel, M., 309, n. 38
Scandinavian jurists, 9; 275, n. 23
Scanlon, T. M., 276, n. 40
Scepticism
Conceptual, Ch. 3